The History of European
Conservative Thought

The History of European Conservative Thought

Francesco Giubilei

Translated by Rachel Stone

REGNERY GATEWAY

Regnery Gateway™ is a trademark of Salem Communications Holding Corporation
Regnery® is a registered trademark of Salem Communications Holding Corporation

Cataloging-in-Publication data on file with the Library of Congress

ISBN 978-1-62157-909-0
ebook ISBN 978-1-62157-910-6

Published in the United States by
Regnery Publishing
A Division of Salem Media Group
300 New Jersey Ave NW
Washington, DC 20001
www.Regnery.com

Manufactured in the United States of America

10 9 8 7 6 5 4 3 2 1

Books are available in quantity for promotional or premium use. For information on discounts and terms, please visit our website: www.Regnery.com.

Ai miei genitori Clara e Giuseppe per tutto il tempo dedicato alla mia educazione e istruzione quando ero un bambino.

Contents

Introduction

The primary difficulty in accomplishing a *History of European Conservative Thought* has been identifying authors who can be defined as conservative, who regard themselves as part of the conservative vision. Many conservative scholars referenced throughout this book never defined themselves as "conservative" in their lifetime. But if we retrospectively define conservatism with the values that we know characterize it, we can identify their work as belonging to conservative schools of thought.

Considering the extensiveness of the topic at hand, as well as the text selections that have been made in writing this book, this work does not claim totality. It rather aims to amply organize a philosophy that began with the French Revolution and continues to the present time. The book you hold in your hands is the product of years of study and in-depth analysis. And although the selection of thinkers for this book could be open to debate, it is supported by thorough research and verified sources.

The first part of this book is structured around a general analysis of conservatism, drawing on its values and historical origins. Then, a comprehensive look into various conservative thinkers in national and supranational contexts—including Britain's heir, the United States—make up the second part of the book. Particular attention is dedicated to my own country, Italy.

This study of conservatism has been achieved through a cultural lens rather than a political one. But history interweaves political content and philosophical theories; it therefore would have been an error of insufficiency and inaccuracy to disregard the relationship between politics and conservative philosophy in certain parts of the book.

As an Italian, dealing with Italian conservatism, as well as choosing which theorists define it, was the most complex part of this work. Despite increased progressivism established in recent years, Italy remains more conservative than any other European country. Excluding its Fascist digression, in which there was an indisputable conservative component, the conservative stamp of Italy is mainly due to the strong influence exercised by the Catholic Church, politically known as the Christian Democratic Party. Some of the most important voices in Italian journalism of the twentieth century, from Indro Montanelli to Leo Longanesi, discuss conservatism with native enthusiasm. And much of nineteeth- and twentieth-century Italian literature draws on conservative content. Some of the most important Italian writers owe their intellectual formation to their conservative cultural education; look no further than Nobel Prize-winning author Luigi Pirandello, or Giuseppe Tomasi di Lampedusa's novel *The Leopard*, from which come these immortal lines: "If we want things to stay as they are, things will have to change."

The decision to omit an analysis of the biographic profiles of liberal-conservative scholars such as Tocqueville or Hayek derives from the decision to trace a path of writers that abide by principles of traditional conservative thought. This is not to say that in certain passages of *Democracy in America* or *The Old Regime and the Revolution*, Tocqueville does not express opinions that are within the realm of conservatism. Although the influence of counter-revolutionary authors brought him to an elitist detachment from the masses and direct democracy, a thorough analysis of his stance reveals one more closely linked to liberal-conservatism than traditional conservatism. As for Hayek, it is sufficient to cite his essay "Why I Am Not a Conservative," published in 1960 in *The Constitution of Liberty*, to justify his absence. However, even this may warrant contest: J. Arthur Bloom aimed to explain reasons for which Hayek actually can be counted among conservatives in the article "Why Hayek is a Conservative," published in the *American Conservative*. Nevertheless, his work will not be explored in this book.

So what is the purpose of this book? It is to ensure that the word "conservative" takes on a positive meaning that overhauls the discriminatory conceptions held in the collective imagination. To many, conservatism is a stale and declining concept; but this notion demonstrates a scarce understanding of true conservative thought. Beginning with the most important European conservative philosophers, this book aims to highlight distinctions between conservatism and other schools of thought—including reactionism and libertarianism, which are too often confused with conservatism. This book provides a solid, well-characterized cultural foundation for contemporary society, in which the centerpiece of progressivism has cunningly and tragically marginalized traditional conservative values.

It is my hope that this book will articulate and inspire gratitude for the indisputable values that have animated—and continue to animate—conservative philosophy.

CHAPTER ONE

Conservatism: Interpretations, Ideas, and Principles

W hat is conservatism?
In contemporary Italian society, the term conservative has taken on an at worst negative or at best anachronistic connotation. Almost no one in the country would define him or herself as conservative; at most, some claim to be "right-wing," but this classification has become almost meaningless, due to the twentieth century's political transformations and dissipating lines of traditional oppositions.

Etymologically, a conservative is one who is "averse to rapid change" and represented by a political party. This political party is "disposed to maintain existing institutions and promote private enterprise."[1]

With this definition in mind, it could be said that the rationale dominating much of the twenty-first century could not be further from conservative principles. As Leo Longanesi expressed in a piercing aphorism: "I am a conservative in a country with nothing to conserve."

To further understand what being conservative means, Gennaro Malgieri includes a short definition of conservatism in the introduction to his book, *Conservatori: da Edmund Burke a Russell Kirk.*[2] Conservatism, he writes, is "more than a political doctrine, conservatism is a spiritual feeling and cultural calling."[3]

Conservatism was born in response to the French Revolution. It aims to protect the human person and his intermediary groups, groups that might be

1

crushed by powers of centralized governments. Such governments tend to erode and sometimes intentionally attempt to destroy traditional values, as well as the idea of community itself. And they might succeed in doing so, were it not for conservatism and the strength of "the increasingly essential values, such as tradition (opposed to progress), prejudice (opposed to reason), authority (opposed to power), freedom (opposed to equality), private property (opposed to statism), religion (as opposed to morality), community (opposed to individual)."[4]

Moeller van den Bruck asserts that a conservative does not look to the past, but rather to eternity:

> Conserving is not receiving to hand down, but rather innovating the forms, institutional or ideal, which agree to remain rooted in a solid world of values in the face of continuous historical setbacks. In the face of modernity as an era of insecurity, opposing the securities of the past is no longer enough; instead it is necessary to redesign new safety by adopting and taking on the same risky conditions with which it is defined.[5]

Conservatives defend the established order while attempting to maintain the social and political balance of a deteriorating society. They ask what might be lost in the name of "advancing" modern society, a society that substitutes tradition with reason.

As the stability of society splinters, conservatives aspire to maintain values and rules of tradition in the face of revolution and unrest. They are the guardians of their culture's foundation. In their book *Il pensiero conservatore. Interpretazione, giustificazioni e critiche*, Carlo Mongardini and Maria Luisa Maniscalco divide the study of conservatism into three different perspectives:

1. The analysis of conservatism as *an ideological principle*. This includes justifying the conservative standpoint, examining the relationship between conservative tendencies and certain historical conditions, and considering general reasons for conservatism's success.

2. The analysis of conservatism as *a political philosophy*. This is properly conceived as a *theory of the limits* of transformation and change.

3. The analysis of conservatism as *a political practice*. This includes studying its application in various political regimes as well as the forms through which it is possible to preserve a social and political system.[6]

Why do we need conservative thought now? The changes and problems of a new social order, following an advent of the masses, present a role worth pondering:

> Conservative thought is an *undercurrent of modern society* and serves as a way to express the need and value of continuity in a complex culture, and has taken on this change as a top priority. Continuity can no longer be entrusted to a mere repetition of tradition, unreflective of the past. It must be continuously constructed in the face of the shifting complexities of society and changing historical situations, and in the face of different economic and cultural trends and emerging needs. These are the issues that conservative thought presents. Every time there is a tendency toward change, every time a check on reality is missing, the principles of conservatism reappear as way to revive continuity and the strength of tradition in the face of change.[7]

Conservatism is linked to universal values stretching beyond a single era, valid in every historical period. Categorical conservatism must be, therefore, not only historical, but ideal, universally functional, sociological, and transcendental.

However, things being as they are in contemporary society, conservatives risk falling into a paradoxical situation. What if a conservative does not see any values worth conserving? Might he then have no other choice but to be drawn toward a progressive rationale with the objective of overcoming laws that govern society? Georg Simmel acknowledged this point of view, but he

believed the preservation of conservatism could be achieved through a principle of "preserving innovation." For the inclination toward progress itself,
the desire to improve the world, is, in fact, *worth conserving*. This poses the
question, then, of the role of conservatism in a changing world:

> To maintain faith in nonnegotiable values, undoubtedly; however,
> also being open to the adventures of a new time, not sternly oppos-
> ing them but rather participating in them with the spirit of one
> who does not want to renounce the idea of establishing civil cohab-
> itation, founded on the dignity of the person and the irrevocable
> project of building different yet converging communities...the idea
> of universal order founded on natural rights, respect of the people
> and of the culture, on sovereignty and on the authority that pro-
> tects liberty.[8]

Roger Scruton has dedicated a large part of his life to the study of conservatism, publishing various books on the subject, including *A Political
Philosophy: Arguments for Conservatism* and *How to Be a Conservative*.[9] In
chapter seven of the latter text, Scruton discusses the birth of conservatism
and its connection to the Enlightenment:

> Conservatism as a political philosophy came into being with the
> Enlightenment. It would not have been possible without the sci-
> entific revolution, the overcoming of religious conflict, the rise of
> the secular state, and the triumph of liberal individualism. Con-
> servatives for the most part acknowledged the benefits contained
> in the new conception of citizenship, which vested power in the
> people, and in the state as their appointed—and in part elected—
> representative. They also recognized the great reversal in the
> affairs of government that this implied. Henceforth, they saw,
> accountability is from the top down, and not from the bottom up.
> The rulers must answer to the ruled, and responsibilities at every
> level are no longer imposed but assumed.

At the same time, conservatives sounded a warning against the Enlightenment. For Herder, Maistre, Burke and others, the Enlightenment was not to be regarded as a complete break with the past. It made sense only against the background of a long-standing cultural inheritance. Liberal individualism offered a new and in many ways inspiriting vision of the human condition; but it depended upon traditions and institutions that bound people together in ways that no merely individualistic worldview could engender. The Enlightenment proposed a universal human nature, governed by a universal moral law, from which the state emerges through the consent of the governed. The political process was henceforth to be shaped by the free choices of individuals, in order to protect the institutions that make free choices possible. It was all beautiful and logical and inspiriting. But it made no sense without the cultural inheritance of the nation state, and the forms of social life that had taken root in it.[10]

According to Heidegger, conservatism "is called to protect the existence of a democracy based on essential elements: *Fuhrung*, the command; *Volk*, the people; *Erbe*, the heritage; *Gefolgschaft*, loyalty; *Bodenstandigkeit*, the roots of one's own land," and is characterized as a countermovement in opposition to the destruction of the values carried out by nihilism. Therefore, a comparison between Ernst Jünger and Heidegger can be made in which:

> The diagnosis of the nihilistic "disease" leads to foreshadowing a new frontier of "resistance" and "anarchy," a "wild" opposition to the "devaluation of values" that precisely corresponds to the diffused and dangerous condition of nihilism. The individual is called to oppose the "fall of old systems" and the "consumption of every traditional resource."[11]

In contrast to traditionalism, conservatism serves as a link between different generations. A conservative allows for the maintenance of heredity as well as the transference of it to those who will come after us:

It is valuable to us because it contains people, without whose striving and suffering we ourselves would not exist. These people produced the physical contours of our country; but they also produced its institutions and its laws, and fought to preserve them. On any understanding of the web of social obligation, we owe them a duty of remembrance. We do not merely study the past: we inherit it, and inheritance brings with it not only the rights of ownership, but the duties of trusteeship. Things fought for and died for should not be idly squandered. For they are the property of others, who are not yet born.

Conservatism should be seen in that way, as part of a dynamic relation across generations. People grieve at the destruction of what is dear to them, because it damages the pattern of trusteeship, cutting them off from those who went before, and obscuring the obligation to those who come after.[12]

Progressivism is the antithesis of conservatism. It dominated Western thought between 1750 and 1900, when the idea of progress was tightly bound to economic development. The beliefs of progressives not only derive from capitalism, but also from Communism. Scholars are still in disagreement about when the concept of progress was born. In his book *The Idea of Progress*, J.B. Bury claims that it was not before the seventeenth century and the Scientific Revolution; other scholars, such as Ludwig Edelstein and E. R. Dodds, believe it to reach as far back as ancient Greece. Robert Nisbet, in his 1980 book *History of the Idea of Progress*, asserts that progress was acquired from the Christian philosophy of history. The progressive doctrine derives from classical liberalism (which emphasizes the concept of a free market), statism (the concept of the welfare state), and socialism, thus creating polarities between puritans, classical liberals, and Darwinists—each of which subscribes to various tenets of progressivism—and reactionaries, traditional Catholics, and conservatives, who generally oppose this concept of progressivism.

Progressivism as an ideology rests on the idea that historical and economic progress is inevitable and we will eventually enter into a historical era characterized by absolute freedom and social and economic equality. Social progressivism is similarly optimistic, advocating that the human condition can be improved through political reform. Francis Bacon, Jeremy Bentham, John Stuart Mill, Jean-Jacques Rousseau, Karl Marx, Auguste Comte, Edward Bellamy and Nicolas de Condorcet are progressivism's founding fathers.

How do you transform an undesirable society into a desirable society? According to progressives, you bring about a centralized government that holds enough power to do so. Ask a conservative about this, and he will tell you that progressive reforms originate from a fundamental misunderstanding of the human condition: namely, that progressives fail to give the devil in man his due.

The German philosopher Hermann Lübbe explored "rules" of conservative behavior:

1. Cultures are born and progress at the expense of heritage. The cost of this progress and the pain of loss does not—or rather, should not—create a blind aversion to progress on the part of the conservative.
2. The practice of defending what one must not give up against current or foreseeable threats *is* conservative. Those who consider such an act to be just and indispensable and are intent on saving what needs to be saved under menacingly changing circumstances are conservative.
3. The practice of creating a valid, distributive rule in both science and politics to determine what progress must be justified and what traditions must be saved is a conservative practice.
4. Prioritizing disaster prevention over the creation of utopia is conservative. Being oriented toward evils that must be eliminated is politically safer than pursuing an image of unknown happiness.[13]

Conservatives are not against the French Revolution in and of itself. Rather, they are against the changes it wrought on economic and moral order. The origins of conservatism are based on medieval European society; the achievements of modernity have not been caused by the emancipation of the individual, but by the alienation of the individual. Conservative thought is opposed to the rationalism and individualism advocated by Voltaire, Diderot, and Kant:

> In remarkable degree, the central themes of conservatism over the last two centuries are but widenings of themes enunciated by Burke with specific reference to revolutionary France. He himself was clearly aware that the French Revolution was at bottom a European revolution, but that truth had to await the writings of such ardent traditionalists as Bonald, de Maistre and Tocqueville for its detailed statement. In Burke and in them we find the outlines of a philosophy of history that was the diametric opposite of the Whig or progressive philosophy; and we find too a perspicuous statement of the importance of feudalism and of other historically grown structures such as patriarchal family, local community, church, guild and region which, under the centralizing, individualizing influence of natural law philosophy, had almost disappeared from European political thought in the seventeenth and eighteenth centuries. In the writings of Hobbes, Locke and Rousseau, traditional society and its historically evolved groups and traditions was recognized dimly at best, almost always with hostility. What alone was central was the hard reality of the individual; institutions were penumbral. Burke, above any other single thinker, changed this whole individualistic perspective. His *Reflections*, by its denunciations of both Revolutionaries and the line of natural rights theorists leading up to the Revolutionaries, played a key role in the momentous change of perspectives involved in the passage from eighteenth-century to nineteenth-century Europe. Within a generation after publication of *Reflections* a whole *Aufklärung* blazed up in the West, at its core nothing more than an anti-Enlightenment. Such voices as Bonald, de Maistre and Chateaubriand in France, Coleridge and Southey in England, Haller, Savigny and Hegel in

Germanic thought, and Donoso y Cortes and Balmes in Spain
were resonating throughout the West. In America, John Adams,
Alexander Hamilton and Randolph of Roanoke issued their own
warnings and proposals. And all voices, European and American, were rich in respect to Edmund Burke as prophet.[14]

Jünger described what it means to be conservative by borrowing the words
of Albrecht Erich Günther: "To be conservative is not a life of what was yesterday, but a life of that which is eternal."[15] He also referenced Rivarol in his
book dedicated to the French thinker when he describes the ideals that characterize conservatism:

An author who has been dead for a hundred and fifty years, who
tried to confront as an individual the Revolution in its nascent
state, what significance does he have in our time, that is, for a
time in which this Revolution has been reinforced, triumphant,
in all its consequences and across the board, territorially and
globally, theoretically and practically, in habits and institutions?
The kingdoms that derived from these new ideas have long
since faded, Prussia, Austria, and Russia, and among them Turkey
could also be counted; the fact that they have been undermined
in one day on both sides of the chessboard offers an idea of the
leveling strength of the attack. While in this case the attack incites
mechanical images, such as that of the broken crowns, in other
kingdoms opposed to change it seems to operate rather chemically,
by means of a more subtle distinction. It is all to be seen spatially,
but the triumph of the ideas of 1789 even repeats temporally in
the great pressures against conservative powers and personalist
regimes, against empires formed by the masses, against the
restored monarchy, against the bourgeois royalty and the conservative land bourgeoisie. Castles are destroyed or transformed into
museums, even where kings still meet. The word "conservative"
does not belong to happy creations. It encompasses a personality
that refers to time and binds the resolve to restore forms and

conditions grown unsustainable. Today, those who still want to conserve something are *a priori* the weakest.[16]

In the third edition of the journal *La Destra*, Mohler published an article in 1972 titled "Perche non conservatore?" in which he expresses the so-called paradox of conservatives:

> Surprisingly, a conservative no longer agrees with the status quo. According to current opinion, a conservative either clings to the status quo or even wishes to restore the past: the left, however, is the one who would like to change the status quo and therefore throws open the door to the future.

What is the paradox today? It lies in the fact that contemporary conservatives are dissatisfied and long for change, whereas progressives, who were at one time revolutionaries, strive to maintain the status quo:

> [Conservatives] consider current foreign and economic policy to be catastrophic, they approve neither the current state of the military nor that of universities and schools, and do not accept barren and industrialized sex that one wants to foist upon them as a tranquilizer.... Even the least conventional conservative would never dare think—until recently—that he would suddenly find *himself* to be the true revolutionary, the only one, actually, who does not accept the status quo, but thinks that there should be a better way than the one on which we drag ourselves like sheep.[17]

Is Conservatism an Ideology?

Robert Nisbet's book *The Quest for Community* was a breakthrough for conservative thought, making him one of the main scholars of conservatism in the last century. In an essay published in *Policy Review*, Nisbet outlines the essential and founding principles of conservatism:

What are these elements? *First*, the indispensability of religion, of a rooted awareness of the sacred. *Second*, the need for family, nuclear and extended, and its autonomy from political regulation. *Third*, the vital role of social rank, of hierarchy in the social order, irrespective of whether such ranking be by birth or achievement through merit. *Fourth*, the crucial importance of property, above all landed property, but property in any form that is private and tangible. *Fifth*, the necessity of intermediate social bodies— churches, guilds, corporations, social classes, and so forth—each valuable in its own right to society, but having the added function of serving as a buffer between the individual and the power of the state. *Sixth*, the importance of local community and region, with maximum autonomy to be granted them by the central or national government. *Seventh*, the value of tradition in contrast to prescriptive law or administrative decree in the workings of a society. *Eighth*, the indispensability of the highest possible degree of decentralization and diffusion of political power.[18]

Scholars who have analyzed conservatism often ask themselves if conservatism is an ideology. While prevailing schools of thought do not consider it one, opposing opinions do exist, the most acclaimed being that of Robert Nisbet, who explains his reasoning in his book *Conservatism: Dream and Reality*.[19] Nisbet considers conservatism one of the three most important ideologies in history, along with socialism and liberalism. He accuses scholars who do not consider it an ideology of having "a stunted view of the world."[20]

Anyone who denies that conservatism is an ideology, he explains, does so because they consider conservative thought to be "lacking the elements of activism and reform which supposedly go into a genuine ideology," offering a definition of ideology that, in his opinion, embraces both the political and cultural realms:

> any reasonably coherent body of moral, economic, social and cultural ideas that has a solid and well-known reference to politics

and political power; more specifically a power base to make possible a victory for the body of ideas. An ideology, in contrast to a mere passing configuration of opinion, remains alive for a considerable period of time, has major advocates and spokesmen and a respectable degree of institutionalization.[21]

Michael Oakeshott disagreed, suggesting that conservatism is less an ideology and more a *disposition* of someone who has neither the character nor the intention to "navigate unexplored seas," an inclination of thought that leads to rejecting aprioristic change. As the main anti-Enlightenment English philosopher of the mid-twentieth century, Oakeshott's most well-known work, *Rationalism in Politics and Other Essays*, is indispensable. Unlike Nisbet, he considered conservatism to be a disposition of the heart and mind, a behavior, rather than an ideology. He was also a strong opponent of rationalism, the child of progressivism.

Russel Kirk's critique of conservatism as an ideology is even more explicit. In an interview with Marco Respinti for the magazine *Cristianità*, he maintained that "every ideology, including a democratic one, carries its own intolerances. This is due to that fact that ideology entails fanaticism and unreality; democratic ideology, which is far from preserving our freedom, weakens the constitutional structure."[22] Kirk considers conservatism to be a school of thought that combats ideologies, as opposed to being an ideology itself. Ideologies, such as Communism or Nazism, are collections of political ideas that promise a transformation of the world, starting with a set of laws to be achieved.

Kirk promotes conservatism as anti-ideology because ideology brings society to feats of disorder, the opposite of what conservatives value. He develops a synthesis of these differences in his book, *A Program for Conservatives*:

If you want men who will sacrifice their past and present and future to a set of abstract ideas, you must go to Communism, or Fascism, or Benthamism. But if you want men who seek, reasonably and prudently, to reconcile the best in the wisdom of our ancestors with the change which is essential to a vigorous civil social existence, then you will do well to turn to conservative principles.[23]

Ideology is an attempt to overthrow order, as the ideologue wants to overthrow God and the divine order. Kirk defines—and Burke affirms—anyone who classifies conservatism as an ideology as incoherent:

> The triumph of ideology would be the triumph of that which Edmund Burke called "the opposite world," the world of disorder, while conservatives try to conserve the world of order that we have inherited, although somewhat tampered with, by our ancestors. The conservative mentality and that of ideologies are to be found at opposing poles. And the fight between these two mentalities will be no less fierce in the twenty-first century than in the twentieth century.[24]

Socialists and conservatives are opposites in the way they operate in individual-community-state relationships. Conservatism has always considered the rights of the church, family, and property; socialism has not. Nisbet lists the differences between conservatism, socialism, and liberalism as they connect to conceptions of history and tradition; he rightly posits conservatism as the only political philosophy that highlights the value of the church and Judeo-Christian morals.

Conservatives believe a strong church is a necessary. It is a check on the powers of the state and exalts the individual toward a higher purpose. Interestingly, the church's critique of capitalism is even graver than the one put forth by Communists at the beginning of the nineteenth century.

Finally, as Spartaco Pupo writes in his book *Robert Nisbet e il conservatorismo sociale*, Nisbet emphasizes the differences between conservatives and liberals by highlighting the distance between conservative thinkers and classical philosophers like Locke, Montesquieu, and Adam Smith:

Nisbet's main goal which, on closer inspection, has finalized this comparison between liberals and conservatives, is that of stabilizing the "primacy of politics" on the economy, demonstrating that while libertarians push in favor of the dogma of free market, and therefore of the economy, conservatives tend to subjugate the latter to politics, which must take priority along with culture and history.[25]

The Birth of Conservatism

Robert Nisbet begins his book *Conservatism: Dream and Reality* with a reflection on the origins of conservatism, and he acknowledges that Edmund Burke played an essential role in the birth of conservative thought. The major conservative themes of the last two centuries, Nisbet notes, correlate to Burke's anti-Jacobinism. Burke's philosophy underlines the importance of traditional institutions like patriarchal family structures, the church, community, and guilds based on a feudal system.

Although François-René de Chateaubriand first used the term "conservatism" in 1818 to indicate "respectable people" who ascribe to religious values, monarchy, and freedom, the philosophy associated with conservatism was born with Burke, whose many ideas were reflected in Tory standpoints despite his being part of the Whig Party.

Burke's break from his own party in reaction to the French Revolution was consistent with his idea that the French deserved the same protection he had fought for years earlier on behalf of the Americans, the Indians, and the Irish. Furthermore, Burke accused Jacobins of being the authors of a "leveling in the name of equality, nihilism in the name of liberty, absolute power in the name of the people" and overthrowing the history and traditions of France.[26]

Aware of the indivisibility of the French Revolution on the world stage, he states in his *Reflections*: "Many parts of Europe are in open disorder. In many others there is a hollow murmuring underground; a confused movement is felt, that threatens a general earthquake in the political world."

He also does not hesitate to name an instigator of the French Revolution: Jean-Jacques Rousseau. Tocqueville, on the other hand, is more cautious when mentioning a precise reference and instead accuses the "men of letters" of having incited fantastical ideas of freedom, absolute justice, and equality in the minds of French citizens. Either way, glimpses into the changes determined by the French Revolution were quickly made evident, and in 1791 guilds were abolished:

> Inevitably the patriarchal family felt the power of the Revolution. The general belief of *philosophes* had been that the traditional kinship structure was 'against nature and contrary to reason.' Clearly, many Jacobin governors agreed. In 1792 marriage was declared a civil contract, and a number of grounds for divorce were made available (in 1794 the number of divorces exceeded the number of marriages). Strict limitations were placed upon the paternal authority, among them the disappearance of this authority when the sons reached their legal majority. The traditional laws of primogeniture and entail were set aside forever, with implications to property as well as family.[27]

Another goal of the French Revolution was the right to property and the seizure of large landowner estates. While the key concepts of the French Revolution were *individualization* and *nationalization*, a plan of *de-Christianization* was also implemented in 1793 to erect reason as the new religion of the state. The enactment of this plan could be seen in everyday life with the new Republican calendar, which served as the instrument through which these changes were achieved. The goal was to extend the revolution to the rest of Europe: "The true total and boundless character of the Revolution was best observed, Burke thought, in laws designed to obliterate or seriously cripple the traditional social order and at the same time to fill whatever vacuum might be left with new arms of the state."[28]

The Revolution also led to the upheaval of the social ladder, in which a new mobility became possible. This mobility, though perhaps attractive to our modern minds, contributed to the disintegration of ancient society and the victory of individualism.

Around this same time, the Industrial Revolution in England was transpiring and was destined to change mankind's way of life forever. The conservative response to the Industrial and French Revolution's changes is entrusted to the words of Benjamin Disraeli: "I see no other remedy for that war of classes and of creeds which now agitates and menaces us, but in an earnest return to a system which may be described generally as one of loyalty and reverence, popular rights and social sympathies."[29]

The French and Industrial Revolutions also brought about the separation of political and religious powers, introducing the births of political and philosophical movements not viewed positively by conservatives of the time. One of the most significant movements was John Wesley's "Wesleyanism" (or Methodism). His "religious revolution" shared many of the ideas associated with the other two revolutions, as well as the utilitarian philosophy of Jeremy Bentham, a theorist whose philosophical principles were based on individual interests, hedonism, and a centralized authoritarian structure to ensure a collective good. Bentham believed the study of the past was useless, which was in direct contrast to conservative wisdom; Nisbet writes, "We cannot know where we are, much less where we are going, until we know where we have been."[30]

Clearly, conservatives rejected Bentham's mechanical vision of history, and Burke's conception of history is undoubtedly anti-progressive. The English philosopher considered these revolutions the result of society's decline starting from the medieval period, a time characterized by cavalry, religion being central to life, and the emergence of universities and guilds, all of which were united by a corpus of homogenous ideas. According to Nisbet, Burke thought the Revolution was supported by a diabolical design:

> It was to the past, especially the medieval past, that Burke and Bonald looked for historical exemplification of the good society. In the feudal code of chivalry, in the perfection of the gentleman, and in the proper establishment of religion, Burke found the glory that the liberals and radicals of his day reserved for the future.[31]

For conservatives, the French Revolution marks a catastrophe on par with the barbaric invasions. Therefore, as Joseph de Maistre noted, an adversary to revolution is more important than revolution itself.

The Principles of Conservatism

In *Conservatism: Dream and Reality*, Robert Nisbet analyzes conservative dogma and identifies a few essential categories necessary to understanding conservative thought: history and tradition; prejudice and reason; authority and power; liberty and equality; property and life; and religion and morality.

History and Tradition

Conservatives view history as experience and not as a mere concept. In *Reflections*, Burke notes: "People will not look forward to posterity who never look backward to their ancestors."[32] Rather than being linear, conservatives consider history a continuous series of cycles in which structures and routines repeat themselves and are handed down from generation to generation.

Nisbet addresses a point fundamental to comprehension of conservatism: conservatives are not opposed to *tout court* change, but rather they dispute the "spirit of innovation," the veneration of change for the sake of change. Conservatives revere tradition not only because they believe addressing the past is valid; they believe it is necessary for contemporary society.

Prejudice and Reason

In the nineteenth century, conservatives had a renewed interest in pre-rationalism and the values preceding the Enlightenment era. Drawing on Burke's conception of the word, "prejudice" is a way that conservatives unite citizens against political rationalism:

> Burke, and conservatives generally, have seen that almost all of
> the will to resist that is commonly claimed to result from inner
> knowledge of natural rights or from inner instincts to freedom,

results instead from prejudices slowly built up historically in people's minds: prejudices about religion, property, national autonomy and long-accustomed roles in the social order. These, not
abstract rights, are the motive powers in the struggles of peoples
for freedom which we honor.[33]

Authority and Power

Conservatives believe it is important for societies to have responsive tools
for containing the passions of mankind. Authority, therefore, becomes fundamental. Natural law, Burke asserts, is indifferent to the traditional and hard-won
moral conceptions of civilization, and ignores the entities of family, religion,
guild, local community, and all structures required for collective freedom.

According to conservatives, modern history has been in steady decline
since the Middle Ages. Corporatist conceptions of history, which view society
as composed of groups, have given way to the lonely individualist conceptions
we see today. Louis Gabriel Ambroise de Bonald promoted a feudal vision of
authority in his book *Theory of Religious and Political Power*, which proposed
a philosophy of authority and power that recognized God's sovereignty above
all else. According to Bonald, oppression consists of the transgression of one
sphere of life upon another; that freedom and autonomy of family are the
sacrosanct, supreme values of society, and as such, must be protected by means
of authority. Conservatism aims to act in accordance with the authority of
God by protecting the family, local community, economy, property, and powers of government from the hands of ideologues.

In *Democracy in America*, Alexis de Tocqueville makes a clear distinction
between the concepts of government and concepts of administration that align
with conservative thought. "The former," Tocqueville wrote, "must be strong
and unified. It is the latter that must, in the interest of liberty and order alike,
be as decentralized, localized, and generally inconspicuous as possible."[34]

Similar to Burke and Bonald, the nineteenth-century philosophers such
as Newman and Disraeli also demonstrated an aversion to ideas of individualism and natural law. They held bureaucracy in contempt, lamented the
legacy of the Revolution, and knew that "once the state begins to substitute

its own authority and distinctive pattern upon the myriad forms of society, there is no alternative to an ever-widening bureaucracy."[35]

No exercise of power and authority can exclude the masses. Tocqueville considers these masses as presenting the most significant threat to democracy, chiefly by bringing a negative leveling to the majority via a fanatic egalitarianism. Although Ortega y Gasset was the one who most deeply analyzed this in his 1929 book *Revolt of the Masses*, other well-known philosophers such as Burckhardt, Nietzsche, and Kierkegaard were also concerned with the power of the masses. If the masses view the power of the state as their own, who will check the masses? "How can the state not be total in its power and responsibility," Ortega asks, "when the population it governs has become denuded of all the forms of authority and function which once made a social organization of it?"[36]

The totalitarian state derives from the destruction of the old order, filling the vacuum that would be filled by a new order. This phenomenon caused Hitler's rise to power, a position Hannah Arendt most eloquently expresses in *The Origins of Totalitarianism*.

Liberty and Equality

The tension between equality and liberty is one of the most important underlying principles of conservative thought. The ends of each are seemingly irreconcilable:

> The abiding purpose of liberty is its protection of individual and family property—a word used in its widest sense to include the immaterial as well as the material life. The inherent objective of equality, on the other hand, is that of some kind of redistribution or leveling of the unequally shared material and immaterial values of a community. Moreover, individual strengths of mind and body being different from birth, all efforts to compensate through law and government for this diversity of strengths can only cripple the liberties of those involved; especially the liberties of the strongest and the most brilliant.[37]

When Burke compares the French and American Revolutions, he explains that while the American Revolution was born from the desire for freedom, the French Revolution was born from the desire for equality. The French saw tyranny as a potential tool for their aim; the Americans identified and fought against it. As the Frenchman Rousseau wrote in his *Social Contract*, to obtain freedom, one must "strike off the chains"—and those include the chains of possessions and rights. Interestingly, the main victims of the French Revolution were not individuals, but groups—communities, guilds, associations, classes—that functioned as the intermediates between single individuals and the state. Without these groups, individuals were left to face the state alone.

Conservatives are therefore aware of the need for societal inequality. Without inequality, social and familial orders cannot be maintained; not all relationships can be of equal rank if we are to experience a variety of meaningful relations. Burke synthesizes this concept with an aphorism: "Believe me, Sir, those who attempt to level, never equalize." In modern times, we see the push toward equality grows stronger and stronger, but it is actually natural and good that man has a hierarchy above him, which reaches its peak in God. In his work *Recollections*, Tocqueville dedicates much attention to this, highlighting how the desire for equality provokes envy, greed, and resentment that eventually manifests in revolutions.

Property and Life

In *Reflections*, Burke describes Jacobins as enemies of private property, because they use the state to appropriate property. He criticizes the Jacobin approach of invasive politics, which uses an increasingly dynamic government to intervene economically, socially, and morally in the private lives of the people, as opposed to a *laissez-faire* approach.

Conservatives consider property to be part of the human spirit. It represents superiority in the natural world; therefore, property is rendered almost sacred. Hearkening back to Roman law, the concept of family is equated to that of property, and the role of the family represents such an essential element of conservative thought that Tocqueville thought "the death of primogeniture and entail, to be replaced by 'equal participation of property,'" could have only one result: "the intimate connection is destroyed between family feeling and the preservation of the paternal estate; the property ceases to represent the family."[38]

As highlighted by Russell Kirk, economic leveling does not equate to progress, and property separated from private possession—and from freedom—is worthless. Once again, attention is drawn to the importance of the intermediary groups of society: family, church, and neighborhood all play an essential role. Their defeat by centralized, state-funded social assistance would cause the individual to be discriminated against; the state must be the glue, the bond that holds various organizations together by property, not bureaucracy. Otherwise the human element of governance is lost.

Conservatives have historically criticized socialism, capitalism, trade, and technology; but interestingly enough, the criticisms of capitalism are even sharper than the criticisms of Marxist socialists:

> In France, the conservatives, with Bonald leading the way, saw commerce, industry, and large cities as just as subversive of "constituted" society as the natural rights doctrines of the Jacobins. In an interesting essay on the comparative effects upon the family and neighborhood of rural and urban life, Bonald rejected the latter on the ground that it increased the social distance between individuals, loosened the bonds of marriage and family, and gave a moneyed character to all life that was not present in a landed-agrarian rural society. In traditional society, Bonald stressed, the very nature of work required an unconscious strengthening of family and cooperation among people.[39]

Charles Maurras's consideration of capitalism is even more extreme; he considers it, along with socialism and radical democracy, to be the reason for the end of traditional society.

Religion and Morality

From a conservative perspective, religion represents a fundamental aspect of the state and society, and recognizing the authority of the church is just as important as governmental and social order.

Conservatism is unique among major political ideologies in its emphasis upon church and the Judeo-Christian morality. All of the early conservatives, and no one more deeply than Burke, were horrified by the Jacobin blows to the Church in France.[40]

Bonald credits Catholicism with a primary role in his book *Theory of Political and Religious Power*, particularly the Catholic Church's return to autonomy during the pre-revolutionary period. Lamennais is even more forthright: without a Catholic state religion, Europe would have dissolved into the obscurity of atheism.

In Kaltenbrunner's book *Der schwierige Konservatismus*, he writes that although a Christian minority of conservatives remained in Germany during the Weimar Republic, most moved away from official positions of the church. "Due to this march by a large part of official churches and important theologians leading toward the shores of current leftist mentality, toward the *cliché* of the latest trend, today we find ourselves in the middle of fundamental ideological-political change," he writes.[41]

With this in mind, we can see how the separation of some conservatives from Christianity is not necessarily linked to a change in the conservative's viewpoints, but rather a change in the church's viewpoints:

The radical lack of orientation and guidance in our society, with its incapable establishment of authority, the disoriented mass media and the fixation of that which is currently fashionable, is not criticized by the church.... The churches and theologians do not denounce (as would be their duty) the psychosocial intoxication of our society, operated by distributors of the system and all the slander of all of those who do not understand themselves in a complicated society.... The churches do not recall our attention to the systematic worship of the obscurantism and the intolerance that flourishes in our schools, on the abstract and scholarly arrogance that reigns in them.... The church, becoming prey of the *Zeitgeist*, does not warn against the deadly sins of society: the ruthless principle of competition and performance, the genetic decadence and the demolition of tradition.[42]

It has become increasingly difficult to find conservative standpoints in the church that counterbalance the mass, liberal, industrial society.

The modern-day conservative then attempts, often without the help of the church, to defend rights and freedoms against totalitarianism. This defense can be found in the limits that conservatism places on the progress of democratic ideas devoid of reason, and in the distance it takes from all that is associated with the Enlightenment:

> The critical conservative stance has its natural and legitimate function within the "dialect of the Enlightenment." In the actions of the fathers of critical theory, it sees the destruction of the Enlightenment progress—in the alarming image of leveling in the East and West, in the "cautious relationship" of Western capitalism just as in the doctrine of socialism, approved as the religion of the state and founded on the presumed possible liberation from all alienation.[43]

At the center of the Enlightenment was a science, designed as an exact theory, that aimed to free mankind from so-called prejudices, customs, and traditions—all considered essential by conservatives. Conservatives contested then and contest today the leveling of society, which is particularly evident in universities where the democratization of teaching methods has reduced quality in favor of diffused mediocrity and egalitarianism, which leads to envy. In 1796, Gracchus Babeuf orchestrated a conspiracy against the French government, the "Directory." Historically known as the "conspiracy of the equals," its objective was to abolish private property and eliminate social differences among men. The plot, though it failed, nevertheless preceded certain prerogatives that would later spread throughout society in the years following:

> It was also expressed in its cultural politics, which did not tolerate superiority in the spiritual or moral aspect. Reading, writing, and

arithmetic had to be sufficient: to the conspirators, this seemed like the most reliable way to guarantee social equality. Thus, resentment against spiritual autonomy and moral superiority would be appeased, simultaneously preventing the birth of an elite that could have endangered the position of the elements that dominate in the name of equality.[44]

Envy is born from the need to discredit anything that reminds a person of his own inferiority, based on the mere fact of its existence. "It is not so much external goods that provoke similar passions in the most vigorous way, but rather the personal values, such as beauty, personality, intelligence, or artistic creativity, values that cannot simply be taken away from others to appropriate them...."[45]

In this way, egalitarianism generates a leveling down of society, in which no individuals with strong qualities have an advantage. To those who would like to have such qualities but do not possess them, however, egalitarianism is certainly advantageous.

Types of Conservatism

The myriad of standpoints among conservatives tends to impede the creation of precise classifications and demarcations. Nevertheless, we will try to identify and sort out a few important categories.

The main differences among conservatives exist in an economic context. Fiscal conservatives follow similar principles to liberalism in that they advocate for reduced government spending and a balanced budget. They also call for the privatization, deregulation of the economy in favor of a self-regulating free market, and reducing public debt and taxes.

In *Reflections on the Revolution in France*, Burke argues that the state does not have the right to accumulate large amounts of debt and then place the burden on taxpayers by increasing taxes.

In the UK, Margaret Thatcher applied fiscally conservative principles to UK policies, balancing the budget through strict spending cuts. The true birthplace of fiscal conservatism, however, is the United States. While American fiscal conservatism reached its peak during the Reagan administration, it was during the twentieth century that Herbert Hoover opposed Franklin Roosevelt's New Deal, calling for government intervention in the economy.

As fiscal conservatism is primarily widespread in the UK and US, so is *libertarian conservatism*. Its defining qualities consist of a combination of libertarian economic principles and conservative cultural principles, often coinciding with right-libertarian policy, based on a free market and limited government. The main difference between left-wing and right-wing liberalism lies in the varying conceptions of collective ownership opposed by right-leaning liberals. These stances were found in a key conservative American figure: Barry Goldwater. He expresses these ideas in his book *The Conscience of a Conservative*.

Aligning almost perfectly with the values of modern society, the exponents of this form of conservatism aspire to economic freedom and base their ideas on Locke, Smith, and Mill, whose main reference was Friedrich von Hayek.

The social stances of *liberal conservatism*, on the other hand, are more closely related to progressivism than traditional conservatism. But this branch of conservatism lines up primarily with classic fiscal conservatism, because it prioritizes the protection of the free market and private property. Liberal conservatism is prevalent throughout countries in which the liberal concept of economy is considered integral and therefore worth conserving.

While liberal conservatives tend toward progressive social viewpoints, *social conservatives* take positions against same-sex marriage, abortion, and euthanasia, and also believe in the increase of "zero tolerance" policies for infractions of the law. They also uphold standards of social justice and, from an economic perspective, favor egalitarianism. Although conservatives are not necessarily Christian, the egalitarian stances of social conservatives put them in close connection to Christian socialists.

In considering the relationship between Christianity and social conservatism, the distinction between Christian and non-Christian conservatives must be made, although both groups contribute to the protection of the Christian traditions of Western civilization.

There are thinkers, who can be defined as Christian atheists or "Christianists," who defend Christian values insofar as they are the foundation of the
Western world and are taken for granted at a time in which secularization and
Islam are increasingly pronounced. Therefore, the protection of Christianity
can be considered as a kind of conservatism, due to the awareness that a lack
of Christian values could lead to the vanishing of traditional European civilization. Christianity is worth conserving.

Prominent European Christianists include Italian journalist Oriana Fal-
laci, who represented herself as a "Christian atheist," and Christianist forerun-
ner Charles Maurras, who considered himself an *athée catolique*.

National conservatism, on an entirely different note, is a conservative
variant based on nationalist stances that clash with multiculturalism, unlim-
ited immigration, and globalization. While concepts of country and national
identity are important to every type of conservatism, national conservatism
is distinct in that these concepts are placed at the very center of the doctrine.
Thus, family plays a preeminent role in identity, along with religious, cultural,
and linguistic traditions. When compared to every other type of conservatism,
national conservatism varies the most from one country to another. This is,
of course, because every nation is characterized by different traditions, so a
variety of stances emerge, particularly in economics. Some thinkers and
politicians want to be part of a free economy; others want major intervention
by the state; others still desire a mixed economy.

One-nation conservatism is a British political conservatism originating
with Benjamin Disraeli, who coined the expression "one-nation Tory" and
achieved a number of social reforms during his time as prime minister. Disraeli initially expressed his form of conservatism in his novels *Sybil* (or *The
Two Nations*) and *Coningsby* (or *The New Generation*), in which he distances
himself from the individualism that dominated contemporary society in favor
of a system based on social obligations among all classes. In *How to Be a
Conservative*, Scruton defines one-nation conservatism (also known as "Tory
Democracy") as a form of conservatism that "sees society in an organic perspective and appreciates paternalism and pragmatism."[46]

One-nation conservatism is directed toward the working class. Each
citizen has an obligation to his or her fellow citizens, and the elite social classes

have a paternal responsibility to the inferior classes. Everyone has a social obligation. This organic model is based more on hierarchy than egalitarianism, since the duties of privileged classes are greater than those of the less privileged. Disraeli's political philosophy borrows from the French concept *noblesse oblige*, the "obligations of nobility." Disraeli feared the widening social gap, so he promoted social reforms organized around the working class and emphasized that dominant classes must recognize the suffering and poor conditions of weaker members of society. The connecting power of obligations, he hoped, would unify the country.

One of the most important legal acts was the Employers and Workmen Act of 1875, which regulated the relationship between workers and employers, rendering both more equal in the eyes of the law. This was one attempt to unify peoples of different classes. The Conspiracy and Protection of Property Act was another one, guaranteeing one's right to picket without being accused of conspiracy. These acts went beyond theoretical knowledge—following the historic Reform Act in 1867, which gave the working class the right to vote, Disraeli knew that in order to win elections, the Conservative Party needed to continue to be more open to social reforms. It was not enough to criticize liberal individualism; laws must be passed in order to bring about true unity.

Around the end of the nineteenth century in England, conservatism underwent an evolution that caused economic stances to be abandoned for a more liberal economic approach. During the two world conflicts, one-nation stances were restored, for fear that Communism would be diffused across the Channel. These one-nation standpoints remained at the center of the Conservative Party until Margaret Thatcher came to power in the 1970s and the New Right political movement, which considered welfare policies to be one of the causes of societal decline, began to take center stage in the party.

While one-nation conservatism is considered an English experience, *neo-conservatism* originated and developed in the United States with Ronald Reagan's presidency. While this form of conservatism shares ties with liberal conservatism, the two viewpoints diverge from an economic perspective, as neo-conservatism opposes government intervention in the economy.

In 2004, Adam Wolfson wrote an article for *The Public Interest* in which he states:

Generally, the neoconservative label has been applied to a particular group of intellectuals who moved from what might be
called a neo-liberal politics in the 1960s and 1970s to what became
known as neoconservatism. It now seems more likely that something like neoconservatism represents a natural conservative
response to modernity, at least in America, one with its own distinctive qualities, its own style and substance, its own strengths
and weaknesses.[47]

Wolfson goes on to explain the distinction between the three types of
conservatism: traditionalism, libertarianism, and neoconservatism, with three
different "ideologies" attributed to Burke, Hayek, and Tocqueville, respectively:

Those of us who regret much of modern American life and find
solace in old, inherited ways will cling to traditionalism. Others,
who celebrate the new freedoms and new technologies, will turn
to libertarianism. As for those who see in modernity admirable
principles but also worrisome tendencies, their persuasion will be
neoconservatism.[48]

Neoconservatives do not long for a pre-industrial, pre-Enlightenment era.
They consider the appeal to tradition, at least in the case of the United States,
to be useless and unneeded. Neocons believe that traditions and customs of the
past have little effect on a democratic population; they therefore believe it is
necessary to value and protect democracy before these other things. Neoconservatives have their own characteristics and prerogatives:

Contrary to general impression, neoconservatism never was sub-
sumed into a broader conservative intellectual movement. This
was in fact unlikely to happen, since neoconservatism represents
less a mere reaction against the 1960s counter-culture than a
recurrent conservative impulse in our democratic age, perhaps its
most vital. Conservatism's other strands are strangely anti-democratic. Traditionalists pine for aristocracy; libertarians look to

limited government technocracy; while paleoconservatives dream vaguely of postmodern utopias.[49]

The defining quality of neoconservatism is the belief in using military force in foreign policy to "export democracy" or take down dictatorial regimes. This deviates from the maxims of conservativism that uphold the protection of popular sovereignty. As denoted by the "neo" prefix, neoconservatism is defined by its innovative positions that often disassociate it from traditional conservativism; it can be defined as a doctrine in its own right. As an almost exclusively American school of thought—with the exception of individual personalities in Europe who also have diverging stances from traditional conservatism—we will not take the opportunity to analyze this further, though interested readers are encouraged to delve into *Neoconservatism: The Autobiography of an Idea* by Irving Kristol, published in 1995.

Another form of conservatism, mostly unique to the United States, is *paleoconservatism* (the "Old Right"). With Pat Buchanan as its most important political figure, paleocons are opposed to neoconservatives economically and politically. They also break from traditional conservatives by completely despairing of the contemporary American lifestyle. Buchanan expressed economic ideas against the free market and globalization; socially, he opposed immigration; and in foreign policy, he argued for the isolationism of the United States. Paleocons are not generally cheerful:

> Unlike traditionalists, the paleocons contend that we have become irrevocably cut off from a living, sustainable tradition. In their view, the acids of modernity have left us entirely disinherited from old customs and ways, and conservatism's project of conservation is but a glittering illusion.[50]

Paul Gottfried's book *The Search for Historical Meaning* is useful in understanding paleoconservative thought. "Paleocons" borrowed their ideas from the Founding Fathers, who supported ideas of neutrality in foreign policy. Their aversion to the neoconservative stance on foreign policy is due to their understanding and disapproval of the neocon's aim to create an

American global empire matrix, with particular influence in the Middle East, while also favoring Israel's interests.

Anti-Communist sentiment is central to the paleocon's ideas for two main reasons: one, they consider Communism to be against both Western order and political freedom, and two, they consider Communism to be a consequence of the French Revolution. In their book *The Conservative Movement*, Thomas Fleming and Paul Gottfried write that paleoconservatives are the number one opponents of neoconservatives—even more so than liberals or progressives. Nevertheless, both neocons and paleocons, unlike traditionalists, believe that the past is no longer salvable. Both groups look to the future for answers:

> The complaint about the loss of tradition drives paleoconservatives to search for new gods, new heroes, and new myths. They are full of contempt for that which they consider the democratic ideals of equality and well-being, they do not try to save democracy from itself, but rather try to accelerate its collapse, thus opening the way to a new post-modern and post-democratic era. On the contrary, neo-conservatives intend to give life to the founding principles of America and democratic lifestyle. They are perfectly aware of the defects of democracy (its often low aspirations and its alienating tendencies), but they also recognize the fundamental justice of democratic equality. Neoconservatives try to guarantee authentic freedom and human dignity in the era in which we live, the democratic era, and not in a futurist utopia.[51]

The Differences between Reactionaries and Conservatives

In his *Manifesto dei Conservatori*, Giuseppe Prezzolini writes:

> First of all, the True Conservative will be careful not to be confused with reactionaries, retrogrades, traditionalists, and nostalgics, because the True Conservative "maintains to continue," and does not wish to go back and redo failed experiments. The

True Conservative knows that new problems require new solutions, inspired by permanent principles.[52]

The differences between conservatives and traditionalists are based on different ways of interpreting history. Karl Mannheim provides a synthesis of these differences in his book *Conservatism: A Contribution to the Sociology of Knowledge*:

> By virtue of its formally specifiable quasi-reactive nature, traditionalist action has no history, or at least none that can be clearly traced. 'Conservatism,' in contrast, refers to a *continuity, historically and sociologically comprehensible, which has arisen in a specific sociological and historical situation and which develops in direct conjunction with living history.* That traditionalism and conservatism are different phenomena, and that conservatism first arises in a specific socio-historical situation, is already indicated by its language, the most reliable guide to history.[53]

Traditionalists, as their name suggests, focus more on tradition than history; conservatives wish for a society based on the history of a people in order to preserve its customs:

> The relationship with history is the crux of Prezzolinian conservatism. History must be evaluated because useful teachings for the present can be gathered from it, but the meaning of history also has a unifying value: we are a nation, country, community because there is a past that unifies us.[54]

The difference between conservatives and reactionaries must also be noted here:

> First and foremost, a conservative should not be reactionary, or rather one who thinks of turning back to past social solutions....

> A conservative is realistic and is opposed to anyone who dreams
> of political, social, or economic solutions that have never been
> tried in and true to reality. The past belongs to history.[55]

Unlike reactionaries, conservatives do not wish for a complete and per-
functory return to the past. Instead, they look toward the future with the
understanding that there are institutions from the past that must be "conserved." As Gerd-Klaus Kaltenbrunner wrote in *Der schwierige Konservatismus*, a conservative is "ready to faithfully conserve that which history has
passed on and to cope with innovation without panicking, and can be seen
as the true revolutionary of the times, as opposed to the purported ones."[56]

Conservatism is a cultural-political current that can be embedded within
the Right. In his book *The Right Wing in France from 1815 to de Gaulle*, René
Rémond identifies three divisions: the traditional Right, the conservative liberal Right, and the nationalist Right. Claudio Quarantotto, alongside Prezzolini in his book *Intervista sulla destra*, defines a classification of various
people on the Right with a dutiful premise:

> the classification of a writer (or thinker or politician) among con-
> servatives, reactionaries, or even revolutionaries is debatable, both
> because the limits between these Rights are uncertain, the ideas
> of these limits are confused, and because the transfer, evolution,
> or involution of writers and politicians from one Right to another
> is far from rare.[57]

These classifications include: right-wing conservatives, right-wing elites,
right-wing nationalists, right-wing reactionaries, right-wing revolutionaries,
the historical Right and right-wing traditionalists.

Right-wing reactionaries originated in opposition to innovations introduced by the French Revolution. In time, they took on a broader meaning
and opposed reforms and innovations, adopting a general hostility to progress. Counterrevolutionaries who pushed for a return to monarchy were
reactionaries, whose school of thought was compiled in Ploncard d'Assac's

book *La Réaction*, and is summarized in Panfilo Gentile's presentation of the Italian edition:

> There are eras in history in which one can only go forward by going back. These are the eras of decadence, in which a supposedly acquired civilization unravels before our dismayed eyes. When an organism begins to decay, nothing can be constructed from its miasmas. One must start from the beginning, going back and recuperating that which was lost. Therefore, today's progress can only be reaction. The only way to be progressive is to be reactionary.[58]

Ploncard d'Assac, pupil of Charles Maurras and Édouard Drumont and adherent to Action Française and the French Popular Party, moved to Portugal and became Salazar's advisor, for whom he also wrote a biography. His most well-known books are *La Réaction*, published by Edizioni del Borghese in 1970, and *Doctrines du nationalism*.

While discussing totalitarian democracy, d'Assac cites *The Origins of Totalitarian Democracy* by Jacob L. Talmon:

> In the past, ideas mattered little in political change. Deeply rooted respect for traditions and precedents worked for stability and continuity...but the replacement of tradition by abstract reason, ideology, and doctrine has become important. Ideologies came to the fore; ideas had reached the masses.[59]

Talmon credits philosophers for the diffusion of revolutionary ideas. Revolutionaries, thanks to the works of philosophers of the time, perceived the nation as a collective entity whose primary public enemy was the "common spirit," or rather, the interests of guilds and civil societies that laid claim to a situation different than the one nationally assigned. Jacobins wanted to single-handedly embody the will of the people without sharing the power with the people.

Society had regulated itself through the laws of experience. But with the changes following the French Revolution, ideological conceptions were introduced into daily life. These upheavals disrupted the societal structure, and Ploncard D'Assac took up what Rivarol had already affirmed in his prediction of the consequences: socialism and the emancipation of the colonies.

Moeller van den Bruck believes reactionaries to be the degenerate form of conservatives. From his counterrevolutionary perspective, reactionaries, who position themselves in opposition to the revolution, are actually causes of revolution itself. Their aprioristic negation of innovation serves to provoke an upheaval of revolutionary forces—forces accepted by conservatives, who simultaneously uphold tradition while respecting innovations of the day. According to van den Bruck, the reactionary's opposition of the revolution risks significant harm and is counterproductive. Nevertheless, commonalities between conservatives and reactionaries are undeniable:

> It can therefore be said, to enclose Moeller's thought in a formula, that a conservative is one who uses redefined objectives of reaction (no longer turning to the past, but rather, with the purpose of conserving that which will always be valuable, thinking independently of time) and makes sure to achieve them in the same newly created context following a revolutionary break. To reactionaries, he says: it's true that a principle of permanence must be affirmed in human and social institutions, but this does not mean that one becomes rigid in unyielding rejection of change. New configurations can easily serve the same objectives of conservation, especially at times in which conserving is only possible through innovation.[60]

Although in common understanding the terms conservative, reactionary, and restorer are used synonymously, there are substantial differences between these schools of thought, beginning with the different conceptions of history:

A conservative looks for a balance between tradition and innovation, and opposes progress that breaks historical continuity. A restorer views history as circular, not as linear. And he does not take change seriously. That which is important and vital is the past, the original moments full of meaning. Finally, a reactionary, like a revolutionary, has almost no relationship with the past. He does not want to know anything about his possible development or even of his past: he wants to stop the present and, if anything, perfect it as a definitive social order that ends history.[61]

Louis de Bonald, a Catholic monarchist, is recognized as one of the counterrevolutionary reactionaries. He is the highest representative of the "ultra-royalists." "Ultra," in this sense, refers to those who, during the restoration in France, wished for a return to an absolute monarchy with powers attributed to the king of the pre-revolutionary period.

In his writings, Bonald attacks the framework that arose after the French Revolution and distances himself from works such as *The Social Contract*, by Rousseau, and the *Declaration of the Rights of the Man and of the Citizen of 1789* on which the new society was founded. Included with Bonald in this vein of thought, albeit with a divergent stance, is Joseph de Maistre. Beyond wishing for a return to the *ancien régime*, Maistre supported the creation of a theocratic government, because he thought the monarchy was divinely inspired.

Prezzolini explains his idea of conservative culture:

Our greatest conservative is Cuoco. He was not just a writer, or worse, Burke's translator. He was the one who taught me that constitutions and laws must respect the character and not contradict the history of the people. They are not goods to be exported at will, good for every country and at any time. Not all nations, for example, are suitable for parliamentary democracy, which is the creation of certain people and gives positive results for them alone.[62]

He proceeds to precisely outline the nature of conservatives and conservation:

> Conservation is common to different religions, societies, and nations because it is not simply a party; before being a party, a movement, it is a structure of the human mind.... Change is the exception; indeed, biologists consider it an "error"...conservation is a vital instinct.[63]

He considers a true conservative different from reactionaries, nostalgics, and traditionalists:

> [The conservative's] end is to "continue maintaining," not repeating failed or depleted experiences. He knows there must be new answers to new problems, inspired by permanent principles. He therefore considers himself a restorer of eternal laws. He does not refuse changes, because he knows how fragile every human organization is and how much effort previous generations put in to be able to create a regime of collaboration and reciprocal respect among men. And, therefore, before changing any social organism, a conservative holds true that he must think seriously, two times, three times, and then perhaps after thinking it over three times, do nothing.[64]

The nature of conservatism consists of maintaining permanent institutions, found in every society and era. A conservative respects that which is natural, including natural inequality, and favors individuality as an essential ideological principle. Being conservative means opposing erratically researched innovation and progress; "in the name of revolutions, whether social, technical, or industrial, mankind has dissipated Earth's resources. We must turn to remedies, conserving that which can still be conserved. Ecology means conservation: conservation of the environment in which mankind lives, to be able to conserve mankind."[65] This is why a conservative society is not equivalent to—and indeed, is a valid alternative for—the consumerist society we live in today.

The difference between reactionaries and conservatives lies in the different ways they approach the past. While a reactionary wants to return to the past by restoring previous forms of government and, with them, all the customs and dynamics that regulated that society, a conservative does not aim to conserve the entire past. Rather, conservatives aim to conserve "the natural and fundamental elements of society, which are: private property, family, the homeland, and even religion... the right-wing conservative is such not because he wants to conserve any regime and any institutions, but rather specific institutions and particular values."

The Differences between Conservatives, Liberals, and Libertarians

Today, there is much confusion and sometimes misidentification of two distinct doctrines: liberalism and conservatism. Certain commonalities between the two are sure to be unmentioned or forgotten, whereas differences between them are substantial, undeniable, and often spoken of.

To understand the differences between conservatives and liberals, one must begin with the origin of the term "liberal," which first entered political discourse in 1812 with the Cádiz Cortes, the Spanish assembly that promulgated the constitution during the final year of the Spanish War of Independence. At this time, conservative and liberal stances were already dissociated: conservatives were in favor of maintaining an absolute monarchy, whereas liberals accepted the "Constitution of Bayonne" drafted during Napoleon's domination, with some liberal modifications.

Liberalism, as written by Giuseppe Bedeschi in *Storia del pensiero liberale*, is "a doctrine that affirms the limit of power of the state in the name of individual natural rights, inherent in every man."[66]

A clear first difference emerges from this definition: both conservatism and liberalism believe in the importance of freedom, but while liberals consider freedom *the* main value for men, conservatives consider it to be *one* of the values.

Another important distinction can be found in conceptions of the individual. Liberals place individuals, and therefore individualism, at the forefront; without individualism (opposed to any form of organicism), liberalism does not exist. Conservatives, on the other hand, put community at the center. They share the same ideas about limits on the power of the state, but their ideas on how to limit that power are different. Conservatives highlight the value of intermediate bodies, whereas liberals highlight the individual.

Furthermore, as affirmed by Norberto Bobbio, "for that which regards philosophical principles, liberalism is the expression of rational individualism, of the Enlightenment philosophy, for which man as a rational being is a person, and has an absolute value, before and independently from relationships of interaction with his peers."[67]

These words synthesize the irreconcilability between conservatives and liberals: conservatives refuse and oppose rationalist philosophy and all that derives from the Enlightenment. The birth of modern liberal democracies occurred in contrast to the typical values of conservatism, through the progressive erosion of the absolute power of the king, the monarchy, and the elimination of traditional forms of government and society. Liberal democracies also brought about the elimination of intermediate bodies that protected the individual from the state—a main trait of conservatism. Differences between the two doctrines also surfaced during the French Revolution. While conservatives markedly condemned the Revolution, so much so that conservative thought originated in opposition to its innovations, liberals were divided between evaluations of the event. Approval prevailed for the first revolutionary phase, but there was also condemnation of the Jacobin deviation and terror. Nonetheless, liberals considered the Revolution to be a good thing, not only because liberty and equality prevailed, but also because the hereditary castes and society based on privilege were abolished: "First it was a political revolution, which abolished the caste division and the privileges connected to it, making all men equal under the law; after, it became a social revolution aimed at the abolition of private property and at substantial equality."[68]

In Italy, as noted by Anthony Louis Marasco in his article "Sono i liberali conservatori?," the Liberal Party's culture did not spread, due to the presence of the church:

> While in the United States the mainline Protestant Church, secularizing itself, placed itself at the center by becoming liberal, in Italy, the Catholic Church placed itself at the center through the Christian Democracy, a party that never completely became liberal. The difference between the two centers is therefore quite pronounced. The American political system was born from the rigid division between church and state, and the mainline Protestant Church, in becoming secularized, could only respect this division. The Italian political system was never able to put liberals at the center because the Catholic Church is not, has never been, and cannot be, liberal. It is either conservative or socialist, depending on whether it follows the letter or the sense of the Gospel. In Italy, liberal Catholics have always been an intellectual minority with little political weight.[69]

Both liberals and conservatives theorize about "minimum state" and contrast the centralization of the powers of the central government. Thinkers such as Alexis de Tocqueville, especially in his most important work *Democracy in America*, implement a series of critiques of democratic society:

> On one hand, the tyranny of the masses and the conformity of the masses (a new, powerful Leviathan); on the other hand, political-administrative centralization. They seem to be two substantially different phenomena, but, upon closer inspection, are deeply connected, and make up two faces (similar and converging) of the same reality.[70]

To avoid a degenerating democracy, Tocqueville advocated for the realization of a decentralized administration that favors local self-government. He highlighted the importance of the freedom of the press and believed freedom to be the main value according to which men must act. In order to protect freedom, the administrative autonomy of local entities, including municipalities and counties, must be guaranteed because:

> Each person is the best judge of what concerns himself alone, and the one most able to provide for his individual needs. So the town and county are charged with looking after their special interests. The state governs and does not administer. Exceptions to this principle are found, but not a contrary principle.[71]

Tocqueville was aware of the importance of a strong central political power, but at the same time, he knew that if this power were to be united with the administrative power, it would limit the possibility of civil society. Centralization necessarily eliminates intermediary bodies, and consequently suppresses a civil society's autonomy, weakening those secondary powers that, historically, have been the link between the state and its citizens.

Tocqueville identified another important problem in democracy when he spoke of the "tyranny of the masses": the absolute rule of the masses offers little to no guarantees to those who hold the minority opinion:

> The moral dominion of the majority is based in part on the idea that there is more enlightenment and wisdom in many men combined than in one man alone, more in number than in choice of legislators. It is the theory of equality applied to minds. The doctrine attacks the pride of man in its last refuge.[72]

The power of the majority is therefore comparable to a tyranny. Unlike the old absolutist regime that exercised material power over the people, the power of the majority reaches the will and the spirit. Democratic despotism uses spiritual violence rather than physical chains, executioners, and material violence:

> Under the absolute government of one man, despotism, to reach
> the soul, crudely struck the body; and the soul, escaping from
> these blows, rose gloriously above it; but in democratic republics,
> tyranny does not proceed in this way; it leaves the body alone and
> goes right to the soul. The master no longer says: you will think
> like me or die; he says: you are free not to think as I do; your life,
> your goods, everything remains with you; but from this day on,
> you are a stranger among us.... Go in peace; I spare your life, but
> I leave you a life worse than death.[73]

In order to prevent democratic tyranny from prevailing, administrative decentralization must be favored by lawmakers who, by protecting order and authority, restrain popular government.

The inherent risk of a democratic society is that it could be transformed into a society in which the citizens identify with the masses by imposing common opinion on every citizen, generating a new despotism that eliminates authority of the spirit and diminishes creativity. In *Democracy in America*, Tocqueville establishes a critique of mass society. It is devoid of original ideas, subscribing to conformity: "The men of democratic centuries love general ideas, because they exempt them from studying particular cases; they contain, if I can express myself in this way, many things within a small volume, and in little time, produce a great result."[74]

A leveling is therefore achieved in the opinions of men, generating such homogenization that anyone with an original thought is marginalized. An equality that exalts materialism, denies spirituality, and favors self-importance and individualism unites with social uniformity to generate the prerogatives of a democratic society where equality becomes more important than freedom.

To avoid the prevalence of a homologous society and to favor a plurality of opinions, Tocqueville highlights the importance of the freedom of the press as "the remedy for most of the evils produced by equality."[75]

Robert Nisbet analyzes the relationship between conservatives and libertarians in his essay titled "Conservatives and Libertarians: Uneasy Cousins."

Spartaco Pupo, a professor at the University of Calabria in Italy, echoes his ideas in a recently published book. Both share a "common dislike of the intervention of government, especially national, centralized government, in the economic, social, political, and intellectual lives of citizens," and both doctrines oppose state control and protect freedom.[76]

However, the differences are more evident than the similarities and, especially in recent years, the gap has widened further, making it such that "by and by, it will be impossible, I would guess, for the phrases 'libertarian-conservative' and 'conservative-libertarian' to be other than oxymoronic."[77]

The first difference is in the conception of the population. Conservatives consider the population to be "composed of not individuals directly, but the natural groups within which individuals invariably live: family, locality, church, region, social class, nation, and so on."[78] Individuals are considered parts of groups or social identities broken up by the French Revolution. Conservatives consider extreme individualism a threat to the social order and freedom; individualism, taken to extremes, pulverizes society into an indefinite number of particles, making it impossible to protect natural rights. "Unlike liberalism, conservatism gives stress to *social authority*, recognizing that apart from the check supplied upon the moral and social lives of individuals, any genuine political freedom is impossible."[79]

Libertarians put the individual at the center of society, and they develop "a state of mind... in which the coercions of family, church, local community, and school will seem almost as inimical to freedom as those of the political government. If so, this will most certainly widen the gulf between libertarians and conservatives."[80]

Conservatives consider authority essential to the protection of order in every sphere of society: familial (parent-child), religious (priest-communicant) and working (master-apprentice). A network constituted by different forms of authority in various spheres of human relationships is therefore created, and it is thanks to the protection of authority that individual freedom can be defined and preserved. By contrast, libertarians view authority extended to different sectors as a constraint on creativity and the free spirit of the individual. Nisbet cites a few traditional societies founded on the principle of authority, such as Athens in the fifth century BC, Augustan Rome, and the Age of King Louis XIV, in which authors, thinkers, artists, and true geniuses flourished. This is confirmed by Shakespeare: "Take but degree away, untune that string, and hark! what discord follows; each thing meets in mere oppugnancy."[81]

Conservatives and libertarians distinguish themselves from each other most definitely in their conceptions of freedom:

> For libertarians, individual freedom, in almost every conceivable domain, is the *highest of all social* values—irrespective of what forms and levels of moral, aesthetic, and spiritual debasement may prove to be the unintended consequences of such freedom. For the conservative, on the other hand, freedom, while important, is but *one of several necessary values* in the good or just society, and [freedom] not only may but should be restricted when such freedom shows signs of weakening or endangering national security, of doing violence to the moral order and the social fabric.[82]

Even the interpretation of Burke's work is contested among libertarians and conservatives. While Burke is recognized as the father of conservatism, his works also include stances that could be defined as liberal. Mauro Lenci, in the online journal *Bollettino telematico di filosofia politica*, dedicated an explicative essay to the topic, titled "Liberale o conservatore? I tentativi novecenteschi di fornire una interpretazione coerente di Burke." It must be said, though, that conservatives borrow much of their conception of freedom from Burke:

> Individual liberty, Burke argued—and it remains the conservative thesis to this day—is only possible within the context of a plurality of social authorities, of moral codes, and of historical traditions, all of which, in organic articulation, serve at one and the same time as "the inns and resting places" of the human spirit and intermediary barriers to the power of the state over the individual.[83]

According to conservatives, there is a major risk in any society, especially the contemporary one, that the authorities of family, religion, and local community will not only be questioned but also eliminated in favor of imaginary freedom. People are left with a loss of social references; the result is chaos. The primary mistake made by libertarians in their understanding of authority derives from the lack of differentiation between the authority of a centralized bureaucratic government and the authority of the family, school, and local community, otherwise known as "intermediary bodies."

Chapter Two

British Conservatism

Although the French writer Chatéaubriand was the first to use the term "conservative," the true birth of conservatism came about with the publication of Edmund Burke's book *Reflections on the Revolution in France*. Though Burke was actually born in Dublin, he and other British thinkers had an essential influence on the Tory Party's definition of conservatism. Burke himself first belonged to the Whig Party, but his conclusions on the experience of the French Revolution were taken from and validated the leading exponents of the Tory Party.

But British conservatism differs from French conservatism; no revolution overturned the entire British society (at least on their soil). British conservatism does not view the French Revolution in the same way it views the American Revolution. Burke considered the American Revolution to be a revolution carried out to *protect* a questioned way of life, whereas the French Revolution arose to *eliminate* the main structures of society.

An analysis of the works of Roger Scruton, especially *How to Be a Conservative* and *A Political Philosophy: Arguments for Conservatism*, which synthesize the main aspects of Anglo-Saxon conservative thought, is indispensable to the study and understanding of British conservatism.

Today in England, conservative culture is represented by the Conservative Party. Although it has diverged, especially in recent years, from certain conservative stances, it has protected the traditions of its society since 1834, the year its founding followed the Tory Party experience: "In England, the nucleus of the conservative party is formed by the rich aristocracy of the landowners...and by the High Church that feeds on state authority.... But the strength of conservatism is especially revealed by a more moral, historical experience."[1]

In *The Conservative Party from Peel to Churchill*, Robert Blake (1916–2003) concerned himself with the history of the British Conservative Party, highlighting its adaptability to different historical periods. Following the first edition of the book in 1970, which ended with Churchill, he expanded the book by first including Margaret Thatcher and then John Major.

In an article published in the British online newspaper The Independent, Kenneth O. Morgan defined Lord Blake as a "custodian of British Conservatism" who knew how to rewrite and redefine the history of the Conservative Party at a time when the major historians were on the left.[2] Blake also wrote a successful biography about Disraeli in 1966, described by The Independent as an essential contribution to the history of literature.[3]

Lord Hugh Cecil (1869–1956), son of Lord Robert Cecil (1830–1903) and three-time prime minister under the reign of Queen Victoria and Edward VII, also devoted himself to the study of British conservatism. In conjunction with his political activity, Cecil dedicated himself to writing and publishing the two-part book *Conservatism* in 1912. Part one consisted of an analysis of conservatism and Burke's school of thought, and part two analyzed specific themes through a conservative lens.

Another indispensable book that contributed to the deepening of conservatism in twentieth-century England was *Ideologies of Conservatism: Conservative Political Ideas in the Twentieth Century* by E. H. H. Green, which begins with the "Edwardian crisis" in the years leading up to the First World War and extends to the final years of the 1900s, with a focus on Thatcherism.

Green's book begins with an analysis of the economic politics of conservative leader Arthur Balfour (1848–1930) and the debate in the Conservative Party on tariff reform, intended to protect British businesses in the empire by creating a "trade preference." In the fifth chapter, Green breaks from his economic analysis and focuses on the development of "Conservative book clubs"

animated by Christina Foyle, and on the "National Book Association" promoted by Arthur Bryant. Both were important initiatives for sharing conservative schools of thought.

Another book which proves useful is *The Conservative Political Tradition
in Britain and the United States*, which, in the same way as *The Nature of the
Right: American and European Politics and Political Thought Since 1789*, has the
honor of producing a parallel analysis of British and American conservatism.

But to truly understand the reasons behind the birth of the Conservative
Party in 1834, it is necessary to retrace the political events beginning in the
final years of the seventeenth century.

With the death of George II on October 25, 1760, the crown was passed down
to George III. It was during his reign that events destined to change the course of
modern history occurred. Under the conservative government of Prime Minister
Frederick North (Lord North), the Boston Tea Party transpired on December 16,
1773. American readers will hardly need reminding, but for those who do: an
English shipload of tea was destroyed by American settlers at Griffin's Wharf,
giving life to a fight against "taxation without representation," leading to a revolt
which led to the American War of Independence. The settlers considered George
III to be a despotic ruler, a tyrant incapable of accepting concessions.

Though the Americans had just had their own revolution, they decided
not to intervene in the French Revolution. And despite pressure from Burke,
the British Empire also decided not to intervene; they waited for events to
develop. But in 1793, following the decapitation of Louis XVI, France declared
war on England. George III gave orders to Prime Minister William Pitt to
prepare for military intervention. The conflict with Napoleon represented one
of the most difficult moments for the British Empire. The risk of invasion of
England was ever more tangible and created the need to leverage a sense of
belonging in England to keep citizens united.

In 1821, George III was succeeded by George IV, whose reign was characterized by anti-Catholic positions, splendor, and ostentation from the time
of his coronation. His brother, William IV, was thankfully very different, and
his politics gained popularity.

Queen Victoria succeeded William IV following his death in 1837, and
she remained on the throne until 1901. Her reign began during the period

following the first Industrial Revolution, which brought radical changes and sanctioned the transition from a feudal and hierarchical society—very dear to conservatives—to a new society characterized by ideas, such as the "common man," typical of the contemporary world.

Queen Victoria's stances were similar to the Whig Party's, and it was no coincidence that in the early years of her reign, her mentor was Prime Minister Lord Melbourne, whose government was characterized by liberal stances. With the fall of Melbourne's government and Victoria's marriage to Prince Albert of Saxe-Coburg and Gotha in 1840, the queen shifted her political convictions to align with the Conservative Party.

The Conservative Party began as a continuation of the Tory Party, whose members—following the Reform Bill of 1832 which extended the right to vote to the middle class—gave life to "conservative associations." Two years after the first conservative government was established, Prime Minister Robert Peel announced his government program with the Tamworth Manifesto, which consisted of more laws and orders, a reform of the taxation system, and a greater importance placed on the interests of trade and industry.

But after public distrust in 1846, conservatives had to wait more than thirty years for a return to stable government. The long-awaited return happened only thanks to Benjamin Disraeli, who was prime minister for a few months in 1868, and again from 1874 to 1880. He had the honor of reorganizing the party, giving it life in 1870 at the Conservative Central Office and the National Union, which united various volunteer associations. His social policies allowed citizens to overcome class barriers and helped to reduce disparities between the rich and the poor.

In 1886, the Conservative Party joined forces with the Liberal Unionists, a faction of the Liberal Party, and was governed by Lord Salisbury (Robert Gascoyne-Cecil), elected prime minister from 1885 to 1886, 1886 to 1892, and finally from 1895 to 1902. The party was then led by Arthur Balfour until the elections of 1906, when Balfour suffered a ruinous defeat.

Conservatives did not return to power until 1915, and then only with a coalition of national unity with the liberals. Following the war, the Conservative Party governed in England (with the brief exception of the Labor government from 1929 to 1931) thanks to the work of Stanley Baldwin, who gave life to the so-called "New Conservatism."

Baldwin was succeeded by Neville Chamberlain who, due to errors made in the early years of the Second World War, lost his leadership to Winston Churchill—one of the greatest statesmen Europe had ever seen.

Despite Churchill's victory in the war, conservatives lost the elections in 1945. This allowed for a reorganization of the party, giving life to new, younger movements, such as the Young Conservatives and the Conservative Political Centre.

But an electoral victory was soon achieved in 1951, and conservatives returned to power until 1964. From that year until 1979, the Conservative Party and Labor Party governments alternated. The critical moment was the defeat of Prime Minister Edward Heath during the elections of 1974, the same year in which Margaret Thatcher rose to power. Her victory in 1979 led the way to a stable government that lasted until 1990. Just as the election of President Ronald Reagan in the United States influenced the history of conservatism, the Thatcher administration also signaled a turning point for British conservative thought.

Thatcher's policies called for a decided reduction of the role of the state in society and can be summed up with one expression: "roll back the state." Welfare programs were reduced, a few of the most important public industries were privatized, and more than a million public housing properties were sold. Thatcher's economic policy, which was accused of operating the "cult of the market," generated discontent not only from the Labour Party, which accused her of disintegrating social order, but also from fringes of the Conservative Party.

Nevertheless, British citizens enjoyed her iron-fist politics, and thanks to the victory of the Falklands War in 1982, she was reelected two more times in 1983 and 1987. Her era ended definitively in 1990 when she decided to resign, due to a series of factors including protests for tax reform. She was succeeded by John Major in the election of 1992.

We could, of course, depart from the historical field and move on to more contemporary concerns in our study of Britain's history. We could examine the decisions of the British Conservative Party in recent years—David Cameron's leadership, his downfall, and—of course—Brexit. But these events are all too recent to be commented on with the objectivity that a study of history requires. Instead, we shall direct our gaze back to the past, beginning with the Oxford Movement.

The Oxford Movement

The Oxford Movement refers to a conservative movement that developed from the Anglican Church's reaction to growing liberalism and rationalism in the Church of England. The birth of the Oxford Movement was initiated on July 14, 1833, when John Keble (1792–1866) gave a sermon against the state, which he believed was guilty of suppressing a large number of Anglican episcopate. Endorsing the discontent brought to light by Keble, John Henry Newman (1801–1890) published the first of a series of tracts to sensitize public opinion. The reform that emerged from these tracts took a conservative mold due to its objective return to traditional Anglican principles.

Despite his passionate writings, Newman grew more and more distant from Anglican stances, and eventually he found Anglicanism to be irreconcilable with his own beliefs. Newman slowly drew closer to Catholicism, and the breaking point came with the publication of *Tract 90*, in which he employed a Catholic perspective to interpret the thirty-nine articles that make up the practice of the Anglican faith.[4]

Of course, the Anglican establishment's reaction caused Newman to leave Oxford the following year, along with his pupils. He continued to distance himself from the Anglican Church until his official break in 1845 (an event that coincided with the end of the Oxford Movement) when he converted to the Roman Catholic faith.

Newman, who was eventually elevated to cardinal under Pope Leo XIII, belonged to the pessimistic Christian school that looks up to Saint Augustine. A collection of his experiences can be found in his autobiography, *Apologia Pro Vita Sua*, published in 1864. In the 1865 edition, an appendix titled "Liberalism" was added, in which eighteen prerogatives of liberal thought are listed which, according to Newman, are worthy of condemnation. The first few lines alone are explanatory: "Liberty of thought is in itself a good; but it gives an opening to false liberty. Now by Liberalism I mean false liberty of thought."

Newman's debt to Burke emerges when he warns against dangerous innovations in his book *An Essay in Aid of a Grammar of Assent*, published in 1870.[5] He links "prejudices"—which are cherished "because they are prejudices; and the longer they have lasted and the more generally they have prevailed, the more we cherish them"—and common sense to rationality.[6] Newman's conversion to Catholicism in 1845 was due to his realization that the Catholic Church was the guardian of traditional values. Its capacity for change in response to changing conditions was in accordance with the principle of making old principles resurface in new forms; it was in opposition to secular progressivism, and Newman defended Christian civilization against the ignorance of modern liberal ideology.

Edmund Burke (1729–1797)

Edmund Burke was the first philosopher to theorize about the conservative sentiment in his book *Reflections on the Revolution in France*, published in 1790, the year after the Revolution.

Unlike Maistre, to whom conservatism resembles mere reactionism, Burke is open to evolution: "A disposition to preserve and an ability to improve, taken together, would be my standard of a statesman."[7] According to Burke, a statesman must preserve and simultaneously reform, creating an intermediate position between Jefferson's democratic liberalism and Maistre's authoritarian conservatism.

Burke's entire philosophy is supported by the idea that society is based on a contract, not only between the current generations but also with the preceding and future generations. In his writings, he rebukes the philosophies that inspired the revolutionaries, stating that the birth of the French Revolution ignored the main principle of social order: differences among social classes. Far from being oppressive, these classes allowed for stable social harmony—it is radical social equality that leads to chaos and, consequentially, military autocracy.

In 1758, Burke signed a contract with editor Robert Dodsley to "write, collect, and compile" an annual register of the most important political and cultural events in Europe of the previous year. This annual register was issued from May 1759 until 1765–66. On July 10, 1765, the marquess of Rockingham became prime minister and designated Burke as his personal secretary. Burke thus identified himself with the Whig inclinations linked to Rockingham, a decision which eventually led to his election to the House of Commons in December 1765. Most of his political career was characterized by his opposition to King George III and his ministries.

Burke's political principles are made up of classical studies and the natural law of Christian morality; he also defends private and corporate property as necessary conditions for societal freedom. Natural law, he argues, provides a moral foundation for other important political principles. Burke's notions of constitutional law, human nature, the role of history in human affairs, social contract theory, and the significance of morality all played a part in his practical policies.

Is society composed of both individuals and meaningful communities, or isolated individuals, grouped together by the necessary conditions of living in the world? In Burke's opinion, society is regulated by a contract between the individual and the group; but in contrast to Rousseau, Hobbes, and Locke, he considers this contract to be between man and God, primarily, as well as among every generation of man, past, present and future.

In his parliamentary speeches, Burke favored autonomy and freedom for the nation. He wrote *Relative to the Laws against Popery in Ireland* with this idea in mind, aware that most Irish Catholics suffered abuse and fewer opportunities to worship under English rule. He denounced the most serious deprivation for the Irish people, which was the exclusion from the benefits of the English constitution, especially in economic and religious aspects.

Burke also directly participated in the debate about the independence of the American colonies. He believed more important compromises needed to be made and that the rights of the Americans should have been equal to those of British citizens. He saw the possibility to preserve and unite American liberty and British sovereignty, and he was convinced that the conflict with the colonies was due to wrong decisions made by the British government, such as exaggerated taxation. In three different books, he collected his ideas on the

American issue: *Speech on American Taxation* (1774), *Speech on Conciliation* (1775), and *A Letter to the Sheriffs of Bristol* (1777) in which he never referred to the "American Revolution" but rather to the "American war"—as the conflict was considered a civil war within the British Empire.[8] Burke's speeches in favor of the American Revolution include *On Conciliation with the Colonies* (1775) and *On American Taxation* (1777). In this manner, he attacked the stances of King George III. In May 1788, he requested complete abolition of slavery.

As an expert on French society, years before the Revolution in 1769, Burke predicted that "France was heading toward 'some extraordinary convulsion' because of its serious financial problems," an opinion that was confirmed during his 1773 visit to France when he was struck by the widespread atheism present among philosophers.[9] He was convinced that the economic crisis in France, combined with the radicalism of intellectuals, would lead to a considerable subversive event. At first, he was not against the French Revolution; he waited expectantly for the situation to evolve. However, when Jacobins assumed power, tearing down the entire political, social, and religious orders of the country, Burke became aware of the diabolical revolutionary strength. In January 1790, British radicals presented the French Revolution as a model to be exported overseas. From February to June of the same year, Burke articulated a series of speeches in parliament that would make up the prelude to the draft of *Reflections on the Revolution in France*. His book was a genuine "Manifesto of a Counter-revolution," as the Irish scholar Conor Cruise O'Brien titled the introduction of a modern edition of the book. "For Burke," writes Marco Respinti, "the revolution constituted the advent of barbarism as well as the subversion of every moral law and every civil and political custom."[10]

Burke's stances grew clearer and even more contrary to the Revolution with the killing of Louis XVI of the House of Bourbon in the Place de la Révolution, where he was publicly beheaded. Shocked by these events in France, Burke used his parliamentary position to encourage British military intervention. He predicted that "the onset of the Jacobin Terror and the killing of the king, an image of true deicide" would be the future of Napoleonic military despotism (which he would never live to see). The Anglo-Irish thinker and statesman was deeply disconcerted by these things.[11]

He therefore wrote a letter to the interior minister recommending a war on the Jacobins. This, he felt, was the only way to save Europe from a terrible revolution, using the counterrevolutionaries of Vendée as an example. The letter proved unsuccessful. Following the Battle of Quiberon and the surrender of the Vendéen, Burke was left strongly disappointed.

"Burke introduced a cultural tradition founded on reverence for historical continuity of social and civil traditions that represent the human (and therefore fallible, but nevertheless worthy of deep respect) attempt to embody normal moral law," writes Malgieri.[12] This frame of mind pushed him "to go head on against the French Revolution that, in the Burkean view, amounted to the pinnacle of absolutism and tyranny, united for the first time, to the positive, radical, and violent negation of Christianity and of the bi-millennium cultural heritage of Europe."[13]

Indeed, Burke exercised an essential influence on both British and American conservative thought:

> The influence exercised by Burkean thought on North American conservatism is more broad than explicit. Its numerous and precious references reveal the thought and even the literature of Burke: so much so that in the English-speaking world, in some of its articulations and "schools," a decidedly, although not official, Burkean conservatism shines through—even if at times (and perhaps because of an incomplete understanding of the core of Anglo-Irish thought) hostile toward Burke. These forms of conservatism, partially or fully anti-Enlightenment, often drink from (and maybe while grasping the importance of the structural nexus) the same fountain from which, more or less directly, Burke's thought derives. British culture in many ways "produced" Burke: Samuel Johnson (1709–1784), Giovanni Altusia (1557–1638), Richard Hooker, and behind all of them Saint Thomas Aquinas (1225–1274) were impressed deeply upon his psyche. The references to them, used often enough by non-Catholic conservatives, shows how the school and the classical ethos based on Greek, Roman, and Hebrew worlds live on.[14]

If Burke can be considered the father of conservative thought, the two main antagonists of the conservative concepts are Hobbes and Rousseau. Both theorize about a strong centralized state, the antithesis of the ideal community. In *Leviathan*, Hobbes describes the absolute state by identifying traditional associations of society (family, church, guilds) as worms in the human entrails; Rousseau replaces the will of the these intermediate social classes with the anonymous concept of "general will."

Reflections on the Revolution in France originated as a private letter written due to the deterioration following the French Revolution. The text was published as a book, received immediate success, and contributed to the development of a robust debate on the consequences of the Revolution. Correspondence with a Parisian aristocrat Charles-Jean-Francois Dupont, who wrote Burke to ask for his opinions on the events in France, make up part of the content of *Reflections*. There was no delay in his answer in two separate letters, the second of which provided the basis for the epistolary book. While the French Revolution was the main motivation for *Reflections*, certain consequences connected to all revolutionary movements convinced Burke to publish his work. Specific events included the nationalization of ecclesiastical assets, the civil constitution of the clergy, and the march on Versailles, all considered true attacks on the church and the monarchy, the foundational institutions of the conservative conception of society.

Burke was profoundly shocked by the events of October 5–6 in Versailles, especially the violence again the queen, Marie Antoinette. Memories of his meeting fifteen or sixteen years before with the queen, when she was the dauphine of France, resurfaced in his mind, and he describes the events in his book with vibrant nostalgia: "Oh! what a revolution! and what a heart must I have to contemplate without emotion that elevation and that fall!"[15]

Burke was not aprioristically against revolutions, but he highlights important distinctions between the French Revolution, the American Revolution, and the preceding Glorious Revolution in England. The Glorious Revolution of 1688 transpired in defense of the constitution and tradition, in order to restore political balance by protecting the founding values of the English monarchy. The first part of the book analyzes the difference between this revolution and the

French one; the second part discusses the dangers of the French Revolution by concentrating on ideas of the National Assembly and the ideology of Emmanuel Joseph Sieyès, a French abbot. Sieyès's main work, *What is the Third Estate?*, is commonly referred to as the manifesto of the French Revolution. It is the polar opposite of Burke's ideas, and Burke accuses Sieyès and the Jacobins of deteriorating rules and traditions by making a *tabula rasa* of the past:

> To make a revolution is to subvert the ancient state of our country; and no common reasons are called for to justify so violent a proceeding.... Passing from the civil creating and the civil cementing principles of this constitution, to the National Assembly, which is to appear and act as sovereign, we see a body in its constitution with every possible power, and no possible external control. We see a body without fundamental laws, without established maxims, without respected rules of proceeding, which nothing can keep firm to any system whatsoever.... All these considerations leave no doubt on my mind, that, if this monster of a constitution can continue, France will be wholly governed by the agitators in corporations, by societies in the towns formed of directors of assignats, and trustees for the sale of church lands, attorneys, agents, money-jobbers, speculators, and adventurers, composing an ignoble oligarchy, founded on the destruction of the crown, the church, the nobility, and the people. Here end all the deceitful dreams and visions of the quality and rights of men.[16]

In his *Reflections*, Burke rejects the rationalist ideas that made up the ideological foundation of the Revolution, including the ideas of Enlightenment philosophers such as Voltaire and Rousseau. "We are not the converts of Rousseau; we are not the disciples of Voltaire," he writes in defense of centralizing private property and preserving tradition. Burke focuses on the importance of "prejudices," understanding them to be forms of knowledge and behavior that characterize the relationships of society.

At a time when the empiricist and rationalist philosophies of Thomas Hobbes and John Locke were ever more diffused, Burke countered these ideas with a vision of the universe and society characterized by a superior order to the reason of man: a universe linked to God.

The importance of Burke's book emerged from its influence not only on his contemporaries, but also on future generations. Shortly after the book's publication, King George III of England defined it as "a book every statesman should read." *Reflections* quickly became the manifesto for every counter-revolutionary thinker.

While there are many followers and fans of Burke's work, there are also those who harbored negative opinions of *Reflections*. James Fox and Thomas Jefferson accused Burke of being a reactionary, and a few works have been published in response to Burke's book, such as Thomas Paine's *Rights of Man* and William Godwin's *Political Justice*. Prime Minister William Pitt stated that there was nothing with which to agree in Burke's book.

In order to have a thorough understanding of Burke's ideas, his book *Essays* is essential, and in *A Vindication of Natural Society* one can read his attacks on philosophers he believes to be guilty of creating governments that fail to conserve the complexities of human nature.

Among the various biographies written about the Irish philosopher, there are two in particular which are worth reading: *Edmund Burke: A Genius Reconsidered* by Russell Kirk and *Edmund Burke: The Visionary who Invented Modern Politics* by Jesse Norman.

Samuel Coleridge (1772–1834)

In 1789, Samuel Coleridge and William Wordsworth published *Lyrical Ballads*. Coleridge's ideas were removed from liberalism and rationalism; he embraced the traditional monarchy and the Church of England. His writings indicate a revolt of the human heart against eighteenth-century rationalism.

Coleridge was a prolific writer; he filled sixty notebooks with his thoughts and opinions between 1794 and 1834. Despite—or perhaps because—he worked on so many various pieces, many are fragmentary and incomplete. His real genius is said to have emerged more from conversations held in person.

Coleridge is considered by many as the "purest" conservative. He never compromised himself with material interests; he had an organic vision rather than atomistic and believed society to be an aggregate of individuals. His expression "people are not things" synthesizes a refusal of rationalism, which aimed to render individuals as equal to objects. His feelings of beauty, antiquity, and mystery encouraged a necessary cultural rediscovery of the collective and sacred aspects of the church.

Peter Viereck collected a series of aphorisms representative of Coleridge's thoughts in works published between 1798 and 1832 in *Conservatism Revisited: The Revolt Against Ideology*. Viereck defended Coleridge's notion of the unity born from living in an organic society as opposed to a mechanical one, and compared the spiritual worth of religion to the spiritual worthlessness of materialism. The difference between an organic and inorganic society lies, he wrote, in the fact that the first consists of a set of single individuals who make up a whole, whereas the second consists of men alone, who are nothing compared to the whole.

Thomas Carlyle (1795–1881)

The last book Adolf Hitler had in his Berlin bunker before he died was the biography of Emperor Frederick of Prussia, written by Carlyle. Carlyle's vision of society contrasts medieval spiritualism with a materialism based solely on the economy. He also compares an organic society with an atomistic one, favoring societal relationships based on honor, loyalty, and humanity—typical of conservatives—versus the vision of capitalists and socialist materialism, which favor societal relationships of an entirely different kind. His main books pay tribute to all conservative ideals: *Sartor Resartus* of 1833–1834, *On Heroes* of 1841, *Past and Present* published in 1843 and *The French Revolution: A History* of 1837.

Benjamin Disraeli (1804–1881)

On June 24, 1872, Disraeli gave his famous speech at Crystal Palace in which he attacked the Liberal Party for stances against the British Empire, kicking off the neo-Imperialism of the Tory matrix. Disraeli founded the Tory democracy by bringing the traditional principles of conservatism to the masses. In 1867, he granted the right to vote to urban workers, and during his period in government between 1874 and 1880, he legalized unions and the right to strike by introducing two important laws: the Employers and Workmen Act and the Conspiracy Act. Disraeli's efforts to protect workers was so impactful that even Alexander Macdonald, a Labourist parliament member, praised him, saying, "the Conservative Party has done more for the working classes in five years than the liberals have done in fifty."

Indeed, Viereck draws a parallel between Disraeli and Winston Churchill in his book *Conservatism Revisited*, describing how both were deeply influenced by the work of Edmund Burke. But both Disraeli and Churchill were less democratic than Burke in colonial situations, and still more democratic in internal politics.

The principles that gave life to Disraeli's administration are characteristically conservative. He knew that it was necessary to facilitate change in a way that allowed for customs, traditions, and the emblematic laws of the nation to be conserved. The founding principles of Tory democracy politics are found consistently in Disraeli's speeches and essays.

The subtitle of Disraeli's novel *Sybil*, "The Two Nations," refers to the upper and lower socioeconomic classes. It denounces the free market capitalism of the middle classes. Like Burke, Disraeli had a genuine veneration for the British constitution, but was also influenced by Coleridge's school of thought and considered the constitution to be an organic union of various classes, each with specific privileges and historical characteristics.

Disraeli deepened his study of the constitution in his 1835 essays *Vindication of the English Constitution* and *Letters of Runnymede* in 1836. In *Vindication of the English Constitution*, typical Tory ethics, including a respect for antiquity, emerged, founded on a profound understanding of human nature and careful observation of public affairs.

Disraeli's 1872 Crystal Palace speech was central to the politics of Disraeli and England itself, ushering in a new era of British imperialism. The speech provided a clear stance against Liberal policies: "If you look to the history of this country since the advent of Liberalism—forty years ago—you will find that there has been no effort so continuous, so subtle, supported by so much energy, and carried on with so much ability and acumen, as the attempts of Liberalism to effect the disintegration of the Empire of England."

Gilbert Keith Chesterton (1874–1936)

Chesterton was a prolific writer who published more than one hundred books, including essays, travel books, biographies, and texts of literary, religious, and social criticism. Widely known for his Father Brown detective stories and his novels *The Napoleon of Notting Hill* and *The Man Who Was Thursday: A Nightmare*, his conversion to Catholicism in 1922 represented the climax of his spiritual journey. His works struck the historical, religious, political, and social imagination by recounting the conflict between Christianity and other religions, most notably in *The Ballad of the White Horse* and *Lepanto*, both published in 1911. Much of his writing consists of attacks on rationalism, materialism, and scientism; he compares industrial capitalism with the Christian economy as envisioned by the medieval world in *The Outline of Sanity* (1926). Chesterton's ideas reflected those of Saint Thomas Aquinas—in 1933, he wrote a biography of him, titled *St. Thomas Aquinas*, and continued to defend the religious idea of man against the Darwinist spirit in his 1925 book, *The Everlasting Man*.

Christopher Dawson (1889–1970)

After studying at Trinity College of Oxford, Dawson converted to Catholicism in 1914 and began an academic career at British and Irish universities. At the end of the 1950s, he moved to the United States to begin teaching Catholic studies at Harvard. Dawson collaborated on a larger number of articles for the journal *Criterion*, created by T. S. Eliot, and subsequently worked as an editor for the Catholic journal *Dublin Review*. He became well-known to the American public after his time at Harvard, and his first book was published in 1928, titled *The Age of the Gods*.

His most important works are dedicated to the study of Christianity: *The Gods of Revolution, The Modern Dilemma, The Formation of Christendom, Religion and the Rise of Western Culture*, and *The Catholic Tradition and the Modern State*. He also wrote several important works analyzing Western civilization, including *The Making of Europe: An Introduction to the History of European Unity* and The *Crisis of Western Education*.

Dawson's entire collection must be framed within the 1930s trends in England. Intellectuals were returning to Catholicism, a phenomenon largely due to the spreading influence of Eliot.

The focal point of Dawson's studies was the relationship between religion, culture, and civilization. According to Dawson, Western civilization, unlike other civilizations, is based on a common culture. Religion constitutes the foundation of culture and enjoys a primary role in the formation of a civilization: "For the existence of the Catholic Church is one of the great objective realities of history. It is impossible to write the history of Christianity without it, and it is equally impossible to understand the history of our own civilization...."[17]

One need not be Christian to recognize the role of Christendom in our society, and there are no aspects of Western society that have not been influenced by its faith or judgments. Simply studying Christian culture provides insight into Western culture and its primary values.

Dawson believed that to overcome the crisis of Western civilization, works were needed to purify cultural memory; a culture can only go on living if it has a valid spiritual foundation. During the era of Christianity, the West experienced maximum splendor and became the beacon of civility in the world. However, in today's world of globalization, despite technological and scientific innovations, we are lacking foundation:

> We have the material conditions for world unity, but there is as yet no common moral order without which a true culture cannot exist. The entire modern world wears the same clothes, drives the

same cars, and watches the same films, but it does not possess common ethical values or a sense of spiritual community or common religious beliefs.[18]

When in contact with the human race, the Catholic ideals of culture, embodying eternal values and the teachings of God, transform mankind's nature with spiritual principles: "The Christian view of history is a vision of history *sub specie aeternitatis*, an interpretation of time in terms of eternity and of human events in the light of divine revelation," wrote Gerald J. Russell in an article dedicated to Dawson on the website Catholic Education.[19]

The philosophers who made the foundation of Dawson's studies were Saint Augustine, Saint Thomas Aquinas, and Saint Ignatius of Loyola. From Dawson's point of view, his era was similar to that of Saint Augustine and Saint Ignatius, the main question being whether the future would bring a Christian civilization or a civilization that would recognize neither moral laws nor human rights.

John Ronald Reuel Tolkein (1892–1973)

There are multiple interpretations of Tolkien's work, along with different schools of thought and analysis of his literary productions that allow for a varied image of his work. However, his life choices, characterized by markedly conservative stances, are exempt from any doubt:

> Tolkien's works are centered on a large canvas, even of a theological character, founded on love, compassion, and charity, as well as courage and strength, including the dedication, selflessness, and heroism of even the "small" ones that the philologist admired in classical literature, epic and mythological tales, and the Bible. He was undoubtedly shaped by the most classical values of British patriotism, of conservatism, and the Catholic faith.[20]

An analysis of Tolkien's work can employ a double reading: the first associates itself with neo-paganism, while the second (and more accredited) associates itself with Catholicism. The best way to understand Tolkien's world-view is to read *The Letters of J.R.R. Tolkien*. In letters addressed to his son Christopher, who was serving in the British Royal Air Force at the time, Tolkien wrote about the Second World War. He was anti-Communist and anti-Nazi. In a letter dated January 30, 1945, at a time of general public mistrust and dejection, Tolkien did not abandon his hope for the future:

> Still I think there will be a 'millenium,' the prophesied thousand-year rule of the Saints, i.e. those who have, for all their imperfections, never finally bowed heart and will to the world or the evil spirit (in modern but not universal terms: mechanism, 'scientific' materialism, Socialism in either of its factions now at war).[21]

Once again, writing to his son, it is impossible not to recognize a conservative mind-set in Tolkien's words written in 1943:

> I wonder (if we survive this war) if there will be any niche, even of sufferance, left for reactionary back numbers like me (and you). The bigger things get the smaller and duller or flatter the globe gets. It is getting to be all one blasted little provincial suburb. When they have introduced American sanitation, morale-pep, feminism, and mass production throughout the Near East, Middle East, Far East, U.S.S.R., the Pampas, el Gran Chaco, the Danubian Basin, Equatorial Africa, Hither Further and Inner Mumbo-land, Gondhwanaland, Lhasa, and the villages of darkest Berkshire, how happy we shall be. At any rate it ought to cut down travel. There will be nowhere to go. So people will (I opine) go all the faster. Col. Knox says 1/8 of the world's population speaks 'English', and that is the biggest language group. If true, damn shame— say I. May the curse of Babel strike all their tongues till they can only say 'baa baa'. It would mean much the same. I think I shall have to refuse to speak anything but Old Mercian. But seriously: I do find this Americo-cosmopolitan very terrifying.[22]

Through his work, Tolkien profoundly influenced conservative culture with his philosophy of life, which opposed the prevailing relativism and the philosophical and political criteria diffused during the Enlightenment. He also gave the church a primary role in his contemporary era. In the book *J.R.R. Tolkien: A Biography*, Humphrey Carpenter summarizes the political and cultural orientation of the British writer:

> His view of the world, in which each man belonged or ought to belong to a specific "estate," whether high or low, meant that in one sense he was an old-fashioned conservative. But in another sense it made him highly sympathetic to his fellow-men, for it is those who are unsure of their status in the world, who feel they have to prove themselves and if necessary put down other men to do so, who are the truly ruthless. Tolkien was, in modern jargon, 'right-wing' in that he honoured his monarch and his country and did not believe in the rule of the people; but he opposed democracy simply because he believed that in the end his fellow-men would not benefit from it. He once wrote: "I am not a democrat, if only because humility and equality are spiritual principles corrupted by the attempt to mechanize and formalize them, with the result that we get not universal smallness and humility, but universal greatness and pride, till some Orc gets hold of a ring of power— and then we get and are getting slavery." As to the virtues of an old-fashioned feudal society, this is what he once said about respect for one's superiors: "Touching your cap to the Squire may be damn bad for the Squire but it's damn good for you."[23]

People's connection with their origins and land, revealed in the description of the hobbits of the Shire in *The Lord of the Rings*, serves as a metaphor for the typically localized conservative community. In an article titled "Romantic Conservatives: The Inklings in Their Political Context," Charles A. Coulombe analyzes the influences of conservative thought on the works of the three most important British authors of the twentieth century: Tolkien,

C. S. Lewis, and Charles Williams. He also highlights the connection between the narrative world Tolkien envisioned and his political reality:

> Arnor itself is very like the Western Empire; counting progressively less militarily as the decades pass, it nevertheless survives in the minds of its subjects, even after the end of its actual existence. Its revival under Aragorn (or Elessar, as we must call him at that stage) bears a striking resemblance to the Carolingian revival. Gondor, on the other hand, reminds one of the Eastern Roman Empire, an analogy expressly made by JRRT in a letter to Milton Waldman in late 1951, wherein he speaks of Gondor's initial glory "almost reflecting Numenor," and then fading "slowly to decayed Middle Age, a kind of proud, venerable, but increasingly impotent Byzantium." As opposed to the mere force of arms and weight of government machinery that Tolkien hated in the pagan Roman Empire, the restored Kingdom under Elessar exemplified the "unity-in-diversity," the preservation of local freedoms under an overarching Monarch, that Medieval theorists ascribed to the Holy Roman Empire. In 1963, he wrote to a fan: "A Numenorean King was a monarch, with the power of unquestioned decision in debate; but he governed the realm with the frame of ancient law, of which he was administrator (and interpreter) but not the maker." Another Holy Roman Emperor manqué was Ingwe, chief of the Vanyar and High King of all the Elves.[24]

Tolkien considered England to be an organic state made up of local communities, one of which was the Catholic Church. While the biography by Carpenter is, without a shadow of a doubt, the best reference for understanding the life of the author of *The Lord of the Rings*, Stratford Caldecott's book *Secret Fire: The Spiritual Vision of J.R.R. Tolkien* is also recommended for a deeper study of a more "spiritual Tolkien." Caldecott uncovers the spiritual intensity and the symbolic power of the Christian message in Tolkien's books. The contrast between Tolkien's Catholicism and the (alleged) absence of

Christian elements in his work is also brought to light in Errico Passaro and Marco Respinti's book, *Paganesimo e Cristianesimo in Tolkien. Le due tesi a confronto*, which explores the reasons for both pagan and Christian interpretations of Tolkien.

Michael Oakeshott (1901–1990)

Following his historical studies, Oakeshott fought in the Second World War on the front lines of the British Army. A professor of modern history at Goinville and Caius College in Cambridge, where he taught from 1926 to 1948, including a brief stint at Oxford, he also taught political science until his retirement in 1968. He spent his final years in a country cottage in Dorset.

In his youth, Oakeshott held socialist views and was moved by the observations of Pierre-Joseph Proudhon; in particular, he held to Proudhon's vision of a social order based on the union of community and equality with individuality and independence. Beginning in 1962 with the publication of his most important book, *Rationalism in Politics and Other Essays,* Oakeshott then changed his views and became part of a leading group of conservative authors. In his book, Oakeshott analyzes the modern political rationalism that led to widespread technical and scientific knowledge, the simplification of modern public life, and an unhealthy aversion to authority and tradition.

An article in *New Statesman* by Jesse Norman, titled "Michael Oakeshott, conservative thinker who went beyond politics", reviewed *Michael Oakeshott: Notebooks (1922–86),* edited by Luke O'Sullivan. The book paints a portrait of the British philosopher while summarizing his most important works. The most representative essay pertinent to our study is "On Being Conservative," which originated as a lecture Oakeshott gave at Swansea University in 1956 and was then published in *Rationalism in Politics.* Oakeshott considered change inevitable and therefore believed it ought to be accepted—but in a gradual way, a way that precluded a loss of identity. He ascribed to a "skeptical conservatism," which differed from Burke's "cosmic conservatism."

When Oakeshott died at the age of eighty-nine in 1990, multiple major British newspapers recognized his contributions, describing him as "the greatest political philosopher in the Anglo-Saxon tradition since Mill—or even Burke."[25]

Roger Scruton (1944–)

While the Thatcher-Reagan hinge of the 1980s was making waves in the political sphere, the main conservative philosopher of culture was Roger Scruton. During this period, the concept of the "New Right" was spreading, and Scruton quickly became a cultural reference for this new idea of the Right. Born to a humble family in the county of Buckinghamshire about fifty kilometers from London, Scruton graduated from Cambridge in 1972 with a degree in philosophy and began teaching in England and France. He published his first book in 1974, titled *Art and Imagination*. Around the same time, he began his journey in the Tory Party.

He received a second degree in law in 1978 but never practiced, and he began publishing with magazines and newspapers. Two years later, *The Meaning of Conservatism*, one of his most notable books analyzing conservative thought, was published. Scruton's analysis begins with the exploits of Thatcherism and the pro-Reagan influence on the New Right; he posits a necessary intellectual and cultural foundation to this conservatism. From this analysis, the Conservative Philosophy Group was formed, established alongside Sir Hugh Fraser, Jonathan Aitken, and John Casey. While actively collaborating with anti-Communist Czech resistance groups, Scruton founded the journal *The Salisbury Review*, which challenged not only the key issues of the day, but also Margaret Thatcher's policies.

With his book *The Meaning of Conservatism*, Scruton became one of the leaders of new British conservatism. He unmasked misunderstandings: namely, that "there is no universal conservative policy... there is no conservative thought, no set of beliefs or principles, no general vision of society, which motivates the conservative to act."[26] Scruton proves this is not actually the case; conservative politics try, rather, to achieve the best conditions that reach the conservative *forma mentis* by responding to present needs and the *hic et nunc*.

In his book *A Dictionary of Political Thought*, Scruton writes that the Right can be defined in its opposition with the Left, and says this political definition is characterized by a few main factors:

- doctrines of political obligation framed in terms of obedience, legitimacy, and piety (rather than contract, consent, and justice)
- belief in private property—not as a natural right, but as an indispensable part of the condition of society
- belief in elementary freedoms and the irreplaceable value of the individual as against the collective
- belief in free enterprise and a capitalist economy—not only as the only mode of production compatible with human freedom, but as the only one suited to the temporary nature of human aspirations

While Scruton sees in his own ideas Oakeshott's anti-rationalism and anti-modernism, and while he shares his regard for conservatism as an instinctual inclination, his critiques of individualism are more precise. His objective is to demonstrate the unsubstantiated cultural and political grounds of progressivism, and to define the exact political confines that would preclude a reality in which people may fall into progressive liberalism that would aprioristically obey the state.

Scruton considers modern society to be dominated by nihilism and holds that with the death of God, nothing remains. He identifies a series of Western culture's failures, worth reexamining here:

> Our failure to adjust immigration policies to the goal of integration, and the reciprocal assumption that we should be free to travel anywhere around the globe without first learning about the taboos and aspirations of the places that we visit; our acceptance of "multiculturalism" as an educational and political goal, and our habit of denigrating the real national and political culture

upon which we depend; our corresponding commitment to "free trade" conceived as the WTO conceives it, namely, as a way of compelling other countries to remove the barriers that they have erected in defense of perceived local interest; our easy acceptance of the multinational corporation as a legitimate legal person, even though it is subject to no particular sovereign jurisdiction and is able to own property in every part of the globe; our seeming indifference as the authority of the secular law and territorial jurisdiction is eroded by predatory litigation at home, and by bureaucratic legislation from elsewhere; our devotion to prosperity, and the habits of consumption that have led us to depend upon raw materials such as oil, which cannot be obtained within our territory.[27]

In *The West and the Rest*, Scruton identifies the two enemies of Western society: a tyrant dictator, and a religious fanatic protected by tyranny. To take action against the dictator, one must follow his rules; similar major difficulties arise when one tries to act against the religious fanatic. A strong and credible political alternative to the absolute power of both these enemies is necessary.

Scruton sees conservativism as this alternative. His thinking stems from Burke's philosophy, which states that tradition provides certain conditions worth conserving, as society is an organism based not only on those who are living today, but also on those who have lived before and those who have yet to come. Although this conservative idea belongs in some ways to all human societies, only English-speaking countries have political parties that define themselves as conservative. In this sense Scruton distinguishes between two types of conservatism, metaphysical and empirical:

> The first resides in the belief in sacred things and the desire to defend them against desecration.... In its empirical manifestation, conservatism is a more specifically modern phenomenon, a reaction to the vast changes unleashed by the Reformation and the Enlightenment.[28]

Our community inherited conditions from the past that must be conserved: the freedom to live the life we want, the impartiality of the law, the
protection of the environment as a common inheritance, an open and lively
culture, democracy that allows us to elect our representatives:

> Conservatism starts from a sentiment that all mature people can
> readily share: the sentiment that good things are easily destroyed,
> but not easily created. This is especially true of the good things
> that come to us as collective assets: peace, freedom, law, civility,
> public spirit, the security of property and family life.[29]

Scruton admits that conservatives in contemporary society seem like bor-
ing people who take on uninteresting standpoints compared to their adversar-
ies. Nowadays, he notes, it is not unusual to be a conservative, but it *is* unusual
to be an intellectual conservative. He perfectly describes the state in which
the conservatives of contemporary society live: they are cautious in expressing
certain opinions. They are forced to move quietly and discretely in the days
of their lives; and why shouldn't they? Ordinary conservatives, Scruton writes,
who are really just ordinary people, are constantly told that their ideas and
sentiments are reactionary, prejudiced, sexist, or racist.

Moving to France was a fundamental event in Scruton's life. In response
to the riots of May 1968, he matured his political understanding; the alternative to revolutionary socialism, he discovered, was conservatism, and he
embraced it. In his opinion, the 1968 protest could only come about in a
context of freedom such as that French democracy. The intellectual environ-
ments of the time considered conservatism to be an evil for society; Marxist
humanism was the only intellectually endorsed alternative to Lenin's revolutionary socialism.

The conditions in Europe in the early 1970s, especially in England, gave
way to a surrendering of historic ideals. In a scope of general dejection among
conservatives, Scruton identifies a cultural turning point in Margaret Thatcher's political power and dedication to the nation:

She believed in our country and its institutions, and saw them as the embodiment of social affections nurtured and stored over centuries. Family, civil association, the Christian religion and the common law were all integrated into her ideal of freedom under law.... And then in 1979, I wrote *The Meaning of Conservatism*—an impetuous attempt to counter the free market ideology of the Thatcherite think tanks. I wanted to remind conservatives that there is such a thing as society, and that society is what conservatism is all about.[30]

Scruton's ideas about Communism were significantly influenced by his time spent in Czechoslovakia, where he made important contacts with under-ground anti-Communist networks. His time there made him intensely opposed to socialism as a government regime, imposed on the people from above. He also developed an aversion to the Labour Party: "I saw that this desire to control society in the name of equality expresses exactly the contempt for human freedom that I encountered in Eastern Europe."

According to Scruton, society is made up of individuals who must be free. The *Salisbury Review*, which he founded, made headlines when reporting on the Honeyford case, in which a middle school principal opined against the multicultural model in an article:

Honeyford's article honestly conveyed the problem, together with his proposed solution, which was to integrate the children into the surrounding secular culture, while protecting them from the punishments administered in their pre-school classes in the local madrasah, meanwhile opposing their parents' plans to take them away whenever it suited them to Pakistan. He saw no sense in the doctrine of multiculturalism, and believed that the future of our country depends upon our ability to integrate its recently arrived minorities, through a shared curriculum in the schools and a secular rule of law that could protect women and girls from the kind of abuse to which he was a distressed witness.[31]

The principal was fired for his viewpoints, and his case drew national attention. Scruton identified him as a victim of the British "establishment," motivated to eliminate any sign of patriotism in schools. The journal in which the article was published, along with its creator, was marginalized and labeled as racist. Scruton describes this as a response commonly used by the Left, always in the absence of a real response to the real change brought about by mass immigration. These types of accusations, repeated on several occasions against Scruton, brought him to abandon his academic career and understand what it means to be part of a persecuted and despised minority. These incidents, along with his return to Czechoslovakia after the fall of the Berlin Wall, instilled certain understandings in him: namely, that the borders of a country cannot be created at a table; they must instead be developed by a national identity. That Islam puts religion before nationality is a threat to political order.

A conservative society, as defined by both Scruton and Edmund Burke in *Reflections on the Revolution in France*, is a sodality of the dead, the living, and the unborn. It is comprised of a chain of obligations and duties that every citizen must respect on behalf of future society. By looking down on the past and the heritage of the deceased, the revolutionaries of history deprived the unborn of their rights. A fair and just society, on the other hand, is based on mutual loyalty and on individual interactions in families, clubs, schools, churches, and small communities. This sense of responsibility is weakened when societies are organized from the top; societies must be free to organize organically, from the bottom up.

Traditions provide a means for conserving the social fabric. Scruton writes, "The important social traditions are not just arbitrary customs, which might or might not have survived into the modern world. They are forms of knowledge."[32] Burke defined these traditions as "prejudices" that belong to the capital, that constitute the society and permit every citizen an understanding of how to behave in the company of others, and without which this sense of understanding would crumble.

Hobbes, Locke, Rawls, and other political philosophers of the Enlightenment found such rules of order in "the social contract," and their way of viewing man has largely prevailed and remained dominant. The modern man is a *homo oeconomicus* who has lost the sense of certain values and virtues, such as responsibility and respect, prudence and abnegation. That is modern man alone; but the concept of "us" can only emerge by means of a shared will of the citizens:

> Conservatism is the philosophy of attachment. We are attached to the things we love, and wish to protect them against decay. But we know that they cannot last forever. Meanwhile we must study the ways in which we can retain them through all the changes that they must necessarily undergo, so that our lives are still lived in a spirit of goodwill and gratitude.[33]

The fashionable distance from the so-called "tyranny of the majority," articulated and embraced by Mill and Tocqueville, weighs heavily on cultural consciousness, and for good reason: the opinions of the majority might be erroneous. It is therefore necessary to defend those in contemporary society who have the courage to disagree with this distance, and guarantee the exercise of this opposition. Scruton uses the example of families that discuss options before coming to a decision: each member expresses their opinion, and while they might not all agree with the final decision, they all accept it, and so the spirit and identity of the community prevails. This same concept should also be applied in politics, Scruton writes—the idea of "we" should prevail:

> The nation state, as we now conceive it, is the by-product of human neighbourliness, shaped by an 'invisible hand' from the countless agreements between people who speak the same language and live side by side. It results from compromises established after many conflicts, and expresses the slowly forming agreement among neighbours both to grant each other space and to protect that space as common territory. It has consciously absorbed and adjusted to the ethnic and religious minorities within its territory,

as they in turn have adjusted to the nation state. It depends on localized customs and a shared routine of tolerance. Its law is territorial rather than religious and invokes no source of authority higher than the intangible assets that its people share.[34]

Protecting and helping one's fellow citizen is not only a duty, but a necessity in the name of a common belonging, which exists for citizens of a nation and is expressed through sovereignty. The European Union was created to surpass the concept of nation and present itself as a supranational body. But it lacks popular legitimacy because it is based on the agreements of bureaucrats, rather than agreements central to a common identity. Scruton explains the failure of the European Union by comparing it to the Federalist model of the United States, which was efficient *because* it was based on a nation state, with characteristics that *united* the citizens, such as a common language. Nations indeed develop from the bottom, from the bond of common habits: "National boundaries can be weak or strong, porous or impregnable: but in all forms they provide the people with an identity with which to summarize their rights and duties as citizens, and their allegiance to those on whom they most nearly depend for civic peace."[35]

Belonging to a nation is ratified by a series of factors: territory that defines the identity of the citizens, history, traditions, rituals, and customs that bind citizens and create a collective sentiment. Each nation has a collective set of stories that make up the foundation of the community. That foundation, religious in the past, grows increasingly secular today. Today, a "culture of rejection" is dominant. Conservatives oppose this idea in favor of a culture based on affirmation of values that must be safeguarded.

While socialism is rooted in equality among citizens, conservatism upholds the idea that social justice resides in the common sentiments of the first-person plural. Formulating social obligations as a contract, like Hobbes proposes, is wrong. The British philosopher is right to consider that life, without any social order, would be miserable for citizens. An obligation of gratitude to order is called for. Order is obtained from social bonds, and must be returned to the community.

Scruton also breaks away from the progressive policies of the welfare state—first and foremost, because they create a dependent social class that benefits from government handouts, eventually killing the motivation to seek out productive and dignified lifestyles. This creates an internalized expectation of subsidies distributed across entire family units that not only represent major costs for the state, but also "directly impacts on the sentiment of membership, antagonizing those who live in a responsible way, and separating the dependent minority from the full experience of citizenship."[36]

Furthermore, welfare states are based on open budgets, so costs for a continuously increasing community generate an increase of the public debt to the state. Today's governments, however, are not able to tackle the topic of welfare in an objective way; the discussion has become so highly politicized that leaders can no longer express their real standpoints. The very nature and role of the state is called into question.

Scruton highlights the biggest misconception on which socialism is based: that one person's success leads to another person's failure. For socialists, and even more so for Communists, the single fact that inequality and a well-to-do social class exists represents an injustice that should be eliminated—an elimination much like what occurred in 1917 during the Russian October Revolution. Such conduct was based on "the widespread belief that equality and justice are the same idea."[37] Scruton stressed that every large-scale economy should be based on private property and free trade. But socialists refuse to accept this assertion, and would prefer to implement governmental redistribution of resources in a limited market. When interpreting conservative thought, it is important to understand that it is open to certain limits on the market, under certain conditions: "Those who believe that social order should place constraints on the market are therefore right. But in a true spontaneous order the constraints are already there, in the form of customs, laws, and morals."[38]

Although socialists subscribe to a *tout court* opposition of the free market, they are not alone in their opposition. In defense of traditions of human life, classical conservatives also distance themselves from certain rationales of the free market. Traditional sexual morality, for example, characterizes a conservative position that is based on the sanctity of the human person. Such a basis leads to a refusal of extramarital sex and rejects the logic of the market that leads to a commercialization of the human body. A conservative's critique of capitalism does not stem from the concept of a free market in itself, but rather from the distortions that capitalism can and even tends to produce. Trade in a free market occurs between free people; every transaction should be based on mutual responsibility and trust. Unfortunately, this does not always happen. "No market economy can function properly without the support of legal and moral sanctions, designed to hold individual agents to their bargains, and to return the cost of misbehaviour to the one who causes it," writes Scruton.[39]

Scruton summaries the conservative view on private property with the help of Disraeli:

> When Disraeli first saw that private property was an integral part of the conservative cause, to be defended with all possible vigour against the socialists, he added an important qualification, which he called 'the feudal principle', that the right of property is also a duty. The one who enjoys property is also accountable for it, and in particular accountable to those upon whom it might otherwise impose a burden. He has responsibilities towards the less fortunate, towards the unborn, and towards the inheritance in which we all have a stake.[40]

A new form of conservatism, which defends private property while simultaneously condemning those who abuse it, and benefits current generations without damaging subsequent ones, must be developed. All of this is possible through a responsible political and business model that prioritizes a sense of responsibility to local bonds.

Scruton also warns readers that an unrestrained market economy will also sell that which should not be sold, and it is up to us to define what should and should not be sold. Since there is no valid alternative to the market economy, we need to articulate so as to eliminate that which we deem non-marketable from the marketplace. Only this project—at once intellectual, spiritual, and intentional—will make order in the marketplace possible.

But a distinction between religious and political order must be made. Political order is based on man-made laws and decisions; religious order is based on divine commandments. Therefore, while religion is static, politics is dynamic. Individual sovereignty is achieved at the moment the state guarantees rights to the citizens; modern democracy consists of a company of strangers that can only function if its citizens recognize themselves in a range of duties to be respected (so-called "social obligations").

In order to achieve proper government, Scruton writes, "the solution is not to impose a new set of decrees from on high, but to re-establish the legitimacy of opposition and the politics of compromise. This was recognized at the Glorious Revolution of 1688, when Parliament was re-established as the supreme legislative institution."[41] The sovereign rights of the people are listed in this revolution's Bill of Rights; in this document, natural rights protecting the individual from power and guaranteeing sovereignty over one's own life are established. Human rights are listed to limit the power of whoever governs.

Scruton continues by addressing multiculturalism. The Enlightenment made it possible for foreign communities to be integrated into Western society by making them assimilate to our way of life. Unfortunately, today, we are marginalizing and renouncing our own customs in the name of multiculturalism, in order to become an "inclusive" society in which everyone can feel at home. Using the justification of inclusion, Scruton rightly notes that we risk repudiating the cultural and political heritage of our nation by abolishing old loyalties and norms of belonging:

> The Orient might have been a genuine alternative to the Western Enlightenment; instead, it is remade as a decorative foil to the Western imperial project. In this view, the old Enlightenment curriculum is really mono-cultural, devoted to perpetuating the view of Western civilization as inherently superior to its rivals. Its assumption of a universal rational perspective, from the vantage point of which all humanity could be studied, is nothing better than a rationalization of its imperialist claims. By contrast, we who live in the amorphous and multicultural environment of the post-modern city must open our hearts and minds to all

cultures, and be wedded to none. The inescapable result of this is relativism: the recognition that no culture has any special claim to our attention, and that no culture can be judged or dismissed from outside.[42]

Those who support multiculturalism perhaps predictably tend to reject Western culture. Still, they become the architects of an obvious paradox: if the Enlightenment eliminated theology from scholastic curricula, dismissing education's goal of searching for truth, an atheist theology has taken its place. This atheism rises to the level of theology in its own self-righteousness, and is founded on the submission to one's own doctrine.

It has long been known that people are afraid of inconvenient truths, and therefore avoid them. Due to this way of thinking, they opt for creations of public doctrines that are guaranteed to be "acceptable" to the community. Legality becomes a convenient source from which to draw opinion, and it is the intellectually lazy and cowardly who benefit. Our modern age undergoes a radical and worrisome process, an attempt to substitute true forms of community with false ones:

> Unfortunately, however, there is no such thing as a community based in repudiation. The assault on the old cultural inheritance leads to no new form of membership, but only to a kind of alienation. It is for this reason, it seems to me, that we must be cultural conservatives. The alternative is the kind of nihilism that lurks just below the surface in the writings of Rorty, Saïd, Derrida and Foucault.
>
> Perhaps the worst aspect of this nihilism is the routine accusation of 'racism', leveled against anyone who offers to endorse, to teach and to uphold the values of Western civilization. Fear of the charge of racism has led commentators, politicians and police forces all across the Western world to refrain from criticizing or taking action against many of the overtly criminal customs that have installed themselves in our midst—customs such as forced marriage, female circumcision and 'honour' killing, and the

growing intimidation from Islamists of anyone remotely critical of their faith.

The charge of 'racism' represents an attempt to turn the culture of repudiation in a religious direction—to make the posture of not belonging into a new kind of belonging, with enemies, banners and an onward march to victory over the status quo.[43]

Citizens of a country share a culture, a language, and a common public sphere. Therefore, the only way to achieve peaceful and beneficial cohabitation with immigrants is to integrate them into the culture. This is the only way to make a nation a home.

Scruton draws his readers' attention to another important, though much-forgotten, aspect of conservatism: the protection of the environment. The love one has for one's homeland makes up the foundation of conservative thought. But modern conservative parties have paradoxically surrendered to the pressure of large enterprises and multinational corporations, abandoning *de facto* pro-environmental policy. There is also another reason that brought conservatives further away from an environmentalist path:

> The truth in environmentalism has been obscured by the agitated propaganda of the environmentalists and by the immensity of the problems that they put before us. When the attention of the world is directed towards global warming, climate change, mass extinctions and melting ice caps—all of which lie outside the reach of any national government, and for none of which does a remedy immediately present itself—the result is a loss of confidence in ordinary politics, a despair at human incapacity, and a last ditch adoption of radical internationalist schemes that involve a surrender of sovereignty.[44]

Scruton explains that the solution to the problems of a free market is not the abolition of the free market, but the regulation of it. Establishing precise rules that incentivize conservation over the exhaustion of collective resources is necessary. By this logic, environmentalists and conservatives should cooperatively protect the land.

Nations, properly understood as communities that take on a political shape via the concept of territory, ought to actively, consistently engage in ecological thought. Rather than believing in global ecological solutions, too vast and vague in ambition to ever be achieved, conservatives must emphasize the necessity of local sovereignty and responsibility to the homeland. Such an approach—an approach that values real loyalties and local customs—is the only feasible way to oppose the centralizing tendency of the modern state.

The tension between Scruton's conservatism and globalist ambitions transcends the realm of the environmentalist. A Scruton conservative will be against any attempt, by international or supranational authorities, to interfere with the decisions of a nation. National sovereignty is to be staunchly defended; sovereign states "should deal with each other through a system of rights, duties, liabilities and responsibilities."[45]

Europeanists that hope for the creation of a united Europe—envisioned as one, large, federal state—refer to the experience of Otto Leopold von Bismarck who, as chancellor, unified German principalities with a homogenous system of laws and a single central bureaucracy. But this experience is not the right reference point for modern Europeans. Bismarck politically unified people who shared a common language and identity, which is very different from the situation of European citizens.

Scruton considers national sovereignty to be a basic condition of democracy, and with it comes the right to determine national borders and to approve who governs the nation. National sovereignty is based on a collective "we" upon which negotiations between states must depend. The task of diplomacy is to maintain order and peace, which can only occur in a state capable of defending its own sovereignty from surrounding states.

Kant originally outlines a "league of nations" in which various nations should be submissive to common laws. The difference between Kant's league and today's European Union is connected to the autonomy of individual nations. In Kant's opinion, a league of nations should be made up of autonomous and sovereign states in which the people have the right and the duty of citizenship. The moment states lose their sovereignty, even the league fails.

Today, however, there is an attempt to eliminate national autonomy in favor of a central government. The best way for democracies to protect themselves from these kinds of threats is to adopt a national rather than transnational outlook.

Such an outlook is boldly articulated and defended by Scruton. In *How to Be a Conservative*, he analyzes the main characteristics of conservatism:

1. *Association and Discrimination*: The freedom of association is necessary because innate human values emerge through work in society, not because an external authority imposes them. People voluntarily choose associations and abide by norms that regulate their behavior. Abiding to such norms allows for true membership to associations—a membership that is different than a membership to a nation. Regimes tend to keep a close and often burdening eye on associations, typically out of fear of not being able to control them. In the face of increasingly frequent attacks that such associations undergo—found often in charges of "discrimination" and "classism"—a Scrutonian conservative perceives these attacks as unacceptable and unjust.

2. *Autonomous Institutions*: In contemporary society, the best solution to resentment is social mobility. To be socially mobile requires quality education. To guarantee quality education for its citizens, the objective of the state is to favor autonomous institutions and provide accessible opportunities for even the most impoverished people. But today, desires to control the habits of citizens has led to attacks upon autonomous institutions that do not conform to the directives of political correctness.

3. *The Conversational Model*: Conversation takes place between rational beings and there is a substantial difference between a

       conversation conducted according to good manners and one
that does not. A conversation that is guided by certain rules is
rare and can only happen among people of a certain caliber.

4. *Work and Leisure*: Free time is only beneficial if it has a positive
effect on the workplace and creates a satisfying political order.
This is how Scruton affirms the "feudal principle" articulated
by Disraeli, according to which responsible relationships should
be the foundation of our life in such a way that our activities
have an intrinsic, rather than merely instrumental, value.

5. *Friendship, Conservation, and Value*: As Aristotle divided
friendships into three kinds—friendships of utility, of pleasure,
and of virtue—so Scruton applies this division to conversation.
Conservatives believe that free association, which enables free
conversation, is the bedrock of civil society, but can be appreciated only if it is of value and brings personal fulfillment.

6. *Defending Freedom*: Conservatives have always emphasized the
connection between the country and the military because "the
true citizen is ready to defend his or her country in its hour of
need, and sees in its military institutions an expression of the
deep attachment that holds things in place."[46] They consider
soldiers to be the guardians of civil order and the military to
be an expression of social cohesion.

The economy deals with the values of society by putting the *homo eco-
nomicus* at the center. But real values are created by traditions, customs,
institutions and, *in primis*, religion. For this reason, there was a particular
anti-religious zeal—which characterizes every type of revolution—during the
French Revolution. Revolutionaries considered the church to be the number
one enemy, because it was and is the bearer of true values and a competing
authority to the state:

Burke foreshadowed what was to become the normal conservative
position in Britain during the course of the nineteenth century.

He held that an established religion, tolerant of peaceful dissent, is a part of civil society, attaching people to their home and their neighbours, and enduing their sentiments with moral certainties that they cannot easily acquire in another way; but he also recognized that it is not for the state to impose religion on the citizen or to require doctrinal conformity.[47]

The conservative's notion of the state is halfway between the socialist's, who expects great public intervention, and the liberal's, who theorizes about a "mild state." From the beginning, conservatism has preserved and defended institutions, customs, and life-forms threatened by new social movements and political aspirations. According to conservatives, religion has a role of primary importance in contemporary society as the bearer of the sacred and the transcendent, but in an eventual conflict between religion and the state, the principle of citizenship and the duties of a citizen must emerge. Although Christians profess their faith in society, they do not mandate that people convert to their religion. The case is different, albeit with various facets, with certain radical Islamic fringes and the so-called "human rights" fanatics who want to limit the freedoms of Christians professing their religion.

Scruton outlines the relationship between conservatism and religion:

We regard religion as the root of communities and a consolation in the life of the individual. But we allow it only a ceremonial role in the life of the state, which is built upon purely secular principles, including the principle of religious freedom. The realm of religious value is open to all of us: we can join churches and temples, learn the ways of holiness and righteousness, and enjoy the peace, hope and consolation that religion brings. But we must concede to others the right to be different.

This does not mean that conservatives are fully secular in their approach to civil society. On the contrary, they recognize that much that we value is marked by its religious origins. Many of the most important conservative causes involve the attempt to maintain an

inheritance of consecrated things, whose aura is precious to us even
if we no longer regard it as divinely bestowed. Hence conservatives
are active in the defence of the countryside against the engines of
progress, in the conservation of historic towns and buildings, in the
defence of the forms and ceremonies of public life, and in maintaining the high culture of Europe. We depend on the realm of sacred
things even without necessarily believing in its transcendental
source—which is why culture matters to us.[48]

Conservatives uphold the importance of religion in society because
removing religion from public life makes moral education the prerogative of
families, the place in which primary bonds are found. Once religion is eliminated, nothing else remains but the family, which was already considered an
enemy of revolution by Lenin and attacked by Marx and Engels. But despite
being subject to attack, the institution of family is still the primary place in
which the groundwork of life is constructed and in which home is identified.
This is why conservatives, in a secular society such as our contemporary one,
are increasingly concerned about protecting the family more than religion.

Family law was based on the union between a man and a woman. The
moment this union was reduced to a simple contract between two partners,
the laws that govern those rights of union lost their meaning. Scruton distances
himself from gay marriage and emphasizes the harassment of anyone who
expresses opinions either against gay marriage or for traditional marriage:

> The whole idea of sexual and reproductive norms has been dis-
> missed as offensive by the advocates of the open lifestyle, and it is
> fair to say that the old-fashioned two-parent family is increasingly
> under threat as an institution, as people try to find other ways of
> living together, and other ways of bringing up children.[49]

Conservatives believe religion and family represent two realms of values.
By now, religion plays a marginal role in the lives of the people, and even the
family is losing its status as a peace-finding entity.

According to Scruton, one of the main social concerns of the majority of people is how to correctly spend free time. The spread of so-called "virtual reality," even during free time, to the detriment of *real* reality, brings people to avoid the risks of real human relationships: "Risk-avoidance in human relations means the avoidance of accountability, the refusal to stand judged in another's eyes, to come face to face with another person, to give yourself in whatever measure to him or her, or to expose yourself to the risk of rejection."[50] The progress of logic that characterizes modernity also emerges in the fields of art and culture:

> So far as the critics and the wider culture were concerned, the pursuit of beauty was increasingly pushed to the margins of the artistic enterprise. Qualities like disruptiveness and immorality that previously signified aesthetic failure became marks of success; while the pursuit of beauty was regarded as a retreat from the real task of artistic creation, which is to challenge orthodoxy and to break free from conventional constraints.[51]

Today there seems to be an aversion to beauty, an attempt to hinder it and take away from its charm. Scruton distances himself from the phenomena of pop music, video clips, and other forms of modernity which "record a habit of desecration, in which life is not so much celebrated by art as targeted by it."[52] Beauty continues to have a role in culture, thanks to the artists and writers who try to emancipate themselves from the prevalent transgressive culture. These artists of culture, regardless of their political affiliation, are the true conservatives of our time; they recognize the value in the traditions of the artistic world, allowing it to be conserved and diffused. They clash with "the haste and disorder of modern life, the alienating forms of modern architecture, the noise and spoliation of modern industry—these things have made the pure encounter with beauty a rarer, more fragile and more unpredictable thing for us."[53]

Conservatives believe that the culture of transgression will achieve nothing other than the defeat of beauty and the values connected to it. With the

disappearance of social order, there is no idyllic kingdom like the one imagined by Jean-Jacques Rousseau; rather, there is a bitter and impervious world.
Our political class prefers to delegate the most difficult political decisions to
European bureaucrats and supranational bodies. In the hands of these agents,
ideologies regulate life—not accountable, local people. The economy, therefore, becomes its own ideology, as insane as Marxism or Fascism.

Another battle which conservatives fight today is the battle for free
speech. Today, the main censure does not come directly from the state, but
through cultural intimidation. There are a few subjects considered taboo about
which conservatives cannot express opinions unless they wish to face bitter
critiques and harassment. Regarding the use of certain terms, Scruton believes
conservatives should go back to "observing the world from the beginning and
describe it using the natural language of human relationships" and overcoming the "newspeak" described by Orwell in *1984* and used in modern Marxist
language. A "heretic hunt" is thus born; unaligned thoughts are deemed as
heresies to be eliminated rather than errors to be criticized.

Scruton writes:

> Locke's essay on Toleration of 1689 argued for the toleration of opin-
> ions and ways of life with which you do not agree, as one of the
> virtues of a liberal society. But many who call themselves liberal
> today seem to have little understanding of what this virtue really is.
> Toleration does not mean renouncing all opinions that others might
> find offensive. It does not mean an easy-going relativism or a belief
> that 'anything goes'. On the contrary, it means accepting the right
> of others to think and act in ways of which you disapprove. It means
> being prepared to protect people from negative discrimination even
> when you hate what they think and what they feel.[54]

As these heretical opinions are scorned and attacked, so are our inherited
traditions. The diffusion of the liberal Enlightenment spirit has affected every
sphere of society, including architecture and the structure of our cities. We
have "achieved" a new type of urban space in which traditional architecture is
ridiculed, where we witness the triumph of "non-places" and "satellite cities":

The wastelands of exurbia—such as those which spread from Detroit for 50 miles in every direction—are places where past and future generations have been disregarded, places where the voices of the dead and the unborn are no longer heard. They are places of vociferous impermanence, where present generations live without belonging—where there is no belonging, since belonging is a relationship in history, a relationship that binds both present and absent generations, and which depends upon the perception of a place as home.[55]

Roger Scruton's Arguments for Conservatism

While the French Revolution of 1789 represented a turning point for Burke, the moment Scruton matured his conservative conscience was in 1968. The Anglo-Saxon model, according to which customs prevail over reason and social relationships are regulated, was an inspiration to him. Conservatism, he realized, was the way to protect the social ecology:

> Individual freedom is a part of that ecology, since without it social organisms cannot adapt. But freedom is not the sole or even the central goal of politics, even if it is the attribute that, at a deep level, makes politics both necessary and possible. Conservatism and conservation are in fact two aspects of a single long-term policy, which is that of husbanding resources. These resources include the social capital embodied in laws, customs and institutions; they also include the material capital contained in the environment, and the economic capital contained in a free, but law-governed, economy. The purpose of politics, on this view, is not to rearrange society in the interests of some overarching vision or idea, such as equality, liberty or fraternity. It is to maintain a vigilant resistance to the entropic forces that erode our social and ecological inheritance.[56]

The main difference between socialism and liberalism compared to conservatism lies in the globalist reach of the first two ideologies and in the local disposition of conservatism. Such a local disposition is able to defend even the smallest capital social systems against unbridled change. Scruton rightly suggests that solutions to international problems are born at a local level through loyalty to one's own nation. However, today we eliminate the national systems and sovereign states in favor of supranational organisms that do not have popular legitimacy: "the nation state has proved to be a stable foundation of democratic government and secular jurisdiction, we ought to improve it, to adjust it, even to dilute it, but not to throw it away."[57]

Territory is at the base of government. Today, more than ever before, that which was affirmed by Goethe in *Faust* is true: "buy that which you have inherited from your fathers to possess it." It is therefore necessary to reacquire the sovereignty of the preceding generations born of Christianity, Roman law, and the imperial government in order to regain true possession of our countries.

Membership in a nation originates through citizenship, which serves as the link between the state and the individuals and creates a reciprocal responsibility of rights and duties. Citizenship means belonging to a common concept, to a "we"; losing such membership leads to social disintegration.

Scruton classifies societies as:

1. *Tribal societies*, in which individuals consider themselves part of an extended family and an enforced hierarchy rules social life;
2. *Creed communities*, in which a religious membership is enforced and there is a link between the individuals who share the same gods and divine precepts; and
3. *Nations*, based on criteria antithetical to that of tribal societies and creed communities. Scruton gives his definition:

By a nation I mean a people settled in a certain territory, who share language, institutions, customs and a sense of history and who regard themselves as equally committed both to their place of residence and to the legal and political progress that governs it. Members of tribes see each other as a family; members of creed communities see each other as the faithful; members of nations see each other as neighbours. Vital to the sense of nationhood, therefore, is the idea of a common territory, in which we are all settled, and to which we are all entitled as our home. People who share a territory share a history; they may also share a language and a religion. The European nation state emerged when this idea of a community defined by a place was enshrined in sovereignty and law—in other words when it was aligned with a territorial jurisdiction.[58]

Scruton explains the difference between nationalism and national loyalty: while loyalty brings peace, nationalism has historically brought war in Europe. National loyalty allows the creation of a system based on consensus and the respect of sovereignty and rights of the individual.

Today, however, a repudiation of the national idea is increasingly widespread, along with a disparagement of the customs and culture of one's own country that can be summarized by the term "oikophobia" (which literally means the "repudiation of inheritance and home").

Oikophobia can go beyond the repudiation of national loyalty and can be energized by feelings against the nation. Support of supranational institutions and the imposition of laws from above can turn distaste to hostility; "the domination of our own national parliament by oikophobes is partly responsible for the assaults on our constitution, for the acceptance of subsidized immigration and for the attacks on customs and institutions associated with traditional and native forms of life."[59] The arguments of oikophobes are always the same: a multicultural society and minority rights trump loyalty to the country.

Furthermore, the unrestrained pursuit of free international trade damages already deteriorating national sovereignties. Scruton points the finger at the World Trade Organization (WTO) as guilty of annihilating local economies, not protecting land ownership, and favoring multinational societies that work to destroy national jurisdictions through transnational institutions. In this sense, an important distinction must be made between a transnational assembly and a national parliament that, in theory, should protect its citizens and serve the interests of those who elected them.

Scruton dedicates great attention to economic issues. How should conservatives respond to free trade? "Not to advocate economic freedom at all costs, but to recognize the costs of economic freedom and to take all steps to reduce them. We need free enterprise, but we also need the rule of law that limits it."[60]

Democratic governments all too often encourage economic growth without considering the repercussions it can have on the environment. Conservatives must try to unify social balance with ecological balance; environmental balance is an integral part of the lasting social order. Both conservatives and environmentalists look for the most suitable ways to defend common legacies of society under threat. Protecting the environment requires finding motivations that encourage citizens to protect it, and it is the role of the conservative to generate respect for one's own territory through the development of the concept of national loyalty.

Attachment to territory and the desire to preserve it in the name of love is therefore of the utmost importance. The elimination of national sovereignty carried out by globalist institutions brought on not only the disintegration of the environment but also a lack of useful ecological policies. Conservatives are against NGOs and international pressure groups that base their ecological policies on the acquisition of power over the world rather than on what would actually be useful to the world. Scruton writes:

> In such examples we see how environmental activism, divorced from national sentiments that can carry the people with it, and expressed through unaccountable bodies that follow self-chosen global agendas, does little or nothing to further the environmental cause. And conservatives will see this as an inevitable result of the radical mindset. Radicals prefer global ideals to local loyalties, and rather than making bridges to their opponents, prefer to demonize them.[61]

Therefore, Scruton hopes environmentalists will separate themselves from the "witch hunting" mentality that characterizes the work of globalists and identify human greed as the main enemy of environmental protection:

There is a tendency on the left to single out the big players in the market as the principal culprits: to pin environmental crime on those—like oil companies, motor manufacturers, logging corporations, agribusinesses, supermarkets—who make their profits by exporting their costs to future generations. But this is to mistake the effect for the cause. In a free market these ways of making money emerge by an invisible hand from choices made by all of us.... The solution is to rectify our demands, so as to bear the costs of them ourselves. In short, we must change our lives. And we can change our lives only if we have a motive to do so—a motive that is so strong enough to constrain our appetites.[62]

Even though our modern societies are ones of foreigners, conservatives still consider the nation to be an institution capable of keeping citizens united amongst themselves, even for future generations:

Conservatives are not in the business of conserving just any law, institution or custom. Their desire is to conserve the institutions that embody collective solutions to recurring problems, and which pass on socially generated knowledge. In Burke's view (and mine) the common law is such an institution; so are political institutions like representative government, and social institutions like marriage and the family. These are institutions that foster the habit of sacrifice, and which therefore generate the motive on which the husbanding of resources depends.[63]

The focal point of conservative thought is the hereditary principle that Burke claims disappeared with the French Revolution, causing a loss of social capital—conceptions of justice, scholastic and educational systems, and public facilities. In a society that tries to deny death, a true conservative recognizes its value. Respecting the dead is a way to safeguard those yet to be born and to pass on legacies to future generations.

Beyond recognizing death as a natural human process, conservatives protect institutions such as marriage that, apart from being a commitment of love between a man and a woman, consist of a division of roles and a form of social and economic cooperation between spouses. Nuptials are an explicit rite that establish the transition from one social status to another, involving an entire community.

The desacralization of marriage began with the French Revolution, when the state declared itself to be the only institution capable of annulling marriages, therefore bypassing the role of the church. The situation has worsened in today's society, to the point that "social constraints that tied a man and wife to each other through all troubles and disharmonies have been one by one removed, to the point where marriage is hardly distinct from a short-term agreement for cohabitation."[64]

It is this idea that conservatives oppose in civil unions and gay marriages. These are antipodes of the traditional function of marriage, which is to create an existential link rather than a series of obligations and duties to be respected. Conservatives consider marriage to be a lifelong unity, not a contract of cohabitation. While the institution of marriage is partly based on sexual attraction, it also has important and essential functions, such as ensuring social reproduction, the socialization of children, and the transfer of social capital.

The loosening of the bond of marriage occurred at the moment the state took over marriage, which used to be a rite based on divine law: "it has, therefore, found it expedient to undo the sacrament, to permit easy divorce, to reduce marriage from a vow to a contract and—in the most recent act of liberalization—to permit marriage, or its civil 'equivalent', between people of the same sex."[65] Today, marriage is no longer a rite of passage from one lifestyle to another, but rather a mere bureaucratic formality deprived of the set of values that are passed on at the moment in which two people marry.

The goal of reaching a condition of complete equality, the Enlightenment utopia, is also alive and often achieved in the context of marriage. But the destruction of the bond of marriage has led to disastrous social results. One of the nefarious consequences of the disappearance of marriage is the sharp decline of new births in Western countries. Where are the future generations? For whom do we conserve, if not them?

Scruton notes that the sinister relativism of modern society was born because of the decline of religious faith. A new, nonreligious form of belonging is thus sought based on the systematic rejection of religion: "in place of objectivity we have only 'inter-subjectivity'—in other words, consensus. Truths, meanings, facts and values are now regarded as negotiable."[66]

The new theology of relativism has emerged and aims to limit every claim of absolute truth by convincing us that traditional Western culture is ethnocentric, racist, and patriarchal. Enlightenment thinkers argue that religion is a set of beliefs now disavowed and discredited by science, which gives one the consolation that religion used to offer to mankind. While religion is threatened by scientific skepticism and social disorder, citizens still actually need it—it is rooted in the social nature of people and carries out an essential social function by defending marriage and family from sexual temptations and ensuring the transfer of social capital to future generations.

Finally, Scruton turns his attention to totalitarianism. Conservatives, he writes, must only distance themselves from totalitarian governments—understood as centralized governments—that limit the constitution and every aspect of the social life of citizens. Soviet Marxism is not the only modern-era totalitarian ideology opposed by conservatives:

> The ideology of the French revolutionaries was one of enlightened optimism, popular sovereignty and human rights; the ideology of the Nazis, although based on socialist theories, had an important racial and nationalist component that is alien to the central tenets of Marxism. All three ideologies, however, were adopted in the pursuit of power, and are to be explained in Marx's way, as power-seeking rather than truth-seeking devices.[67]

Totalitarian regimes are characterized by their abolition of institutions that give power and freedom to individuals, including independent information, private property, and religious affiliation. Totalitarian regimes also identify certain social groups as enemies against whom they orient propaganda and repressive actions—for example, the Jacobins singled out the aristocracy during the French Revolution; Nazis the Jews; Russian Communists the middle class.

These regimes derive power from hate and social spite by dividing human beings into two groups: guilty and innocent.

But the disappearance of political totalitarianism does not lead to diminished social resentment. Rather, such resentment is diffused in different forms and manners not even linked to the state's actions. Therefore,

> we should not resent the fact that we resent, but accept it, as a part of the human condition, something to be managed along with all our other joys and afflictions. However, resentment can be transformed into a governing emotion and social cause, and thereby gain release from the constraints which normally contain it. This happens when resentment loses the specificity of its target, and becomes directed to society as a whole, and to the groups that are thought to control it. In such cases, resentment ceases to be a response to another's unmerited success and becomes instead an existential posture.[68]

Propaganda is the main tool of totalitarianism, realized through special language that, paraphrasing Orwell in *1984*, we can define as "newspeak," a new language that takes the place of a regular one which aims to describe reality not as it is, but in ways that affirm power to a state, political party, or ideology:

> One can disagree with anything the Party says or does, but provided that one uses its terminology, as the scope of said terminology is precisely to make agreement and disagreement, conviction and doubt, truth and falsehood, indistinguishable. The newspeak eliminates reality even as it describes it.[69]

CHAPTER THREE

German, Austrian, and Prussian Conservatism

Austro-Hungarian Empire and Austria

Before they suffered defeat in the First World War, the Austrian and German Empires were founded on traditional values and norms of a clear conservative mold.

The principles of their conservative policy emerged from a book titled *Die Elemente der Staatskunst* by Adam Müller (1779–1829). Published in 1809, the book, with its defense of the empire against reforms, was met with immediate approval by the Austrian court and Klemens von Metternich. According to Müller, recuperating medieval principles of government was the only way to return to the great Austria. At that time, Austria and Prussia had undergone a progressive decline due to the rise of liberal individualism at the expense of the elite, leading to a collapse of feudal values. Likewise in France, the destruction of medieval organic society took place well before the arrival of Napoleon, who established liberal reforms to increase his own power: all citizens are equal before the law but must also be equally without power. In his work, Müller not only wishes to defend the status quo but also hopes to restore medieval order. He points his finger at the clergy and the aristocrats, all of whom were guilty of provoking the revolution by progressively abandoning medieval and feudal Christian morality in favor of the liberal spirit of individualism.

The liberal spirit of individualism does not acknowledge that men are born from social groups such as the family, tribes, clans, or nations, and that their rights and duties derive from these institutions. The only way to find social harmony is to look to the state as an aggregate of communities that performs social functions of which each citizen is a part, rather than as a collection of single individuals.

At the end of the eighteenth century, Joseph II of the Austrian Empire restored traditional institutions and assisted the nobility against philosophers led by Voltaire. With the advent of Napoleon's power, liberal reforms were proposed in the Austrian Empire with the intent to mobilize the people against him. However, Emperor Francis II actually avoided going through with them. No concession was granted to the various nationalist characters; even making small concessions in an empire based on feudal values would have meant giving space to demands that could have culminated in revolt or requests for independence.

Following the immediate defeat at the Battle of Wagram in 1809, the emperor was forced to begin negotiations with Napoleon to avoid the disintegration of the empire. He relied on Klemens von Metternich who, through diplomatic channels, looked for a political solution to stem French expansion. A man of conservative training, Metternich collaborated with Friedrich von Gentz: Burke's translator, reader of Justus Möser (1720–1794), and writer who defended stability and the feudal spirit by denouncing modernity. Metternich was convinced of the need to impose counterrevolutionary values and defend imperial institutions; he did not allow himself to be seduced by the sirens of liberalism. Besides being opposed by the aristocracy, liberal reforms were also opposed by the church; the Austrian clergy was one of the most conservative and reactionary in Europe, and an authentic campaign denouncing liberal atheism unfolded from the pulpit.

Metternich implemented repressive measures to keep liberal proposals from spreading to the general population, but nationalist and liberal ideas were only ever limited to a tight circle of intellectuals in Austria. Dozens of people were arrested, and, thanks to the church, careful measures on education and censorship were employed. In 1819, Metternich approved the Carlsbad Decrees, which aimed at repressing liberal and nationalist aspirations, thus leading to a crackdown on free expression. In the following years, the defense of restored order continued to be defended through political action, cultural initiatives, and propaganda.

But the events of 1830 were the preamble to the subsequent revolution of 1848, which proved to be bloody and widespread. Revolts of citizens and students in Vienna led to Metternich's dismissal and the enactment of liberal legislation. Ferdinand I of Austria was open to and carried out the demands of revolutionaries, causing the court, the clergy, and the high officers of the army to run for cover, and the emperor to abdicate his throne to his nephew Franz Joseph.

The reaction of Austrian conservatives was immediate. In the 1850s, the aristocracy not only resumed their positions of power but put out publications such as the *Kreuzzeitung*, a newspaper with clearly conservative, if not reactionary, stances. The aristocracy also enacted repressive policies against liberalism and nationalism, declaring such sentiments enemies of the empire. Franz Joseph authorized a Germano-centric policy by canceling liberal concessions of previous years and granting more power to the church.

The Austrian Empire's fate was linked to fringe conservatives of society. During Metternich's administration, traditional conservatism prevented the prevalence of liberalism or Slav nationalism. In the nineteenth century, economic innovations and the rising awareness of Slav ethnicity led to detrimental changes for the Germanic constituency; they increasingly abandoned the moderate conservatism of the Habsburgs for extreme right stances, in an attempt to protect the status quo.

Thanks to industrialization, even the Slavs obtained more important positions in society, boosting aspirations of national independence. Despite a short period of time in the 1860s when liberal tendencies emerged in favor of anticlerical stances and *laissez-faire* economic policies, a conservative order was soon reestablished. This was despite the stances of the House of Habsburg growing more and more fragile: if they were to endorse the requests of the

Germanic constituency, they would generate discontentment among the Slavs, and if they allowed for certain concessions of the Slavs, they would create strong resentment on the part of the Germanic ethnicity. Therefore, they had to alternate between a policy of repressions and very small concessions, though middle-class pressure to use force against the Slavs grew increasingly apparent.

Georg Heinrich von Schönerer (1842–1921), who founded the Pan-Germanism party in 1885, intercepted these resentments through a program that proposed the unity of the Austrian Empire and the German Reich. Such a unity would make the Slavs a minority. Its prescription called for adopting Protestantism and breaking away from the Catholic Church, which would reinforce discipline and Prussian virtue; legislation to protect small business owners; and abolishing socialism by removing Jews from positions of power or prestige. In 1897, Prime Minister Kazimierz Badeni made Czech the official language of the empire along with German, which provoked violent protests that led to the closure of the parliament in Vienna.

The elections of 1907—the first with universal male suffrage—introduced Karl Lueger (1844–1910) as leader of the conservative Christian Social movement, and on the other side, the Marxist Social-Democrats, polarizing the votes of citizens. Lueger was elected to parliament in 1885 and mayor of Vienna in 1897; the key to his electoral success was his fervent Catholicism. The Austrian Church, other than being the most conservative in Europe, exercised strong influence on the aristocracy and on the lower-middle classes, thanks to a monopoly on education. Lueger's policy was characterized as anti-Semitic but was actually based on the background of Catholic intellectuals, thinkers, and supporters such as Karl Freiherr von Vogelsang (1818–1890)—who, after converting to Catholicism from Protestantism, took over the newspaper *Das Vaterland* in 1875. The paper refused democratic liberalism in favor of the Christian Social Party, articulating stances later adopted by Pope Leo XIII in *Rerum novarum*. Lueger's electoral victory also coincided with the arrival of a young Hitler in Vienna, which faced a tense social-political climate ready to explode at any minute.

The breaking point was brought on by the murder of Franz Ferdinand and the declaration of war on Serbia, marking the Austro-Hungarian Empire's final attempt to preserve and reaffirm its unity and traditional imperial strength. Russia took a similar direction in response; to avert a crisis in the tsarist society and preserve Russian order, a test of strength and military victory was necessary to restore the morale of the people. Germany's involvement, on behalf of its Austrian allies, was the result of intentions to stimulate central Europe and the Germano-centric East, to affirm Prussian values, and to oppose liberal democracies and socialism.

Following military defeat and the collapse of its empire, right-wing groups such as that of Heimwehr di Ernst Rüdiger Starhemberg (1899–1956) spread throughout Austria, feeding vengeful sentiments focused on defending the homeland from socialist enemies and foreigners. Austria withdrew from conflict as a reduced state, destined to be absorbed by Germany in just a few years. The terms reached in the Treaty of Versailles in 1919 brought independence to Hungary, but also alleviated the European chessboard from strategic protagonists such as the Austro-Hungarian Empire. The empire was reduced to a subordinate state of Germany, and it became incapable of balancing German economic and demographic capacity.

Prussia, the German Empire, and Germany

Compared to other European countries, Prussia was governed by an extremely conservative ruling class. Its existence in 1807 was thanks to Napoleon's decision not to annex it to the French Empire. Independence, however, came at the cost of large parts of territory and population, as well as significant economic damage.

Due to the strict conditions imposed by Napoleon, the call for liberal reforms began to emerge throughout the population. King Frederick William III promised to devise a constitution that would represent every social class and surmount the rigid Prussian caste system. Noblemen immediately withdrew support from the proposed reforms and, with the Prussian army officer Friedrich von der Marwitz as their spokesman, expressed their disdain for a reform that essentially imported French liberalism to Germany and eroded cohesion in the Prussian community. Such liberalism brought materialism

and individualism along with it, and opposed the established patriarchal society based on centrality of the family.

Napoleon's defeat put a halt to reform proposals and brought about a
restoration of ancient principles. Prussia continued to be governed by the
Hohenzollerns and the nobility, and ancient institutions remained intact while
liberal constitutions were abolished. At the Congress of Vienna in 1815, Austria, Prussia, and Russia restored the previous order by putting an end to
liberal and nationalist demands. Starting from the assumption of the sacred-
ness of their alliance and justifying political and military actions as guided
by God, the allies highlighted the need to attack countries in which revolutionary movements were gaining leverage to restore order.

Beginning in the 1850s, industrialization and urbanism transformed
rural Europe, in a way that coincided with the diffusion of nationalism in
large parts of the populations. At first, nationalism was considered the result
of liberal revolutions, especially by central empires. It was also associated with
Jacobin radicalism.

During this time, the role of the statesman Otto von Bismarck began to
emerge, giving life to an opportunistic conservatism based on political power
and devoid of a philosophical basis. Thanks to his policies, founded on Prussian military force, he achieved unification of greater Germany. William I,
king of Prussia, became kaiser of Germany. He opposed liberals who tried to
limit both his political and military power. Bismarck was nominated prime
minister of Prussia in September 1862, in an attempt to stem proposals of
liberal reform in the Prussian parliament. His goal was to achieve and maintain real unification based on conservative values.

An assembly of princes, aristocrats, and generals proclaimed William I
emperor of Germany in January 1871. Subsequently, to demonstrate Germany's military power, he incited the Franco-Prussian War. At the same time,
Bismarck's policies grew increasingly authoritarian; in 1878, he used the
excuse of two attacks on the emperor's life to pass several anti-socialist laws.

In 1888, William II became kaiser. From the beginning, he wanted complete decision-making autonomy, deeming Bismarck a cumbersome figure.
Bismarck's system protected him from everyone except the kaiser—Bismarck

resigned in 1890. William then took rule of the country into his own hands, starting with the educational system.

Beginning in 1850, educational policy of the feudal approach was increasingly removed from the old lower and higher humanistic gymnasiums in order to establish the modern *Realschulen*, which transformed schools into technical-professional institutions. Classical instruction, such as ancient Greek, was gradually perceived to be anti-monarchic and neo-pagan. The imperial courts were also afraid of the consequences of in-depth teaching of natural sciences in high schools, and such lessons were therefore reduced. Rational thinking, they thought, could induce atheism and materialism in the youth, and critics of the bourgeois educational system affirmed their fears. A true modernizer, William II proposed a sort of middle ground by assigning a central and decisive role and task for a specific subject—German language and culture. This took the focus off the problematic subjects, and German schools were thus transformed. In the 1892–93 scholastic year, students learned about "Germany and history," or rather, "historical narration." These lessons were emphasized over all others, and at that precise moment in history, such emphasis had the purpose of reinvigorating the love for people and the homeland.[1]

The highest literary and cultural expression of the Bismarckian government emerged from the writings of Heinrich von Treitschke (1834–1896), member of the Reichstag from 1871 to 1884. His studies were oriented toward preserving the power of Prussian rulers and gave a voice to the conservative issues of the Reich. After 1848, when German conservatism embraced nationalism, Treitschke represented the conservative wing of the national party that supported Bismarck from 1866 to 1878. His *History* of *Germany in the Nineteenth Century*, the first volume of which was published in 1879, represented a nationalist conservatism that distanced itself from Metternich's traditional conservatism, which Treitschke considered too pacifist, too internationalist, and too tolerant toward Slavs and Jews.

Without a state based on feudal particularism, which had disintegrated since the century of enlightenment, there was no social stability in civil life. Bismarck therefore had to resist liberal individualism. The German Reich, as professed by William I, was born as an extension of Prussia and was based on Prussian values of sacrifice and harsh discipline. William viewed Bismarck's antisocialist laws in a positive way; he believed the growing influence of the societal masses would lead to the decline of traditional morality and of the Prussian character found in patriarchal families and rural villages, where life was marked by the laws of tradition. Cities, on the other hand, incited the loss of the social identity and, consequently, the sense of community and morality.

His writings exalted the "German race" as virtuously superior to other populations. He also endorsed certain anti-Semitic positions of Bismarck's out of fear of losing the support of the left-leaning middle. In foreign policy, Treitschke was in favor of an alliance with the Austrian Empire, because Eastern Europe should have been under German rule. Following the German defeat in the First World War and the abdication of Emperor William II, the kingdom of the Hohenzollern family, a dynasty that had governed Prussia for centuries, came to an end. They had reigned without interruption from 1701, the year the Kingdom of Prussia was founded, until the subsequent unification of Germany and the creation of the German Empire in 1871. The family's story is told in Walter Henry Nelson's book *Soldier Kings: House of Hohenzollern.*

K. L. von Haller (1768–1854) hoped for the return to the medieval union between church and state and revival of pre-1789 legitimism; Joseph von Radowitz (1797–1853) influenced the pro-medieval vision of society of Frederick William IV of Prussia; Friedrich von Schlegel (1772–1829), considered one of the founders of the Romantic movement, became a close associate of Chancellor Metternich and one of the biggest theorists of the Restoration. Karl von Vogelsang (1818–1890) was the intellectual father of Austrian conservatism and the Christian Social Party at the end of the 1800s—the same party that came to power in Austria in 1934 and gave life to a clerically Fascist corporate state before Germany's annexation of Austria. All these thinkers, despite being originally Protestant, converted to Catholicism.

Patriotism was on the rise. In 1932, German chancellor Heinrich Brüning (1885–1970) refused to pay further war reparations, due to economic stagnation and the political paralysis of his government. Engelbert Dollfuss (1892–1934) was the founder of *Vaterlandfront,* the "Fatherland Front," a political organization joining the main right-wing Austrian parties, drawing inspiration from Italian Fascism. Dollfuss was killed in 1934 by the SS.

Kurt Alois von Schuschnigg (1897–1977) was nominated as chancellor with Mussolini's support, continuing policy developed by Dollfuss defined as "clerical Fascism," which aimed to reconstruct Austria as a corporate Catholic state. Supported by the clergy, the policies condemned Marxism, materialism, liberalism, and individualism. Unions were suppressed and punitive measures were implemented against Democrats, Socialists, and Jews. While Schuschnigg was trying to preserve Austria's independence by embracing Fascist stances, many Austrians began to view Hitler as the only figure capable of asserting German supremacy in central and eastern Europe. On March 12, 1938, Austria was invaded and occupied by the Germans.

The role of conservatives in the Nazi takeover of Germany can be described as a mix of political errors, an underestimation of Hitler's influence, and an inability to understand the changes of the time. At the beginning, German conservative elites were characterized by nationalist, conservative, and elitist stances. During the elections of 1932, votes for their party fell from 28 percent to less than 10 percent; Nazis were the makers of a true electoral boom, reaching 35 percent. But the most worrisome figure was the percentage achieved by Communists and Marxist Social Democrats, whose sum of votes reached 34 percent. German conservatives hoped to exploit their methods and Nazi violence in order to marginalize Socialists and put an end to the Weimar Republic, but the situation got out of hand: by trying to exploit the Nazis for their own purposes, they were instead overpowered. The most obvious case was that of Kurt von Schleicher (1882–1934), the last chancellor before Hitler took power, who declared a few months before he and his wife were brutally assassinated by the SS: "If Nazis did not exist, we would have to invent them." The error made by German conservatives was not realizing the danger of Nazis, and undeniably having the same enemies as Hitler: the allies, the Jews, the Communists, the Socialists, and the liberal democracies.

The upper classes of Europe took it upon themselves to protect the status quo in these moments of intense social change and major uncertainty. Such protection led to the advent of authoritarian regimes; in Spain and Portugal, such regimes were characterized by basic repressions of freedoms. But the German situation was different from every other European country—because Hitler took power.

In order to reach their goals, the Nazis immediately looked for support from militarist and ultra-conservative fringes. The army played an important role in supporting Nazi policy, and the aristocracy had a monopoly on the official body. The Nazis succeeded in attracting the children of the most important aristocratic and upper middle-class families to its ranks, as well as small landowners, historically linked to the conservative party. Such subscribers guaranteed a strong base for the party's work.

The relationship between the Catholic Church and Nazis was complicated from the beginning. Initially, cardinals and bishops viewed Hitler as a leader capable of preserving the church's traditional values by opposing secular liberalism, materialism, and anti-Christian bolshevism. However, fearing the church could influence citizens more than he could, Hitler forbade meetings of Catholic groups and accused Christianity of Jewish corruption and a penchant for paganism.

In order to understand the German Conservative Party post-1945, it is necessary to retrace the evolution of conservative thought to the beginning. After the war, there was an attempt to return to the origins of conservative thought, which was faithful to the idea that conservatism is in constant change. Unlike Marxism and liberalism, whose doctrines, although slightly changed, remained mostly consistent, conservatism adapted and changed in every historical period. If a current conservative—a pupil of Carl Schmitt or Arnold Gehlen, for example—suddenly found himself faced with one of the predecessors of the middle of the last century, the two would not have much to say to each other; they might even feel like clear antagonists.[2]

After 1945, conservatives in Germany tried to restore the bygone era and the status quo prior to the Nazi dictatorship. The period between 1945 and 1949, when the Federal Republic was founded, was rather chaotic, and conservatives were the architects of a "repair conservatism." They considered Nazism to be nothing more than a plebeian uprising and favored the restoration of an ancient pre-Nazi hierarchy.

In the early years after the war, this German conservatism was extremely—and somewhat problematically—tame. It could hardly understand reality and had become completely apolitical; in the end, it was nothing more than nostalgia. The connection with the Third Reich, in which conservatism flourished for the last time, was abruptly broken, and it seemed almost impossible to build a bridge to the past.³ From 1945 onward, German conservatism ignored one of the two characterizing elements of conservative thought prior to the Nazi dictatorship: nationalism. Although the second element, anti-Communism, was maintained, German conservatives recognized themselves in their home but no longer in their country. In a period of uncertainties for the nation's future, in which disorientation reigned, anti-Communism became the sole glue of conservative strength.

Beginning in the mid-sixties, parallel to the political stabilization of the country, a new form of conservatism developed, characterized by "overcoming the past," or the recovery of values prior to 1945 that were lost due to the "axial period." The term "axial period" is understood as the moment in which conservatives realized that "other political groups gave rise to a status quo that was no longer acceptable, and that previous situations could no longer be restored."⁴

Karl Ludwig von Haller (1768–1854)

Karl Ludwig von Haller was the Swiss author of the book *Restauration der Staatswissenschaften*, in which the term "restoration" was introduced for the first time. His hope was to return to a traditional state in opposition to the Revolution, according to the slogan "in alliance with the throne and the altar." For him, the term restoration "indicates a state of mind, a mentality, a commitment that transcends the strictly political fact of becoming a principle and idea, in which all the manners that facilitate the design of *reductio ad unum*, the fusion between man and the divine, between body and soul, between authority and freedom, between State and society, can join together."⁵

Haller condemned the Revolution and Protestant reforms that originated from the theories of Enlightenment philosophers. In his opinion, the revolution contradicted its own initial objectives, giving life to a dictatorship. Therefore,

> pressured by the need to stop the spread of revolutionary ideas and pushed by the will to bridge the cultural gap that he believed existed between the ranks of counterrevolutionaries, he felt the need to develop "a more solid opposing doctrine, capable of bringing down all the bad apples, of reconciling experience with reason and serving as a life support for the people with common sense."[6]

In his reflection, Catholicism plays a central role and is considered the only religion with an anti-subversive and hierarchical character.

Klemens von Metternich (1773–1859)

Metternich began his career as a Hapsburg diplomat at twenty-two years old. Cosmopolitan, anti-revolutionary, internationalist, and anti-Jacobin, his book *Memoirs of Prince Metternich* denotes the influences of Burke and Maistre. He accused the liberal revolutionaries of the '20s and '30s from Italy, Spain, and Germany of being unhistorical and unrealistic.

He played a central role in the Congress of Vienna of 1815 as a representative of the Austrian Empire. Along with the British delegate Robert Castlereagh (1769–1822), French delegate Charles Talleyrand (1754–1838), and Alexander I of Russia (1777–1825), he redrew the boundaries of Europe, reestablishing those that had existed prior to the Napoleonic wars. The goal of the congress was to establish a Europe based on well-defined principles:

1. Conservatism as a response to the French Revolution
2. Traditionalism against the changes that occurred at the end of the '20s
3. Legitimism to reestablish the principle of the hereditary monarchy
4. Restoration of "Ottantottisti" to restore power to the monarchies who governed before the French Revolution
5. Peace in response to the Napoleonic Wars

The alliance among rulers, sanctioned by the congress, gave life to the so-called "Holy Alliance" of Christian powers inspired by Tsar Alexander I's plan. Part of the aftermath of the Congress of Vienna included the suspension of nationalist demands in Italy, Spain, and Germany. Between 1815 and 1848, Jacobins and Republicans were not the only groups considered to be revolutionaries; nationalists were also included, because nationalism was considered a destabilizing element of the social order. The historical consequences of the Congress of Vienna on one hand included the abolishment of democratic progress, and on the other hand the creation of peace, excluding the local conflict of the Crimean War, which lasted a century thanks to a model based on diplomacy.

But Metternich's world definitively faded with Bismarck's rise to power; his "iron and blood" policy opposed diplomatic policy. After 1848, Metternich meet Disraeli in England and, due to their like-mindedness, became fast friends and cofounded a conservative newspaper. It was largely thanks to Metternich's influence that Disraeli renamed the Tory Party "Conservative."

On December 15, 1820, Metternich sent Tsar Alexander I a "secret memorandum" to fight the infiltration of Jacobin thought in society. Part of the text was published in the *Confession of Faith* collected in *Memoirs,* in which Metternich denounces the societal changes taking place at the time. Religion, morality, economy, policy, and administration were becoming accessible to anyone; modern man did not recognize the value in experience; faith did not represent anything to him; he substituted traditional values with individual beliefs, without truthfulness. The most important need of society, Metternich knew, was to be governed by a strong authority and to have a stable system of laws.

Johann Joseph von Görres (1776–1848)

Görres was a dedicated Jacobin, to the point of leading the most revolutionary German newspaper, the *Red Sheet* (from 1790 to 1799), which criticized religion and endorsed the ideology of the French Revolution. Despite all this, he too became a staunch defender of traditional German principles. As a professor of history at the University of Munich, he created the Görres Society, active from 1837 to 1848, which enjoyed significant influence over political and religious life at the time.

German conservatism was also diffused through the works of certain German historians such as Friedrich Carl von Savigny (1779–1861) and Leopold von Ranke (1795–1886). Savigny thought history was the only way to understand current conditions of mankind; he wrote in his book *The History of the Roman Law during the Middle Ages* that preserved customs and traditions are essential. Ranke's work also considered each society on its own terms and opposed universal Enlightenment generalizations.

Friedrich Julius Stahl (1802–1861)

A political philosopher and constitutionalist of Jewish origin, Stahl converted to Lutheran Christianity at seventeen years old. His most important book, *Die Philosophie des Rechts nach geschichtlicher Ansicht*, is a historical vision of the philosophy of law in which he bases the laws of politics on Christian revelation and refuses rationalist doctrines. In his opinion, hatred towards the monarchy and the aristocracy pushes the middle class toward liberal stances, and the technical-economic thinking that dominated his contemporary society was no longer capable of perceiving political ideas—therefore rendering the state a big factory.

Jacob Burckhardt (1818–1897)

Born in 1818 in Basel, the thinker, historian, and philosopher of history Burckhardt reached notoriety with his publication *The Civilization of the Renaissance in Italy*. As a student at the University of Berlin, he studied under Leopold von Ranke and became editor of the conservative journal *Basler Zeitung*. When Ranke withdrew from teaching, Burckhardt was chosen to be his successor but refused to take the position, due to both the relationship that tied him to Basel and his embroilment in a controversy with what the centralized Prussian government represented. Years later, after time had calmed things down, he did become a professor at the University of Basel, where a young Friedrich Nietzsche attended some of his lessons. The two met but never developed a strong friendship due to Burckhardt's personality and, most likely, the envy the professor had for the young philosopher.

A man of great culture and an admirer of Italy, Burckhardt left for the peninsula in 1846, where he spent a stimulating two-year period being fascinated by Italy's cultural heritage. Italy offered him extraordinary ideas for his work as a writer and historian. His Italian experience resulted in his work *The Age of Constantine the Great* and especially *The Cicerone: An Art Guide to Painting in Italy. For the use of travellers*, a large volume published in 1855 in Basel and reprinted in the 1950s in Italy, as a guide for anyone wishing to visit and understand the *Belpaese*.

He believed that universal suffrage and democratic equality would lead to a total dictatorship, worse than the old monarchies. He also believed that the nineteenth century was inexorably destined to undergo a socialist tyranny, identifying its origins within the French Revolution and the Paris Commune.

Another central work was his *Reflections on History*, published posthumously in 1905, consisting of a collection of his university lessons audited by Nietzsche. They both shared a common skepticism of their era and an aversion for progressives. "Progress," which Burckhardt described as "infamous," was what he was chiefly against. After being so close to liberalism as a young man, Burckhardt developed a clear critique of the Enlightenment, especially Rousseau's philosophy, and "progress" as understood by his contemporaries.

In *Predictions of Totalitarianism*, a series of Burckhardt's writings translated and selected by Viereck, the Swiss thinker explains how the main damages of modern society were created in the eighteenth century, especially by Rousseau, and led to complete detachment from the concept of authority. With the masses taking on an increasingly central role, one value after another was sacrificed: social status, the right to property, religion, and tradition. In a passage from *Gestalten und Machte*, the entire conservative vision of Burckhardt's history emerges:

> Universal history is an eternal transformation of the old into the new. In the continuous cycle of things, everything destroys itself, and the fruit that was able to mature drops from the plant that produced it. However, this cycle must not lead to the rapid end of everything that exists.[7]

Ferdinand Tönnies (1855–1936)

Tönnies is the most noted representative of "communitarianism," a theory summarized in the book *Community and Society*, published in 1887. Nazism never looked favorably on Tönnies, and in 1934 he was dismissed from his role as professor at the University of Kiel. In 1936, the year of his death, a book was published in his honor to remember his activity:

> The conservative German setting, which the regime looked down on with suspicion, hoped for a return to the spirit of community by virtue of the aversion toward the structures of bourgeois liberalism. In Tönnies's work the theoretical foundations arose, which should have presided over the construction of the *Volksgemeinschaft* (the people's community).[8]

In order to understand Tönnies's philosophy, one must begin with the philosophies of Hobbes and Spinoza, which make up the foundation of modern subjectivism. He theorizes about the concept of community as a human group based on the unity of human will, on a common sentiment, and the union of men:

> At the base of the form of the said community, the notion of "common heritage" is always present: blood, culture, religion, history, ethnicity, etc. "Common heritage," contrary to what one would have been led to believe, does not become less extreme by adapting itself to its members, but rather differentiates them as the participants who are naturally differentiated by various "bodies" that contribute to creating the community.[9]

The idea of society as a circle of men is antithetical to this. Even though they live next to each other, in reality, men are separate. In the typically contemporary society, there are no common goods; individualism, personal interest, and a mechanical lifestyle typical of the contemporary world triumph. Tönnies found an organic way of living in the community and compares the peasantry world (one connected to the land) to the trading one. In

1897, Tönnies published *Der Nietzsche-Kultus* in which he identifies, beginning with an analysis of Nietzsche's philosophy, the context for his sociology in reference to nihilism and those disruptive aspects of modernity that not only affect traditional practices but all of Western civilization.

Central themes of his philosophy are found in his book *Community and Society* in which he compares these two concepts, considering society according an organismic model and community according to a mechanistic model. According to Tönnies, community is organic, with bonds developed according to ties of blood, spirit, and place which render men similar amongst themselves and reduce inequality within certain limits. The book includes a true contrast of the two concepts that can be outlined in three dualities: old/recent; lasting/passing; and authentic (private and intimate)/apparent (public).

Stefan George (1868–1933)

If ever there were a need to identify a spiritual father of the conservative revolution, George would assume the role without a doubt, despite being a poet rather than an ideologist. George considered the rediscovery of the *Gestalt*, the manifestation of the *spirit* in *form*, to be the solution to the crisis of Germany's destiny. His book *Der Stern des Bundes*—in English, *The Star of the Covenant*—served as a manifesto for Germany's moral and material devastation. George believed that a German rebirth could only come from the constitution of a new empire capable of combining the German warrior spirit and Greek-Latin virtues. In this work, George opposes materialism and militarism, hoping for a spiritual renewal of society.

George was born in a small town in the Rhineland to a middle-class family. He spent most of his life traveling, hosted by friends and writers in Germany, Italy, and the major capital cities of Europe. Thanks to his wanderings, he came into contact with the symbolist school in Paris at twenty years old and embraced the concept of "pure poetry" theorized by Mallarmé and Verlaine. A few years later, he founded the literary magazine *Blatter fur die Kunst*. Even though Nazis highlighted him as a nationalist poet after his death in 1933, George immigrated to Switzerland to distance himself from the violence of Nazis and refused the accolades the regime wanted to attribute to him.

In all his works, beginning with *Hymnen* in 1890 and *Algabal* in 1892, which catapulted him to fame, there are moments of controversy regarding the middle class. Written from the point of view of an aristocrat, George's writing speaks of a hope for the birth of a new society based on an intellectual elite, led by a true leader; he identified and glorified heroism and personal sacrifice as the means to achieve these important results.

In 1892, he gave life to the "George-Kreis" society, a social circle for artists and intellectual friends, with the objective of proposing a *Gestalt* (the German spirit) resurrection through a precise ceremonial aestheticism to be repeated at every meeting. The members of the society were chosen by George, and each had to have a spiritual commonality: among those who stood out were Rilke, Hugo von Hofmannsthal, and Klaus Mann. The George-Kreis represented the first phase of the German and European spiritual rebirth, completed with the realization of the *Bund*, a spiritual brotherhood that served as a community from which the foundations of the future Reich were born.

Thomas Mann (1875–1955)

Born in 1875 in Lübeck to a bourgeois family, Mann was one of the most important and profound voices of twentieth-century German literature, and the author of true literary masterpieces. His youth was devastated by the death of his father, a senator, in 1891. His family was forced to sell their import-export business and move to Munich before Thomas could finish his high school studies. Between 1895 and 1898, he spent a lot of time in Rome with his brother Heinrich. Over time, their relationship deteriorated until its final split during the First World War; the brothers had very different views of the war, and very different ways of understanding society. During the same period, he began publishing his first books:

> As the successor of eighteenth-century German realism and one
> fascinated by the teachings of great French and Russian authors,
> Mann leaned into the problems of the isolation of the individual
> in bourgeois society; problems that soon thereafter, in *Tristan* and

all the more in *Tonio Kröger* (both published in 1903), specify how the artist and the creative spirit survive in the face of the society. Prior to his creative work, it was Schopenhauer, Wagner, and Nietzsche, his declared mentors, that informed him.[10]

In 1898, he wrote *Little Herr Friedemann* for the Fischer publishing house, and in 1901 he published *Buddenbrooks*, which gained him notoriety. The first edition of the book passed quietly, but the editor at Fischer decided to republish it the following year and quickly sold thousands of copies—a true literary event. Mann's novel is conservative in every sense and, as the author himself writes, the bourgeoisie identifies itself in the contents:

> It came to my mind that the bourgeois of other countries would feel touched and affected by the decadent story of a family and that they would be able to recognize themselves in the story; that...while I sent a very German book to the presses, in both form and content, at the same time I had also created a European book, a piece of history of the soul of the European bourgeois.[11]

Buddenbrooks tells the story of the decline of a middle-class family from Lübeck in 1800 over four generations:

> Through the story of the Buddenbrook family, on one side, Mann describes the progressive crumbling of the certainties of eighteenth century positivism and, consequently, the vitality of the bourgeois spirit; on the other side, he describes the arrival of a spirituality much more complex and conflicting, with limits and boundaries impossible to retrace.[12]

In 1929, Mann won the Nobel Prize in Literature, and in 1933 he delivered his last public speech at the University of Munich, titled "Suffering and Grandeur of Richard Wagner." He later decided to leave Germany permanently while on a trip to the Netherlands, due to political instability and the growing support for and power of the Nazis. His decision was also due to the reactions to his speech in Munich, in which he criticized the connections between German art and Nazism.

After a holiday in France and Zurich, he moved to the United States permanently. He was a professor at Princeton University for two years before moving to California, where he spent thirteen years.

Mann's decision to take a public stance against Nazism, as well as his doubts, fears, and reflections, are recounted in Britta Böhler's novel *The Decision*. The book is set in 1936, during his voluntary exile to Switzerland after leaving Munich. At that time, unlike his brother Heinrich and his son Klaus, Mann had not yet publicly expressed anything against the Nazis. Developing his decision, he sent a letter condemning the regime to Eduard Korrodi, chief cultural editor of the conservative newspaper *Neue Zürcher Zeitung*: "Nothing good can come from the present-day German regime, not for Germany and certainly not for the world."[13]

Britta Böhler's novel tells the story of the three-day period between the sending and the publication of Mann's letter.

> Did he make the right decision? Will he know how to handle the consequences? Three days had passed since its publication, and from that point on, nothing would be the same. They will confiscate his assets, he will never be published in Germany again, and his readers will abandon him. And then, what will happen to his diaries left in Munich? ... How difficult is the art of remaining neutral.[14]

He listened to the outcome of the election on the radio from Switzerland, when the Reichstag yielded dictatorial power to Hitler. As he listened, he understood that his time in Germany had definitively ended, at least for as long as Nazis remained in power. The consequences, as Ezio Mauro wrote in *la Repubblica* in an article entitled "Thomas Mann, nella notte d'Europa il dilemma tra silenzio e denuncia del male," were disastrous:

It was then that the attacks by German newspapers began. They suddenly accused him of "staining Wagner," just as the Gestapo arrived to search his house in Munich and the Rotary communicated his expulsion to him via letter. It was clear that he, who had never harmed anyone, could never return to Germany. He who, in *Reflections of an Unpolitical Man*, spoke about his highly sensitive "spirit of solidarity to his era." He who, in *Mio tempo*, wrote of having "always felt the need to be patriotic." That's it. He would never return to his studio; he would never again see his eight thousand books and the grand piano he used to sit behind dressed as a magician from Carnival, with the black cloak and golden stars on his top hat, when Erika and Klaus were children. His house was gone, just like Germany.[15]

Mann's accusations against Hitler were not only political but spiritual. He thought the Führer degraded the German spirit of Goethe, Schopenhauer, Wagner, and Nietzsche.

Mann's most conservative works, other than the already cited *Buddenbrooks*, are the books he wrote at the beginning of his literary journey: *Tonio Kröger* tells the story of a young man who begins to realize how different he is from his peers and is torn between a middle-class lifestyle and his attraction to art—a text with clear autobiographical themes. But his most conservative ideas appear in a collection of essays entitled *Reflections of an Unpolitical Man*, in which he compares the concept of the German middle-class (*bürger*) to that of the French following the revolution (*bourgeoisie*); the incarnations of modernity and negations of tradition as heirs of the Enlightenment age and rationalism.

Reflections of an Unpolitical Man is not to be read as a reactionary text, but rather as the work of a conservative with stances similar to Moeller van den Bruck. The spirit of the book is the escape from cultural homogenization imposed by modernity. To do this, Mann wanted to be above compromises and political agreements, hence the term "unpolitical":

> One who knows how to look at the events of a nation without the
> blinders of the modern spirit rises above the refined intellectual
> suggestions that generally condition and own men of culture,
> enslaving them to the spirit of the time and to the decrees of civi-
> lization. The unpolitical one is one who believes—or rather, *sees*—
> the need for a rebirth of culture, of its regeneration, through the
> rediscovery of original sources. From here, naturally, the critique
> of democracy as a mass regime that, in wanting to defend the
> rights of the individual, actually humiliates the character of men,
> generically annihilating them into a system that transforms them
> into rootless and meaningless atoms.[16]

Mann believed authority should be based on a spiritual standard inspired by traditional principles to be adapted to the contemporary era. He distanced himself from the philosophy of the time, which posited that humanity was characterized by constant improvement and progress. Mann believed in the need for a German democracy founded on differences rather than equality. This critique, summarized in his *Reflections*, is also based on Nietzsche's work and the antithesis between *Kultur* and *Zivilisation*. Mann's *Reflections* can be read as a manual of conservatism, in which the critique of nihilism emerges as the true disease that plagued Europe at the time.

That being said, Mann's thoughts can be divided into two moments: before and after Hitler's rise to power. The first Mann was an advocate of the Konservative Revolution and opposed to Europeanist thought; the second Mann embraced democratic requests. Understanding the evolution of his ideas requires compliance to the juxtaposition of *Kultur* and *Zivilisation*. His earlier works can be counted in the *Kultur* setting, whereas later works are more similar to the values of *Zivilisation* (*The Magic Mountain* and *Confessions of Felix Krull* fall into this latter category).

The qualities of *Kultur* (art and metaphysics) counteract the ideals of *Zivilisation* (egalitarianism, pacifism, and internationalism). Art and meta-physics are connected to eternal, sacred, and transcendental qualities; they conflict with middle-class materialism. The moment sacred values are eliminated from society is the moment consumerism and false ideals prevail. According to Mann, *Kultur* is the foundation of civilization; but in the declining West, void of values, *Zivilisation* has assumed a leading role, creating a time in which the contrast between *"Kultur*, whose essential content is the eternal reality of human existence—love and death in great works of art and philosophy—and *Zivilisation*, the ordinary aspiration to improve the conditions of life," is as striking as it is vexing.[17]

Mann's wish was to blend tradition with modernity by looking for a balance between opposite stances. Modern reason, he thought, must meet ancient wisdom; the Enlightenment must meet Romanticism; and the aristocracy, he knew, must meet democracy.

Arthur Moeller van den Bruck (1876–1925)

Born in 1876 in Solingen, Moeller van den Bruck spent his youth in Düsseldorf. As a boy, he was expelled from the gymnasium. He dedicated his time to self-education, focusing on the main works of German literature and philosophy, with particular attention given to Nietzsche.

His restless and rebellious spirit led him to travel Europe at a young age. At first, he enrolled at the university in Leipzig, which he later abandoned in order to follow his own study of Pan-Germanism, and in 1902 he moved to Paris. It was there that he met the Norwegian painter Edvard Munch and the Russian writer Dimitri Merezhkovsky, who introduced him to Dostoevsky's work. He began devoting time to the German translation of his books, publishing his *opera omnia* between 1906 and 1922. In 1905, he put out his first book, an eight-volume work dedicated to the cultural history of Germany. In 1913, after taking various trips, he published another book dedicated to Italian art titled *Die italienische Schönheit*—in English, *The Italian Beauty*.

At the break of the First World War, he enlisted as a volunteer and was assigned to the Office of Propaganda. After the war, he was among the founders of the Juniklub ("June Club") in Berlin, a national conservative group that influenced young German conservatives with stances opposing the Treaty of Versailles. In 1919, he published *Das Recht der jungen Völker*, a political book in which he compares Russian society, based on Communism, to American capitalist society.

His most important book was published in 1923, two years before he committed suicide at forty-nine years old for personal and ideological reasons. Titled *Das Dritte Reich* (*The Third Reich* or *Germany's Third Empire*),

> it contains a summary of the conservative-revolutionary vision. The book is articulated in chapters, each of which is dedicated to a specific ideology and the person who expressed it. The order is: revolutionary, socialist, liberal, democrat, proletariat, reactionary, and conservative. The entire thing culminates in the final chapter, titled "Third Reich," which does not correspond to any political figure and instead is meant to transcend every other one previously listed and critiqued. It therefore begins with that which is the furthest from the Third Reich in order to gradually move toward that which is most similar to it. The conservative is last and opposes all the other political visions. And yet, the trajectory is not a straight line, but circular and spiraling, revolving around itself to return to the point of departure—but to a more elevated degree the second time around, so much as to, somehow, show that the Third Reich is the synthesis of the conservative and revolutionary.[18]

In *Germany's Third Empire*, Moeller van den Bruck defines a conservative as someone who "refuses to believe that the aim of our existence is fulfilled in one short span; the man who believes that our existence only carries one aim.... The conservative ponders on what is ephemeral, and obsolete, and unworthy; he ponders also on what is enduring and what is worthy to endure. He recognizes the power that links past and future; he recognizes the enduring element in the transitory present. His far-seeing eye ranges through space beyond the limits of the temporary horizon."[19]

He also highlights an important characteristic of conservative thought: the eternal return of lasting and permanent aspects of history and the inseparable elements of human nature. The conservative revolution was linked to National Socialism, by virtue of the common rejection of liberalism and Western democracy. But considering Moeller van den Bruck and the Konservative Revolution theorists to be aligned with National Socialism is a historical inaccuracy. The thinkers who remained loyal to the conservative creed during Nazism were marginalized, forced to leave, or even killed by Nazis. His thoughts were a right-wing critique of National Socialism, and there were two men who influenced him most: Nietzsche and Dostoevsky.

Moeller knew he was living in a historical moment of transition. His main criticism of modernity pertained to the role of the individual in society. Modernity and liberalism had brought about individualism; conservatives like Moeller believed in the importance of intermediary bodies and the *aggregation* of individuals. Moeller also harshly criticized the desacralization of the world; modern man, as a technical man, had lost touch with the scope of the sacred, putting doing before being. However, he opposed not only liberal individualism, but also socialist collectivism, the other extreme; both were guilty of pushing man away from the sacred.

Moeller also recognized a distinction between conservatives and reactionaries, and expressed that conservatism is not "anti-modernity, in opposition to modernity, but rather the way in which modernity must be treated in order to avoid its devastating effects on everything sacred that should be of value to the individual; those inalienable values without which man would end up renouncing himself as well."[20]

One of the enemies of conservativism is liberal modernity, which does not conserve the supratemporal; the other enemy is a left-wing modernity, based on the myth of the manufacturing man, that considers the economy as a collective identity. Actually, Moeller observes, only the transcendent can unite a community.

Modernity destroys every preceding bond that connects individuals. It posits that the only form of aggregation is the nation, considered a pre-modern bond relaunched by modernity itself. Moeller knew every nation is different, and it is therefore not possible to validly export a universal model and form of government; knowing this, he opposed universal values of liberalism that, while useful for British society here, were not useful for Germany or other countries there. Becoming a liberal nation meant, in Moeller's opinion, losing one's own cultural identity in favor of a globalization that led to dividing communities, creating conflict and tension.

Moeller, thanks to his Russophilia—born from his love of Dostoevsky, who considered Russian life capable of bringing paradoxes to light—had his ideas shaped and inspired by cultural revolution, and advocated for a conservative revolution linked to the affirmation of transcendental values:

> He is the man who became the revolutionary for conservatism and this is because he intended to save Russia from the West and the West from its nihilism. It was precisely this yearning for salvation that led Dostoevsky to reject the conditions of current life.[21]

Moeller later distanced himself from the revolution of November 1918, defining it as a failed revolution. A well-designed revolution should lead to a political establishment founded by the people as a nation—in other words, the opposite of what happened with the Weimar Republic. Once the war was lost, "Germany had nothing left to conserve, but concerned itself with a new political, cultural, and spiritual reality worthy of being conserved. Moeller rebuked the revolutionaries of November 9 for not being revolutionary enough and called on conservatives to guide and fully implement the revolution."[22]

His understanding of the revolution was antithetical to that of many other conservatives. He himself was not a counterrevolutionary; he considered revolution a tool for overcoming modernity and the upheaval caused by the French Revolution, bringing "revolution against the revolution." The difference between the conservative revolution compared to other revolutions was the finality: it had to restore lost values and authority. Rather than calling for a return to the past, which would have resulted in a restoration, it must call for a new order.

The conservative revolution had to restore the principle of authority, defending individuals from the increasing homogenization of modernity. The conservative had to defend traditional values against relativism in favor of merit and individual capabilities by putting man's dignity first: "Being conservative is a metapolitical attitude, consisting of extrapolating political stances from dispositions that in themselves are not political, but rather belong to other spheres, such as spiritual or cultural ones."[23]

In his book *Germany's Third Empire*, "he would influence numerous intellectuals in search of innovative thought, especially inspiring the Juniklub, which would later become the famous and influential Herrenklub, which, under his direction, published the revolutionary-conservative periodicals *Das Gewissen* and *Der Ring*. However, it was mostly the young conservatives of the Die Standarte group, including Ernst Jünger, who referred to Moeller's rousing legend of a new empire."[24]

Finally, his book *L'uomo politico*, published in Italy by Settimo Sigillo, must be remembered. This work attacked liberalism's surface; it blamed liberalism for creating a society that no longer exists as a community and for paving the way of the disintegration of humanity, just as the Enlightenment transformed man from a thinker to a mere computer.

The relationship between conservative thought and Nazism is an extremely delicate topic. Although there are more differences than similarities, Hitler did draw ideas from conservative revolutionary thoughts—even though Moeller's opinion of Hitler was anything but flattering:

> Hitler's world was completely different from the world of conservatives. Conservatism never held anti-Semitic racism, or philosophy of vulgar Darwinist power, and would never struggle for a Pan-Germanic *Reich* of the German Nation that overpowered Europe.... After a speech by the *Fuhrer* of nationalists, Moeller observed: "That guy does not understand anything," and did not want to witness the abuse of the conservative concept of the Third Reich for purposes of power.[25]

Robert Michels (1876–1936)

Social classes that tend toward conservative thought are usually privileged. From a political point of view, being conservative means stabilizing the role of privileged classes in society while adapting to changes. Conservatism means maintaining the status quo, which is why the social classes that identify with conservative thought are the wealthier ones. On the other hand, anti-conservative classes hope for the improvement of their own conditions: "Conserving indicates the tendency to maintain the status quo.... In this case, love of authority, discipline, and attachment to tradition constitute recurring elements."[26]

However, conservative ideas also spread throughout the working-class. This is for two reasons: the first is due to a fear of deterioration of their own condition in a revolutionary upheaval. The second is a lack of awareness of how to change their situation.

The link between aristocracy and conservatism originates from various factors, including the stability of an aristocratic system compared to a democratic system, and the understanding that "political capabilities, just as moral or professional capabilities, are often transmitted by blood and education, from father to son: healthy pride, feelings of honor and responsibility, *esprit de famille, noblesse qui oblige.*"[27]

Michels, following this analysis of conservatism in politics, presents a thought that draws more closely to the reactionary spirit than to the spirit of conservatism:

> Often the conservative spirit is also an indication of mental laziness, of misoneism and of inadequate will or meditative and reasoning ability to review old ideas and confront new ideas. In this sense, the most conservative man is a primitive, prehistorical man or that of today's central Africa, whose life is regulated and organized in every detail. He is controlled and conventionally bound from birth. His life is surrounded and circumscribed by innumerable *tabù* that make him a slave to traditions.[28]

Quickly retracing the role of conservatives in history in his *First Lectures in Political Sociology*, Michels cites a book by Giovanni Botero, *The Reason of State*, published in 1589. Botero recalls that the conquest of power is much easier than its conservation. This is why the elites who govern the country must reinvent themselves when new forces appear in society—they must blend with them:

> In history, setting China aside, the most conservative State...was the Republic of Venice. For a certain period of time under Louis XIV, France seemed to have become the most conservative power. But in the nineteenth century, the center of conservatism passed to autocratic Russia, then to bureaucratic and imperialist Germany—with the difference, however, that in Russia, it assumed forms of immobility, whereas in Germany it went hand in hand with wonderful industrial and intellectual development.[29]

Even Michels dealt with the paradox of conservatism, as did other scholars. The conservative, guardian of the status quo, becomes a guardian of the status quo ante. The risk in entering into the present while resisting the *present's* conservation is that the conservative transforms into a reactionary—and, assuming reaction is action, may be in favor of revolution.

It is at this point that a contradiction arises: is a conservative an anti-revolutionary, or can he become a revolutionary at times? The answer is to be found in the ideas of revolutionary conservatives, according to whom the revolution is a means used by conservatives to reach a precise goal: the values at the foundation of conservatism.

In 1911, Michels published *Political Parties: A Sociological Study of the Oligarchical Tendencies of Modern Democracy*, in which he expounds on his theory of the iron law of oligarchy. Every political party, he writes, originates with an open and democratic foundation, but then develops into an oligarchical structure with a limited number of leaders. An elite is created and dominates the party, progressively aiming to reach its own objective, which is not so much the achievement of the party's agenda, but rather its own survival.

Michels's thoughts are summarized in an essay by Professor Corrado Malandrino in the periodical *POLIS Working Papers* of the University of Eastern Piedmont, titled "Il pensiero di Roberto Michels sull'oligarchia, la classe politica e il capo carismatico"—in English, "The thoughts of Roberto Michels on oligarchy, political class, and the charismatic leader."[30] According to Michels, the image of the charismatic leader emerges from the circulation of the elites and their struggle.

Antonio Gramsci challenges Michels's theories in *Letters from Prison*, in which he contests Michels's "classification of political parties." Gramsci's critique derives, however, from a bias against Michels; the part of Michels's theories that Gramsci opposes with the most emphasis is the leader's charismatic role, which seems to coincide with the celebration of Mussolini.

Othmar Spann (1878–1950)

Othmar Spann created the "universal organic school," also known as the school of Vienna. He influenced supporters of the conservative revolution with his critique of Enlightenment and individualist concepts and, more generally, of modernity itself. Named extraordinary professor of political economy at the polytechnic university in Brunn in 1909 and ordinary professor in 1911, he was injured in combat on the eastern front during the First World War. Upon moving to Vienna, he obtained a professorship in political economy and sociology in 1919. In 1921, he published *Der wahre Staat,* in which he criticized liberalism and Marxism and established himself as an essential reference author for the conservative revolution. During the crisis of the Austrian Republic in the 1920s, he declared his support of the union between Austria and Germany, meant to give life to a corporate state.

What led him to criticize modernity was rooted in the historical moment he experienced after the First World War. In his work, he embodies "the profound sense of the crisis of European society":

> It was indeed during this crisis that he was forging both the method that distinguished him and the central objectives of his doctrine.

It was a crisis that was intensely lived and intensely experimented, in a way, perhaps, that only certain Austrian authors on horseback during the two world wars could experience.[31]

With the end of the Austro-Hungarian Empire, the values passed down from the medieval era disappeared, and new states were born according to the will of American president Woodrow Wilson, who redesigned Europe without considering the identity and history of the people. He was the essential author of nations dominated by liberal democracy, with alarming results:

> All the signs of a historic crisis. A crisis to which, according to Spann, adequate responses could not be provided by socialist utopias or even Soviet Communism, which had taken hold in Russia and pressured the "internal" borders of Europe, where it seemed to take over from one moment to the next.... These could not be the responses because of their extreme, pathological structures, emblematic of that "individualism" that was at the root of evil. Spann believed the answer to be elsewhere, precisely in an organic state...seen as a living entity, made up of different "organs," each one different from the other, but nevertheless essential, and inevitably working together for the well-being of the entire organism.... However, his idea never took shape.[32]

Spann's main work was published in three volumes, titled *The True State*. In it, he explains the organic concept of the state, made up of corporations. He did not consider the state to be superior to these corporations, but rather to be organic—each corporation belonging to an expansive community. He simultaneously criticizes the Enlightenment, beginning with an idealistic and romantic vision of society. Thanks to his development of the concept of corporations, Spann's work influenced a few Fascist thinkers, especially Carlo Costamagna, the editor and founder of the journal *Lo Stato*.

Spann preferred to remain unknown in politics, and he opposed "scientific racism," to the point that he was not only barred from teaching by the Nazi regime but also imprisoned.

Like every major conservative, Spann condemned individualism, considering it a complete negation of true human nature; in his opinion, an individualist society is based on materialistic and contractual theories. Spann considered social harmony to be based on the differences among individuals and a balance of the groups and corporations that make up society, representing the societal organism in both physical and spiritual aspects. His goal was to create a society in which the economy, politics, and spiritual strength make up an organic and balanced whole. In his work, he goes beyond positive and materialist thinking to a metaphysical conception of man based on a divine reality. He uses different philosophical proofs that demonstrate God's existence, and he applies metaphysical themes to social and political theory.

In an article titled "Critica dell'individualismo"—in English, "Critique of Individualism"—Giovanni Franchi writes:

At a time of serious symbolic crisis in political order, such as the one our culture is currently experiencing, Othmar Spann's work represents an original and profound effort to renew, through the lexicon of modern social sciences, a set of ancient subjects that are inscribed, in full, in the great tradition of Western metaphysics.[33]

Franchi also writes of what motivates Spann's conservatism:

Spann's position in the so-called "*Lager* conservative," according to a thesis by social science historian Karl Acham, is not only justified by his elaboration, in idealistic terms, of the concept of nation (*Volkstum*), but especially by his most famous political work, *The True State* (1921), which articulates energetic stances in favor of a "corporate state" (*Standestaat*) against Marxist collectivism—indeed, even against liberal democracies and the *laissez-faire* approach to the market economy. However, only a full understanding of the nature of Spann's conservatism, in the historical and political context of Austria between the two world wars, allows for an explanation of the often conflicting relationships of the Viennese philosopher with two different "souls" of his own *Lager* culture: namely, the Catholic world on one side and the nationalist Right on the other side. Such an understanding also sheds light on the causes of his fortune in the academic and cultural spheres.[34]

He hoped for the reorganization of society and the economy with a corporative and professional foundation. This hope clashed with the Catholic world, due to its deviant interpretation of the church's social doctrine. The conflict soon became political, especially because Spann initially welcomed Hitler's rise to power and simultaneously aligned himself with conservative Catholic stances. He thought he could influence Nazism with his own ideas and suffered a tragic fate by being imprisoned for more than a year and a half in 1938 after the annexation of Austria.

The Nazis' aversion to Spann was chiefly due to his opposition to "scientific racism." It was no coincidence that he also clashed with right-wing Fascists and nationalists, due to their Pan-Germanic vision of society. He had hoped for the unification of Germany and Austria, but his idea of a corporatist society was unaligned with the complete state envisioned by Schmitt and Costamagna.

Franz von Papen (1879–1969)

Despite Nazi Germany's Nuremberg Laws, conservatives represented by Papen opposed the fight against the churches and the Jewish religion. In the years in which Hitler gained power, there was a real conservative permissiveness, if not complete approval, of these acts. By the time conservative forces realized the true scale of the Nazi design, it was too late.

Born to a Catholic family, Papen began a military career and, at the end of the First World War, came into politics in the German Centre Party, becoming a deputy of the Prussian Diet and representative for the wealthiest social classes. During the German political crisis in 1932, the president of the Weimar Republic named him chancellor. From the beginning, Papen focused his governmental work on overcoming the constitution of the Weimar Republic as the abolition of political parties. To achieve this goal in anti-democratic and anti-socialist terms, he aligned himself with Hitler.

His conservative politics and reactionary traits generated a political crisis that resulted in the fall of the government, due to General Kurt von Schleicher's decision to withdraw his trust. On January 30, 1933, Hitler became chancellor, thanks to an agreement with Papen, who was named vice-chancellor. His political decline began with his speech at the University of Marburg on June 17, 1934, in which he distanced himself from the regime and the violence of Nazism. Clashes soon resulted and, on the Night of the Long Knives, Papen was saved thanks solely to Göring, who intervened on his behalf. In the years following, Hitler named him ambassador to Vienna and then to Turkey.

After the end of the war, Papen was among those prosecuted in the Nuremberg trials but was acquitted of all charges—a very different outcome than the trial in Germany. In 1947, he was condemned to eight years of forced labor, and he was released in 1954.

Oswald Spengler (1880–1936)

The Decline of the West, by Oswald Spengler, is probably the most well-known work of conservative and traditionalist thought. In the introduction to the Italian edition of the book, Stefano Zecchi writes that Spengler "considered parliamentary democracy, which he saw represented in the Weimar Republic, to be the place of development of a dictatorship of money; a giant market of votes administered by the leadership of numerous parties. He criticized socialism; in his Bolshevik expression, it was 'the stupidest and most vile revolution, without honor and without ideas, in the history of the world,' because it constituted a form of nihilism, just like Buddhism or Stoicism, that denies how much civilizations had designed and built: 'the ideals of yesterday, the religious, artistic, and political forms developed over centuries are being liquidated.'"[35]

The first volume of his monumental work was published in 1918, the second in 1922. While he was initially pleased with National Socialism's rise to power, his hope was soon stifled due to the methods and ideological confusions of Nazism.

In his main work, Spengler studied civilizations as organisms with their own cycle of a beginning and an end, thus making a distinction between the conception of a mechanical world, dominated by chance, and an organic one, in which nature makes room for physiological development:

> He does not read history as a "spiritual journey" that has a begin-
> ning and progresses to an end—that is, to a permanent stage.
> History appeared to him mostly as the co-existence of different
> cultures that, from time to time, embraced a similar evolution,
> but remained autonomous in essence. . . . In Spengler's mind, the
> Middle Ages did not exist: rather an Indian, an ancient Greek-
> Roman, an Arab, and a Western culture existed, all of which,
> from time to time, went through medieval phases that might be
> chronologically distant by hundreds or even thousands of years
> and developed according to similar organic rules, that could be
> metaphorically represented through the stages of spring, summer,
> autumn, and winter.[36]

During the period of *Kultur*, civilization was organized in castes, ordered by hierarchical principles. The moment *Zivilisation* arrived, however, there was a distortion of the instances dominating social life, such as the prevalence of technology over craftsmanship and quantitative principles over qualitative ones. In particular, it prompted the homogenization of society centered on economic principles.

The crux of *The Decline of the West* is the cyclic vision of history, under-stood as a development of humanity through various cultures rather than a linear development that repeats the same cycle of birth, development, and decline. It describes the historical reality that has emerged in eight civiliza-tions: Babylonian, Egyptian, Indian, Chinese, Greco-Roman, Arab, Western, and Central American. While each of these civilizations has elements of diver-sity and differentiation, there are actually many common themes in each, such as their average duration (each about a millennium). Spengler also compares the course of the civilizations to that of living beings:

> Every civilization goes through phases that correspond to differ-
> ent stages of life, resulting in its beginnings characterized by the

same creative passion that enlivens youth: the intermediate period between achieving objectives of positivity, understanding that distinguishes the maturity of an individual, and a decline of physical and spiritual strength in many ways analogous to those which afflict the descending parabola of human life. After completing its own cycle, every civilization emerges, so to speak, from history and, although in certain cases, such as India and China, seems to survive and maintain itself for a long time, its history is considered concluded, taking on the traits of a pure and simple stagnation.[37]

In *Man and Technics: A Contribution to a Philosophy of Life*, Spengler addresses the mechanization of the world, in which "the Lord of the World is becoming the Slave of the Machine, which is forcing him—forcing us all, whether we are aware of it or not—to follow its course." He predicts that triumph of technics in modern society will "have victory over God." For Spengler, technological civilization is synonymous with decline.

With the end of the First World War, Spengler understood that the era of imperialism had reached its end, as well as the true cycle of society. It was no accident that before dying, he affirmed "I shall die with Europe: I am in good company":

> With a Goethean fascination for the physiology of living species, Spengler imagined a "naturalistic universal history" characterized by a string of eight monad civilizations that, like a plant, are born, bloom, produce fruit, wilt, and die: a grandiose deterministic vision, like the nineteenth-century scientist that he was, capable of elaborating on a dense fabric of analogies between different cultures. The pages Spengler dedicates to the comparison between the "decline" of European civilization and the Hellenistic civilization are read with discomfort today, but also with amazement and admiration. Spengler thought human events were not marked by a continuous process, but rather by a process of deterioration: *mundus senescit*. The two pillars of this second reading of history are the Greek and

Nietzschean theory of the "eternal return," deeply opposed to bibli-
cal and Hegelian finalism, as well as the culture of Decadence.[38]

According to Spengler, bourgeois capitalism is the creator of the ruin of
European civilization, and it is therefore necessary to reverse all that was
achieved through a conservative revolution. Spengler's entire worldview is
based on the conflict and dichotomy between the "dictatorship of money"
and "civilization of blood": "the revolt of blood against gold, of work against
capital, was in fact swept away by war, tragedy, and failure, at least in the West.
After the conflict between politics and economy, money was left to dominate
without dispute."[39]

Despite being erroneously labeled as a prophet of National Socialism,
his relationship with Nazism was actually so hostile that Nazis considered
him an enemy for refusing to collaborate on several occasions. But Mussolini's admiration for Spengler was born from the identification of the
Duce in the German thinker's praise of the Mediterranean and Roman
spirit and of young people. It also offered an anti-German reading to Spengler's writings.

The book, published in 1933, is a *j'accuse* of the West as the only one
responsible for its own decline. The author lashes out against places of public
opinion, managing to pick out the main aspects of decline—in particular, the
corruption of the ruling classes and their enslavement to the economy, as well
as the pressure of non-European populations at our borders with a culture
and lifestyle unknown to us. Furthermore, Spengler highlights how "right"
and "left" are two meaningless categories. The very title of the book, *The Hour
of Decision*, is explicative of his idea and his awareness of living in a historical
moment, characterized by choices and strategic decisions to make for the
future of the continent. Counteracting the European decline, caused by American influence, bourgeois values, rationalism, and the Enlightenment, would
require rediscovering spiritual and religious values.

As Marcello Veneziani emphasizes in an article published in *Il Giornale*,
"Il "Tramonto" di Spengler. Alba del (neo) pessimism," Spengler was little
understood and sometimes openly opposed:

Italian idealists, beginning with Croce, considered Spengler an amateur. For the Catholics, he was an author steeped in paganism and devoid of transcendent open-mindedness. The *Treccani Dictionary of Philosophy* dismisses him as a pseudo-philosopher (the author was Felice Battaglia). Evola, however, appreciated him and later translated *The Decline of the West* (De Felice curiously defined Evola an "Spenglerian mystic") and Giuseppe Rensi, Adriano Tilgher, Lorenzo Giusso, and Vittorio Beonio Brocchieri admired him. In Italian culture, Furio Jesi's reading has more recently prevailed, which reduces Spengler to a proto-Nazi and a barbarian scholar, hostile toward culture in the name of life; a galvanizer of radical language, of "ideas without words."[40]

Spengler's autobiographical writings from 1911–1919 are collected in the book *A me stesso*, in which his personality emerges; he was a pessimist, and behind his Prussian spirit hid a melancholy loner of sickly health, confined to living in economic hardship. Not surprisingly, he was called "the hermit of Schwabing," a man of steel with a strong spirit closed in on itself and inclined toward reflection.

Carl Schmitt (1888–1985)

Originally from the Rhineland, Schmitt graduated with a degree in law and later went on to teach at the University of Greifswald and Bonn. In 1928, he became a law professor in Berlin. Despite his initial aversion for the party, he registered with the National Socialists and was appointed councilor of the Prussian State, a decision that would mark his life forever.

As Marcello Veneziani writes in an article in *Il Giornale* dedicated to the German legal expert, titled "Il Machiavelli del '900 contro il potere di tecnici e finanza. Spoliticizzazione e predominio dell'economia e del falso umanitarismo: ecco le profezie (avverate) di Carl Schmitt" (The Machiavelli of the 1900s against the power of technicians and finance. Depoliticization, economical domination and false humanitarianism: the [confirmed] prophecies of Carl Schmitt), being born and raised in a Catholic family had a major influence on his ideas:

> The Roman and Latin Catholic matrix is crucial to his intellectual biography. The tradition recalled by Schmitt is the *jus publicum europaeum*, in which "the father is the Roman law and the mother the Church of Rome"; the faith into which he was born, lived, and died was apostolic Roman Catholic. Hugo Ball noted, "Schmitt's conception was Latin"; the Latin language, for Schmitt, was "a pleasure, a true enjoyment." ... The underlying critique that Schmitt addressed to his Germany was of "the anti-Roman sentiment" that plagued the country's psyche for centuries, and that also substantiates the difference between Evangelical and Catholic culture. This divergence explains many things from the past and even a few things of the present, including the uncompromising harshness of Germans and other Protestant populations toward Greek-Latin and Roman Catholic Mediterranean countries. Schmitt considered this to be the real divide between German and Latin descendants, but he goes even further, capturing the incompatibility between the capitalist-Protestant German "model of control" and the Roman Catholic concept of nature, with its love for the land and its products (which Schmitt calls *terrisme*). Schmitt writes, "A unification between the Catholic Church and the prevailing form of capitalist individualism is impossible. The alliance between throne and altar does not follow that of office and altar or factory and altar." However, it is possible for Catholics to adapt to this state of things, though Schmitt thought Catholicism should have refused to become "a pleasurable complement to capitalism, a sanitary institution to limit the pains of free competition."[41]

Arrested in 1945 by the Allied forces, he was among those prosecuted in the Nuremberg trials. Charged with being a war criminal, Schmitt was imprisoned in Berlin from 1945 to 1946, and was arrested again in 1947. Imprisonment was a traumatic experience; he was forbidden to write. But an American doctor managed to pass him hidden sheets of paper and a pencil on which Schmitt took notes about prison, which eventually became the book *Ex Captivitate Salus.* On March 19, 1947, "Don Capisco," as Jünger called him, was once again arrested and incarcerated for six weeks in Nuremberg, despite already being acquitted of the charges. Robert Kempner was appointed to the interrogation, and in their dialogue, there emerged a Schmitt who preserved his dignity by maintaining coherent philosophical theories, as shown in the article "L'imputato Carl Schmitt" by Antonio Gnoli and Franco Volpi in *la Repubblica*:

> "I followed my idea." And still, "I am an intellectual adventurer. It is the only way to form thoughts and expertise. I am ready to take the risk, and actually I have already paid my bill." Toward the end of the last interrogation, to the question "So you are not ashamed of writing certain things?" he answers with his dignity held high: "Today, obviously, I am. However, I do not find it fair, in the humiliation we have suffered, to continue to rummage through the wound." Kempner, with respectful *pietas*, concludes: "I will try to get you home." As an old intellectual adventurer, convinced that with a love for risk there is no understanding, Schmitt withdrew "to the safety of silence."[42]

Schmitt lived out the trial and incarceration with such shame that, at the end of the judicial proceedings, he retreated to his hometown of Plettenberg and dedicated himself to study and writing there for the rest of his life. A study of the structure of the state was central to his ideas, especially in *The Value of the State and the Significance of the Individual* of 1914, in which he criticized modern civilization as having lost touch with its own soul in search of material well-being. The state, he wrote, is meant to be a sovereign political entity in which the people identify themselves. Studying the state requires an understanding of the social and political changes as well as concrete situations. Schmitt believed in the importance and protection of order and safety:

All the most meaningful concepts of the doctrine of the state are secularized theological concepts. Schmitt highlighted how, in traditionalist Catholicism, the "theocratic" project of the theological re-founding of the principle of sovereignty, based on continuity and intangibility of the spiritual order, is born from the lucid awareness of the de-Christianizing process of politics, introduced by Enlightenment philosophers and by the revolution.[43]

Schmitt also explored the friend-enemy dichotomy in his work. The political "enemy" is the "other," with whom conflict occurs, and it is up to the state to not only determine who is the enemy, but to have and execute the power to declare the *jus belli*. In this way, the state guarantees the order and safety of its citizens. Civil war emerges at the moment the distinction between friend and enemy takes the appearance of an armed conflict within the state's own territory; the state is therefore no longer able to guarantee order. Schmitt also makes a distinction between a personal enemy (*inimicus*) and a public enemy (*hostis*); a personal enemy should be loved, while the *hostis* must be fought.

The state's constitution is a set of laws that sanction political order, differentiated in a monarchy, democracy, or in Communism. No constitution is neutral in its standards; each requires the existence of a superior force, capable of guaranteeing constitutional principles and representing its people with indifference.

Schmitt wrote about constitutional aspects in *Constitutional Theory* (1928) and *The Guardian of the Constitution* (1931); a well-constructed constitution, he thought, must not offer political parties the tools for its own repeal or the ability to make itself void. If an anti-constitutional party were to assume power in a legal manner, it might repeal the constitution. In order to avoid this, the role of the German president of the republic becomes strategic; the president becomes the guarantor of the constitution by indicating which political parties do not respect the document's prerogatives.

The art of governing requires a decisiveness that unites the political and judicial element, giving meaningful order to the chaos. Schmitt cites Hobbes as an example of decisiveness, in which thought becomes the passage from chaos to order. He theorizes that the principle of sovereignty is tightly linked to decisiveness. The sovereign is essentially the secular version of the Christian God; just as God created a world according to his will, the sovereign creates the juridical order from his will.

Schmitt contrasted the model of Germany's terrestrial expansion to the model of maritime England. A dichotomy emerges between terrestrial powers—continental states based on defense of the homeland and the value of the identity of the people—and maritime powers, states based on the values of universalism to the detriment of the state, and in favor of the elimination of private and public law. Based on these differing ideologies, Schmitt wrote, modern war develops.

The partisan fights in the name of his own ideological truth, substituting the public enemy with the private enemy, ratifying the prevalence of the economy and technology in politics. The partisan reduces the role of the state to a purely bureaucratic function at the service of the economic sphere, rather than the service of the citizens. Schmitt was attracted to the thought of Machiavelli on this subject, to the point of taking his retirement in Plettenberg, the same place to which Machiavelli retreated in exile after abandoning his activities as secretary from Florence.

In his works *Political Romanticism* and *Dictatorship*, Schmitt rejects the theoretical basis on which liberalism is founded. He clarifies his support for the unity between the state and the people, criticizing the politics of the Weimar Republic and considering National Socialism to be the fastest way to reach this unity. Schmitt's relationship with National Socialism was long a topic of debate. The French philosopher Raymond Aron summarizes it here:

> Carl Schmitt was never part of the National Socialist party. As a man of high culture, he could never be Hitlerian and never was. However, as a right-wing doctrinaire and nationalist, he was full of contempt for the Weimar Republic, mercilessly analyzing its contradictions and agonies. He interpreted the events of June 30, 1934, the "Night of the Long Knives," presenting the Fuhrer as the supreme judge. At the time, this interpretation could have seemed

like an approval, but Schmitt ceased to be a *persona grata* to the regime before the outbreak of the war. After the war, he recognized his errors and retired to a small town in Westphalia.[44]

Although more aligned with liberal thought, Raymond Aron (1905–1983) covered a few important themes of conservatism, especially in his book *Saggio sulla destra. Il conservatorism delle società industriali* (*Essay on the Right: Conservatism of Industrial Society*), in which he analyzes the relationship between modernity and the Right, focusing on the transformation of conservatism and its relationship with democracy. His book *Il destino delle nazioni, l'avvenire dell'Europa* (*The Destiny of Nations, the Future of Europe*) consists of a collection of essays dedicated to the future of Europe and European nations.

On May 1, 1933, Schmitt joined the Nazi Party. He was asked to testify at the Nuremberg trials after the war. He defended himself with the following words: "If you hold me responsible for Hitler, you should also hold Rousseau responsible for the Jacobins." But compared to other revolutionary conservatives, Schmitt was the one who most openly aligned himself with Nazism.

Schmitt criticizes the parliamentary system and democracy in his books *La Dittatura* (*Dictatorship*, 1921) and *La condizione storico-spirituale del parlamentarismo attuale* (*The historical-spiritual condition of current parliamentarianism*, 1923). While at first he aligned himself in favor of the Weimar State, he soon changed his stance and became involved in the elaboration of National Socialist laws as a lawyer. These decisions also involved his friend Jünger:

At this point, it is no longer possible to avoid the question of whether it is possible to name representatives of the conservative revolution who wanted to save the republic. I answer in the affirmative and intend to begin with the broadest concept possible: even from within the presidential system, conservative revolutionaries wanted to put an end to the Marxist challenge. Despite this, the enigma of Carl Schmitt still remains—shortly after the National Socialists took power, he embraced Hitler's party's cause.

He even accepted, as the only one among conservative revolutionaries, a high state office as "Prussian State advisor" and participated in the legislation of the single-party state.[45]

His ideas bear some similarities to Heidegger's, specifically his thought
that man is unable to construct logical and rational philosophies at a time
when technology dominates. Schmitt also elaborates on his theory of the
categories of politics:

> The Roman Catholic model was an example of how Schmitt
> defended the "political theology" that supported the authority
> of the custodian of the constitution—that is to say, the "deci-
> sion maker."[46]

The year 1796 was important for counterrevolutionary theories, with the
"hot years" of the revolution past and the main works of counterrevolutionary
thinkers widespread (from *Reflections on the Revolution in France* by Burke,
to *Théorie du pouvoir* by Bonald, to *Considérations sur la France* by de Maistre). Counterrevolutionary arguments were solidified:

> The idea that law and the state could result from the methodical
> activity of individual human beings is invariably rejected. All-
> important state institutions, especially the constitutions altered
> so frequently during the French Revolution, are said to result over
> the course of time, from prevailing circumstances and the nature
> of things.... On this point, Burke—in phrases often powerful and
> emotional—stresses the growth of the national community that
> spans generations. De Maistre still sees the individual entirely
> from the perspective of classical theology: he believes in his insig-
> nificance in the presence of a transcendent providential power
> that governs us, and in whose hands the active heroes of the
> Revolution appear as mere automatons. As early as 1797, Bonald,
> a great systematic thinker, had explained what is at stake with

splendid precision: the opposition between liberal individualism and social solidarity.[47]

Concerning European conservatism, Schmitt wrote:

By nature, the conservative element is inseparably linked to historical distinctions.... In Europe, every specifically conservative value, such as religion, tradition, and culture, gave life to ecclesiastical, state, and national distinctions. The romantic matrix of Catholic realism, the dynastic sentiment of evangelical Prussians, and the link between Russian orthodoxy and Tsarist autocracy made up three different conservative powers from a religious and national point of view that would have never been able to give life to such a homogeneous unity as that of the international revolution.[48]

Ernst Niekisch (1889–1967)

Although Niekisch cannot be defined as a conservative in the traditional sense of the word, his critique of Nazism as a southern Roman Catholic closely aligned him with conservatism. Niekisch was one of the members of German National Bolshevism. While on the one hand, he despised the bourgeoisie, on the other hand, he embraced an extreme nationalist stance:

Niekisch revered Bolshevism because he radically refused the West and approved of all it detested, such as anti-liberalism, anti-individualism, and the open recognition of violence. At the same time, however, he proposed an interpretation to which no other Russian Bolshevik would have ever subscribed: the ideal Communist would have been the mantle on which the vital Russian national impulse would be covered in its extreme need to assert itself.... However, the thing that was most deeply imprinted on the public consciousness was the future image of Germany "as a guide, organizer, and integral part of a single block of states that extended from the great ocean to the Rhine," in front of which France would have trembled.[49]

Niekisch was dedicated to his teaching, concentrating on the reading and detailed study of various authors, including Nietzsche, Hauptmann, Machiavelli, and Hegel. Although he enlisted in the army during the First World War, he never fought in battle due to health problems. In 1917, he joined the Social Democratic Party (SPD). The following year, he helped set up the Bavarian Council Republic and the Soldiers of Augsburg. Later, after being sentenced to two years of incarceration for his participation in the Bavarian revolution, he joined the Independent Social Democratic Party (USPD) of Germany because of his opposition to the politics of the SPD. When the two parties were consolidated, Niekisch once again found himself back at the drawing board. He disputed that payments should go to France for war damages, and he supported the resistance in Ruhr that immediately began to emerge. His final break from the party occurred in 1925 when he decided to dismiss himself, anticipating his expulsion for differences with the party leadership. His cultural-political activities continued with the founding of the magazine *Widerstand* in 1926; two years later, he would found the publishing house with the same name.

Niekisch hated the Latin and Catholic worlds, blaming them for the decline of Germanism. Protestantism, by contrast, understood the exaltation of the German spirit, and opposed the Catholic masses. In his writings, he theorized about a Germany which, taking from the Machiavellian lesson of *realpolitik*, prioritizes foreign policy over domestic policy. Conflicts between states were desirable insofar as they presented opportunities to achieve supremacy. He aspired to create a single German-Slavic empire dominated by proletarian people.

From a national perspective, Niekisch considered the Russian Revolution to be an event reacting to and attempting to avoid the prevalence of Western and capitalist values. It was really a revolution against Western imperialism, he thought. Russia, therefore, became the perfect ally for Germany; the enemy of Germany's enemy was Germany's friend.

The attitude against bourgeois democracy was born from the influence of Schmitt's work. He, too, promoted the primacy of politics over the economy and distanced himself from both materialism and individualism. Both thinkers criticized capitalism and the social classes representing it—mainly, the middle class.

The Nazis began to consider Niekisch as a dangerous voice to be silenced because of his large following, made up of the associations from his magazine. They initially suspended the publications of *Entscheidung*, followed by *Widerstand*, the namesake of the publishing house. This escalation culminated in his arrest in March 1937. Two years later, Germany's People's Court sentenced him to life in prison after he was found guilty of high treason and breaking laws which prohibited the establishment of new parties.

After being liberated by the Russians when he was nearly blind, he was named professor at Humboldt University in Berlin, and then director of the Institute of Research on Imperialism. At the same time, he joined the Socialist Unity Party of Germany (SED), where he was elected to the German People's Congress as a delegate of the Cultural League. But because of his criticism of the Russians' politics, he quickly fell from grace again, and decided to definitively abandon politics.

Late in life and poor in health, he dedicated his final years to writing his memoirs, trying to place particular emphasis on his opposition to Nazism. He died on May 23, 1967, and remains forgotten by most German people.

Karl Mannheim (1893–1947)

Born in Budapest, Mannheim began his formative journey teaching sociology in Germany. He moved to London in 1933 due to his opposition to Nazism, and he was named professor of sociology at the London School of Economics. His career climaxed in 1947 when he became the president of UNESCO—it was also the same year in which he died of a heart attack.

Max Weber—whose brother was Mannheim's teacher in Heidelberg— greatly influenced Mannheim's work, serving to distance him from the

Marxist influence of his first teacher, Lukács. He compared relationism to the prevailing relativism, which was incapable of resolving the absence of values in modern society. In Mannheim's book *Ideology and Utopia*, he presents his vision of society, comparing two different visions of the world: ideologies representing the opinions of the dominant classes and utopias representing those of the dominated class. While the first class advocates the preservation of reality, the latter hopes for the transformation of reality.

In the introduction of the book, Alberto Izzo writes:

> While relativism presupposes the futility of absolute valid knowledge and the denial of any truth, relationism upholds the idea that bringing light to relationships between ideas of the world and their historical-social context does not invalidate them; it simply means that these ideas are not absolutely valid, but rather valid only in relation to their context.[50]

Mannheim also distinguishes traditionalism from conservatism in his work. The latter, he believed, identified an answer to sudden changes brought on by the revolutions. He studied conservative thought deeply, writing his thoughts in *Morphology of Conservative Thought*:

> Quite evidently, *traditionalist* refers to a *formal psychic attribute* which is more or less present in every individual, while *acting conservatively* refers to action *in accordance with a structural contexture* which is objectively at hand. To act in a politically conservative way in any given historical period involves a way of acting whose structure cannot be determined beforehand. But how traditional conduct will manifest itself in any given case can be pretty well predicted on the basis of the formal determinants of this "general mode of behavior." There is no doubt what the traditionalist reaction will be when something new—say, the railway—is introduced. But how a conservative, or someone who

is acting in keeping with the political conservatism epoch, will conduct himself can be estimated only *on the basis of our knowledge of the distinctive character and structure of the "conservative movement"* in the country and period under discussion.[51]

The difference between traditionalism and conservatism is highlighted in the reactive conception of the traditionalist action compared to the conservative action, which changes and evolves over the course of a historical era. In some situations, traditional elements can be found in conservatism—which, Mannheim highlights, is not to be understood as an action occurring in an exclusively political structure, but rather as a precise vision of the world of certain sentiments constituting a defined form of thought. Therefore, while traditionalism is outside of history, conservatism has a precise historical and sociological continuity.

With the incongruities between conservatism and traditionalism established, Mannheim in turn distinguishes conservatism from progressivism: conservatives and progressives have different conceptions of time. While progressives consider the meaning of life to be found in what lies ahead (the future), conservatives look to the past. Conservatives adhere to the present and the concrete, interpreting the present as a consequence of the past; progressives fight the concrete, aiming to create a new point of departure, considering the present as the beginning of the future. In Mannheim's philosophy, the analysis of time is divided according to bourgeois, proletarian, and conservative perspectives:

> While conservative thought is oriented towards the past surviving in the present, and bourgeois thought, because it bears the present, nourishes itself on new developments, as they transpire from moment to moment, proletarian thought attempts to consider and to further the future within the present, by putting into the foreground those present factors which herald the future structural forms of social life.[52]

All this being said, what does being conservative mean to Mannheim?

> Conservative experience in its authentic mode therefore means to
> draw sustenance from the foci of experience whose origins are
> rooted in past constellations of history, and which maintained
> themselves relatively unchanged until modern conservatism con-
> stituted itself.[53]

Aware that he was living in an era of social and spiritual crisis, in which idealistic nineteenth-century conceptions were obsolete, Mannheim theorized about the "sociology of knowledge" and believed in the values that emerged from the concreteness of man rather than the abstract. All his work is permeated with the understanding that sociological theories can be a model for understanding the transformations of our times. As Carmelina Chiara Canta highlights in *Ricostruire la società: Teoria del mutamento sociale in Karl Mannheim* (*Reconstructing Society: The Theory of Social Change* in Karl *Mannheim*), he was aware of the frenetic changes taking place in modern society, and he tried not only to understand the dynamics behind these changes but also to propose solutions:

> A reinterpretation of Karl Mannheim's philosophy appears par
> ticularly timely and useful at this moment in history, which, in
> many ways, presents many analogies with the "great society" in the
> crisis analyzed by the author. With foresight and lucidity, he sensed
> the problems that would be caused by the rise of a mass society, of
> the social fragmentation, and that even today remain unresolved
> and are subjects of intense analysis and study.[54]

Ernst Jünger (1895–1998)

A prolific writer—the author of dozens of books and thousands of pages in his diaries—Jünger is perhaps the most well-known modern conservative. Jünger served as an officer in both world wars, and experiencing the main events of the twentieth century firsthand gave a traumatic shape to his life. Not surprisingly, the monumental biography that Heimo Schwilk dedicated to him contains the subtitle *Una vita lunga un secolo—A Century of Life*.

All Jünger's work originated from a continuity of his anarcho-conservative ideas. He managed to make characters of modernity's main players: the Soldier on the frontlines, the Rebel, the Anarchist, and the Laborer. His ideas were driven by a strong anti-modernism, anti-capitalism, and a deep analysis of omnipresent technology.

Jünger was the primary intellectual representative of a generation that actively participated in the First World War, and in the years following the conflict, he provided his firsthand knowledge to political service. His early works include *Storm of Steel* (1920), *Der Kampf als inneres Erlebnis* (*The Fight from Inside*, 1922), and *Copse 125: A Chronicle from the Trench Warfare of 1918* (1925). Each is based on "the intellectual contrast between 'blood' and 'intellect,' in other words, the will to fight, and the meaningful, consoling affirmation: 'you did not fall in vain.'"[55]

In the early twenties, Jünger, like many other German thinkers, looked for a way to forge a new Germany, capable of recovery after defeat. Technology had caused the homogenization of the individual, standardizing customs and traditions imposed by modernity. Jünger moved away from these trends in search of a new type of man, capable of distinguishing himself from mass society: *l'operaio*, "the worker."[56] He searched also for the anarchist, the one who withdraws into the wood and escapes the logic of modernity to find himself.

The choice of the anarchist, Jünger believed, was twofold: fight against the herd or follow it. Fighting means becoming a rebel, and the adventure of such a choice was described by Jünger in *Der Waldgang*, (*The Forest Passage*). The man who "goes into the woods" is foreshadowed as the new elite. Jünger proposes a new plan: the historical juxtaposition of the bourgeoisie and bourgeois, he who dominates technology and he who is dominated by it (and therefore succumbs to it), must be blurred to be overcome. The laborer represents the means by which tradition and modernity are united.

Jünger was an anarcho-conservative, but he had his criticisms. He believed pure conservatism was too focused on the passing of time, pushing the human will toward the restoration of unsustainable forms and situations. For Jünger, reading and enjoying conservative authors meant appreciating the spiritual clarity of their work: "You enter in half-ruined buildings that have become inhabitable: this is the emotion that works by Chateaubriand, Donoso Cortès, and even those by Burke communicate."[57]

In his youth, Jünger felt like he had been born in the wrong era. He did not excel in school, and due to the continuous moving of his family, young Ernst had to change schools eleven times and was never able to have real stability or create lasting friendships. But the absence of stability was compensated by his lifelong friendship with his brother, Friedrich Georg.

Junger's childhood literary interests included classic German writers, such as Goethe and Schiller, as well as ancient writers like Homer, who caused him to idealize heroic war over modern technological warfare. This idealization remained constant throughout his own literary work, echoing Marx's question of 1859: "Would the Iliad have been possible with gunpowder and lead?"

His experience in the First World War marked him for life. He was distinguished by his deeds and obtained various decorations, including the highest honor of the Prussian Empire: the Pour le Mérite. During the war, he kept a notebook in his jacket pocket, in which he recorded daily events. Spanning over sixteen notebooks, these notes would later become extremely precious for writing *Storm of Steel*.

During a period of leave, he immersed himself in Goethe's *Campagna di Francia* (*Countryside of France*), a story of Goethe's experience in the Austro-Prussian army during the revolution of Paris. Writing these experiences provided important assistance during the war for both men. In addition to keeping the mind in shape, writing helped them focus their own experiences as individual soldiers, instead of disappearing into the anonymity of the war of the masses.

With the defeat and collapse of the German Empire, the values that made up Prussian society disappeared. Jünger received the news as an observer, as he was still recovering from a lung injury and preferred to stay out of the public scene. But he wrote to his brother Friedrich defending the democratic government as a transitional phenomenon.

Jünger viewed the Treaty of Versailles as a humiliation for Germans, who were deprived of their colonies and forced to pay an excessive war tax. A humiliation for the nation, he believed, is lived as a humiliation for every single citizen. Once again, he sought refuge and reassurance in his writing at a time of national weakness and transition. In October 1920, he published *Storm* of *Steel*, which not only consecrated him as an officer, but also as a writer. His example was no longer Goethe's *Campagna di Francia*, but rather Caesar's *De bello gallico*, (*The Gallic Wars*) with its "virtus," "dignitas," and "fortune." Just as Caesar's journal was, Jünger's book was written with the intent of facilitating a subsequent political career, and to "concretely show the reader the experiences of an infantryman during the Great War in a famous regiment, as well as the thoughts that accompanied him at that time."[58]

The narratives are based on the values of heroism and patriotism, with the understanding that these values are worth giving one's life to, and Jünger's hero is essentially Achilles in the modern war of the masses. Jünger was a careful and avid reader. Adolphe Thiers's ten-volume work dedicated to the French Revolution was among his primary inspirations, as was Loyola's *Spiritual Exercises*, Baltasar Graciàn's *The Art of Wordly Wisdom*, and Immanuel Kant's *Dreams of a Spirit-Seer*, all of which he read in the years following the First World War.

Jünger continued the literary current he began with *Storm of Steel* with *La battaglia come esperienza interior (Combat as an Internal Experience)*, published in 1923, with clear influence from Spengler. While his metaphysical-historical vision of the world differed from Spengler's, they are linked by their conception of the First World War as a turning point at which the Caesarism era of the masses guided by charismatic leaders began.

The German writer viewed war as an internal and spiritual experience, in which the soldier belongs to a necessary historical process and is the tool of higher reason. This vision is set against the war of the masses, in which man is dehumanized and we see the triumph of technology—the means over the goals and the end of all values.

Thanks to his reading of Maurice Barrès, Jünger became a convinced nationalist. He was struck by the parallels between the situation Barrès describes in France in 1871 and Germany in 1918:

The mysticism of blood, typical of Barrès, the celebration of ecstatic states, the bond between eros and death. Even the titles of the chapters—"Blood," "Horror," "Eros," point out Jünger's closeness to the ideal and conceptual world of the French nationalist.[59]

Just like many other German thinkers, he looked for a solution to give life to a new Germany, capable of resolving itself after defeat. In 1923, he published an article titled "Revolution and idea." Schwilk writes that in it Jünger affirmed:

> The motto of Marxism, long since decayed, was still proposed in the present, but a body that does not know to eliminate "toxic substances from within" was condemned. The idea of the "real revolution" was "the nationalistic one."[60]

On August 31, 1923, he decided to dismiss himself from the Reichswehr and enroll at the University of Leipzig to study natural sciences. The decision came as a disappointment to everyone who had hoped to assign him a powerful role in the army, including Colonel Kurt Hesse, who dedicated an article to Jünger in March 1924, praising his literary work but criticizing his decision to withdraw to a more private life. Having taken his leave from the army, he could openly express his own political opinions. He did this through the press agencies of the NSDAP, of which he was never a member, carrying forward the proposal of a national revolution to overthrow the Weimar Republic, which was dominated by materialism. This was most likely the period in which Jünger most closely sympathized with Hitler's stances and his movement, which he considered a tool to destroy the republic.

On September 26, 1923, when Gustav Stresemann announced that war reparations to France and Belgium would resume and the passive resistance of France's occupation of the Rhineland would end, Hitler became widely popular. It was only two weeks prior that Jünger publicly expressed his approval of a revolution that would establish a dictatorship based on National Socialist principles:

An authentic revolution has not yet taken place, but is relentlessly marching on. It is not a reaction, but rather a real revolution, with all its traits and symbols, with the same idea as the people, refined to the point of obtaining a sort of clarity unknown until now, its banner the hooked cross, its form of expression the collection of will at a single point—dictatorship! It will replace words with actions, ink with blood, rhetoric with sacrifice, pen with sword.[61]

•

Along with his political interventions, Jünger continued dedicating his time to writing. In February 1924, he began drafting *Copse 125*, a chronicle about the combat that occurred in 1918, expanding on an experience described in *Storm of Steel*. A nationalist interpretation of the war is key to reading *Copse 125*: the pages of the book are imbued with spirituality and piety. "The land of our forefathers," Jünger writes, "is a religion, and the soldier is ready for sacrifice because he is driven by unconditional faith in his nation."[62]

On June 3, 1925, he was married in Leipzig to Gretha von Jeinsen, and in May 1926 his first son, Ernstel, was born. They never organized a honeymoon, because Jünger was, once again, at work. A few weeks after marrying, he finished *Fire and Blood* and published various newspaper articles, increasingly marketing himself as a national-revolutionary author.

But these were still halted years from an editorial perspective. In June 1925, the first edition of the weekly magazine *Die Standarte* was put out. The publication, which collected "contributions to the spiritual and intellectual deepening of thoughts from the frontlines," originated in opposition of the democratic "I" of the state and in favor of the national "We."

Jünger's articles were addressed to nationalists and highlighted Germany's need for a spiritual leader. He argued against the democratic system and envisioned politics as a tool to fight, believing political parties represented the bourgeois world that was condemned to decline and had to be overcome:

We want to grow until we become an independent power, that will be increasingly more powerful than the state.... We make up a unity with blood, soul, and memory; we are the "state of the state," the block of attack, around which the masses must gather. We do not keep big speeches in great consideration: a hundred new supporters is more important to us than a parliamentary victory. At times, we celebrate festivities to allow power to be paraded in tight processions and to remember how the masses move. Hundreds of thousands of people already participate in similar festivities. The day the parliamentary state falls under our attack, and on which we will proclaim a national dictatorship, will be our biggest day of celebration.[63]

In 1926, *Fire and Blood* was published, in which Jünger, taking up themes of the Great War, expressed his own nationalism and revanchism. Critics attacked the book for its extremism. In response, Jünger tried to embroil all young nationalists against the "bourgeois press." During the same period, he began having his first disagreements with Hitler:

> Jünger, however, supported the need for a "Council of Central Command" to unite the various scattered and divided groups of nationalists. Hitler, who only wanted to claim the title of national leader, must have been irritated by the fact that Jünger had supported the candidacy of a few national responsibilities a few months earlier. Most likely, Jünger saw Hitler as *a* Führer, not *the* national Führer.[64]

Hitler wanted to persuade Jünger to join the National Socialists and entrusted Goebbels with this task, but Jünger was unyielding and maintained his distance, preferring to be a point of reference for German nationalists. In 1926, his brother Friedrich published a text envisioned as the nationalist manifesto which coincided with Ernst's stances: modern nationalism had no need for parties, parliament, or the right to vote, because parties (which represented only a part of the population) were elements of division. The nationalist state had to be led by an authority capable of bringing the masses together. Jünger compared nationalism to Enlightenment universalism, insofar as nations that take up the Enlightenment spirit are those that achieve their aspirations at the expense of Germans. To Jünger, being a nationalist meant supporting the aspirations of the nation by any means necessary; it meant putting the idea of the nation among the supreme values, to which everyone is subordinate. It did *not* mean being European or "citizens of the world," but considering it more important to be German, British, or Italian:

> It means attributing more value to the specific rather than the universal, putting life above concept and organic bonds above that which does not know any type of bond. It means wanting to be connected to life by way of the grand and mysterious flow of blood, and not through the abstract scaffolding of intellectual construction. Only for true vital unity, and not for that which is useful, practical, or factitious, is life ready for any kind of sacrifice.[65]

His points of disagreement with National Socialism emerged from the differing conceptions of the masses. While Nazis had the mobilization of the masses against the old elites as their goal, Jünger had an elitist vision of society. Nazis believed the nationalist movement should fight against the Jews, capitalists, Free Masons, and Jesuits, whereas Jünger's objective was the fight against the liberal state.

In 1927, the same year in which Hitler asked him to run for the Reichstag with the NSDAP, Jünger moved to Berlin. Jünger's response is well-known: "I consider writing a single verse, one sentence, richer and more deserving than representing sixty thousand idiots in parliament."

Hitler's attempts to convince Jünger to join the Nazis continued, and the writer was invited to participate in the congress of the NSDAP from August 1–4 in 1929 as a guest of honor. But Jünger once again declined the invitation. He was convinced that Germany needed a serious revolution, not one led by Hitler's movement—which, in the meantime, had gained increasing notoriety and had many members in parliament.

Jünger "proposed himself to be the mentor of a national and intellectual avant-garde, that is, a revolutionary elite, guarantor of the purity of means."[66] His objective, even in 1929, was to unite National Socialists and national revolutionaries in opposition to the liberal state and anti-national powers, a project which definitively failed with the election results of September 14, 1930, in which the NSDAP obtained 18.3 percent of the votes and became the second party of the Reich. This result caused major problems for Chancellor Heinrich Brüning, who was only able to govern with emergency ordinances, warranting a crisis for the Weimar Republic.

With the publication of *Der Arbeiter* in 1932, Jünger presented his soldier-worker theory. The book is characterized by its anti-bourgeois tone, and the image of the worker is a recurrent *topos* in his work. Schmitt's participation in the National Socialist Party in 1933 deeply upset him, and on November 16 of the same year, Jünger established his final rejection of Nazism when he refused to join the artistic prose branch of the German Academy of Literature. His decision infuriated Joseph Goebbels, Reich minister for education and mass propaganda, who wanted to make Jünger a model for Nazi culture. His refusal to join the Nazi cause is metaphorically expressed in *On the Marble Cliffs*, a novel with strong spiritual worth.

During the Second World War, Jünger served as an officer in occupied Paris. During his time there, he was praised for his quietness and culture, and was quickly welcomed in cultural circles of the city, thus creating a teeming network that he kept for the rest of his life. It was thanks to these relationships that, following the war, his books became an important channel of diffusion in France.

A large part of the Parisian *état-major* was responsible for the failed attack on Hitler, and Jünger risked involvement in the subsequent repression. While he was not directly involved in the plot, it is likely that he knew enough about it to be culpable. Miraculously, he managed to escape from punishment—as there were no charges brought against him—but the orders he received to abandon Paris were painful. Not only was he forced to leave the city in which he had established such a strong network of relationships, but he also had to face an uncertain future, characterized by a now undeniable defeat that would bring disastrous consequences for Germany. News of the death of his favorite son Ernstel, which occurred while he was in Italy in Carrara, upset him even more and marked him forever. The end of the war and these personal losses represented a moral, material, spiritual, and national catastrophe for him.

Jünger's relationship with Nazism was put under so much suspicion by the Allies that the occupying authorities did not allow him to publish anything in Germany until 1949. News of the atomic bomb drop confirmed the predominance of technology in modern civilization—technology that leveled and erased every aspect of tradition. These were trying times for Jünger.

In the early post-war period, Jünger wrote *The Peace*, dedicated to his son who had died in the war. Shortly thereafter, beginning in January 1946, he started working on the outline of his novel *Heliopolis*:

> This work, stretching from January 1947 to March 1949, is a novel about the future told in a retrospective tone—backwards, so to speak—and therefore a key text and opinion novel, in which the author re-elaborates on his own experiences in light of the political-military fight for power in Paris.... Jünger proposes *Heliopolis* as a continuation and variation connected to the representation in *On the Marble Cliffs*: the eternal struggle between anarchy and order.... In *Heliopolis*, two orders of dominance meet and collide: the democratic formation of the masses (the *podestà*) and the aristocratic-elitist system (the proconsul). Just as in the major utopian novels of the century (*1984* by Orwell was a contemporary of *Heliopolis*), Jünger denounces the inhumane consequences of the technical optimization of man, and consequentially its totalitarian control.[67]

In the early years after the war, Jünger was excluded from the literary field and began to realize German literature's fall toward mediocrity. He therefore dedicated himself to the reading of authors whom he considered classic, such as Léon Bloy and Nietzsche.

Between the end of 1948 and the beginning of 1949, he began a partnership destined to last for years with editor Ernst Klett. During the same period, the French military administration gave him the permission to publish the diary

series *Strahlungen* (*Reflections*), a compilation of four different diaries kept by
Jünger. With *Heliopolis* and *Strahlungen*, Jünger established himself as a prolific
writer. In addition to his writing, he had to take care of his correspondences,
meetings, and appointments. He therefore decided to hire a secretary, a role
taken on by Armin Mohler. Philosopher Martin Heidegger was among the
interlocutors to whom Jünger dedicated his book *Oltre la linea* (*Beyond* the
Line), an analysis of nihilism in modern society which, according to Heidegger,
is no longer an external phenomenon but rather a part of the human praxis.

> Jünger's skepticism toward the democracy underway is made explicit
> in the book *Der Waldgang* (*The Forest Passage*), written about those
> who go to the woods, withdraw into the forest, and go into hiding.
> The text calls the individual into question, along with his range of
> free action, and proposes him as a form of resistance against the
> technocracy and apparent freedom of *plebiscitary democracy*—
> which, according to the author, erases the differences between mass
> dictatorship and parliamentary democracy.... The most evident
> nihilistic symptoms in Jünger's time, within this context, are the
> extreme powers of technology and the loss of the metaphysical. But
> the most exemplary form of opposition is still, and will always be,
> the Rebel.[68]

Jünger considered the Rebel to be an adversary of technology in the modern world and, along with the Unknown Soldier and the Worker, the quintes-
sential mythical figure. His resistance to consumerism and dominating forces
of modernity is an obligation:

> The attitude and inclination toward anarchist existence, the insup-
> pressible tendency to achieve "the highest degree of freedom" even
> under major constraints, and from this an ability to obtain further
> incentive for self-realization, was freed and was manifested during
> Jünger's military service. The "lost position in combat," the "rebel,"

the fugitive in the woods, the "anarchist," are all signs of the transition to uncertainty, related to unforeseen events.[69]

Jünger's final readmission to the German literary circuit came in October 1955, when the federal president Theodor Heuss visited him at his home in Wilflingen. Despite this welcome, melancholy increasingly took the upper hand over Jünger's personality, especially after his visit to the United States. He wrote of the visit in a letter:

Although I have only peripherally encountered it, the New World has truly depressed me. The clocks there go on, and, like Tocqueville at his time, today we can also extract from it what will flourish: a world that knows neither death nor love. This has infinitely appalled me, even if it was only a confirmation.[70]

As he always did in moments of depression, Jünger threw himself into his work. In 1960, despite his wife's illness, he experienced one of his most prolific years. Following his first wife's death, he married Liselotte Lohrer, his long-time editor, on March 3, 1962. From that moment on, Liselotte became a fixed and indispensable point in his life. The two took various trips in Europe and around the world. Nevertheless, his literary activity continued uninterrupted, and he branched into new genres of travel writing and philosophy.

In the spring of 1977, Jünger was shaken by his brother's illness. He therefore went to his bedside to help him. On July 20, at the age of sixty-eight, Friedrich died. The loss was devastating.

More tragedy was to come. On April 22, 1993, he received tragic news: his son Alexander, sick and depressed, had committed suicide before reaching the age of sixty. Later that year, he was hospitalized after being bitten by a tick while taking a walk. It wasn't until the following year that he resumed his writing—a long time for such a man.

He completed the fourth volume of his diary and finished the revision of the five-volume completed edition of his works, to be published in 1995, the year of his one-hundredth birthday. In addition to his writing, Jünger would take long walks in snow-covered forests, refreshing his mind:

> On his walks, he tirelessly reflected on the same themes that can also be found in his diaries: the superhuman, or Nietzche's super-man, the world of the Titans, the history of the land, the spiritu-alization of the earth, and the readings of Oswald Spengler, Charles Darwin, Victor Hugo, and Paul Léautaud.[71]

On September 26, 1996, after thinking deeply about the spiritual experience for decades, and thanks to the parish priest of Wilflingen, Jünger converted to Catholicism. Jünger had shown signs of his advance toward Catholicism when he thought about baptizing his son Ernstel in the Catholic Church (after being influenced by Joris-Karl Huysmans's mystical novel *The Cathedral*), but his then-wife Gretha had refused.

While Jünger continued writing in his final year of life to add a new volume to his diaries, he died of heart failure on February 17, 1998. Germany, and the rest of the world, lost one of the most prominent voices of the twentieth century, one that could recount the events of the century with an anarcho-conservative perspective and an anti-modern, critical eye, the likes of which are rarely seen today.

Leo Strauss (1899–1973)

Born in 1899 to a Jewish family, Strauss first attended the University of Marburg, then that of Hamburg and finally that of Freiburg. During this intensely academic period, he not only received a PhD in philosophy but also deepened his study of theology. Thanks to a research project about Hobbes, he met Carl Schmitt at the end of the 1920s, with whom he established a life-long friendship. After being awarded a scholarship, he and his family moved to London in 1934 so he could deepen his study of Hobbes. He then moved to the United States in 1938, where he continued his philosophical studies at Columbia University. In 1948, he published *On Tyranny* and was named a member of the department of political science at the University of Chicago, where he worked as a philosophy professor until 1968.

During the war, he was called to serve as an interpreter during the occupation of Belgium. After the war, he continued his study and writing, publishing his *Thoughts on Machiavelli* in 1958 and *What is Political Philosophy?* in 1959. In the years following, he published a series of new publications, including a collection of essays and articles titled *Liberalism: Ancient and Modern*. His aversion to modernity was one of the central themes of his work:

> Strauss was inspired by the conviction that modern political thought, from Hobbes onward, tends to be modeled on the paradigm of natural sciences, with liberalism (Locke), democracy (Rousseau), and eventually Nazism (Hitler) and Communism (Stalin) as inevitable outcomes. Strauss viewed the reasons for the tragedies of modernity to be nested in the fatal abandonment of the classical theory of natural rights, clearly formulated for the first time in *Politics* by Aristotle.[72]

According to Strauss, classical studies are the key to understanding the modern Western crisis. Through his reading of the classics, he developed a sharp criticism of nihilism and democracy as enacted in contemporary society. But Strauss was most critical of the nihilism of dictatorships. In his book *On Tyranny*, he looks for tyranny's historical origin, asserting that the duty of political philosophy is to search for the right political order, through the possession of practical knowledge theorized by Plato and Aristotle, which guides individuals in their own ethical and political conduct. His reading of Xenophon's work was central to his analysis of tyranny, the subheading of his book being *An Interpretation of Xenophon's Hiero*. The book is actually a metaphor criticizing the political doctrine of the time, which Strauss accused of not understanding the dangers of Hitler's and Stalin's dictatorships in time. His thoughts are characterized by his critiques of modernity and skepticism toward progress. Although his vision of the state and society is more liberal than conservative, his criticism of progressivism and cultural relativism, his affirmation of natural inequality among men, and his defense of the family as a "good" value are stances that are undoubtedly ascribable to conservatism.

In *Natural Right and History*, Strauss writes:

> The contemporary rejection of natural rights leads to nihilism— nay, it is identical with it.... In order to live, we have to silence the easily silenced voice of reason, telling ourselves that our principles are in themselves as good or as bad as any other principles. The more we cultivate reason, the more we cultivate nihilism, and the less are we able to be loyal members of society. The inescapable practical consequence of nihilism is fanatical obscurantism.[73]

The American nation and the Declaration of Independence were drawn from natural law. However, the policies in the United States then went in a diametrically different direction by embracing relativism and historicism. Strauss favored the classical political philosophy America was originally founded on, asserting the superiority of ancient thought over modern thought due to a series of factors:

> First of all, in the classical vision, moral and political reflections are carried out in light of the perfection of man and his ends, his purpose. Modern reflections, by contrast, draw inspiration from the origins of man and his *state of nature*. Secondly, while according to the classics, man is a naturally social being, or "political animal," modernity says the individual comes before and ought to be prioritized above society. And this is the third point regarding the end of political life: while in ancient philosophy, political activity was primarily aimed at achieving human virtue, the scope of modern political activity involves getting man out of the condition of maximum insecurity—that is, the state of nature. And the fourth difference, regarding the very essence of the social-political phenomenon, is this: according to the classics, the essence of the

government, broadly understood, is that it creates the *way of life of a society....* On the other hand, modern ideas minimize the importance of the concept of government in favor of that which they consider the moral-political ideal of excellence: the right to self-preservation.[74]

By drawing from that which was affirmed by classical authors, Strauss identified the crisis of modern society: the abandonment of natural law.

Eric Voegelin (1901–1985)

Born in Germany in 1901, Voegelin worked as a political science and sociology teacher at the University of Vienna for the beginning of his professional life. In 1931, he published two books against Nazi racism. The publication of *The History of the Race Idea* forced him to immigrate to Switzerland in 1938, and later to the United States. From there, he published *The New Science of Politics* in 1952, *Order and History* between 1956 and 1987, and finally, *Anamnesis*. Returning to Germany in 1958, he taught political science in Munich in Max Weber's place. In 1969, he returned to the United States, where he remained until his death.

The study of political violence was central to his work. By 1938, he was already analyzing totalitarianism in *The Political Religions*, an analysis of the points of commonality between totalitarian structures and religions. In *Order and History*, he aimed to give life to a "history of the order of experiences" by asking if the concept of a "civilization" can sufficiently explain the complexity of history. The book involves a philological-historical analysis of the main works of the West: the Bible, Homer's poems, and writings by Plato and Aristotle. Voegelin's plan was to achieve a six-volume history of civilization based on order. The first three volumes, titled *Israel and Revelation*, *The World of the Polis*, and *Plato and Aristotle*, were published in 1956 and 1957. The fourth volume, *The Ecumenic Age*, came out in 1974 after in-depth study and reflection on his method of investigation. It does not follow the chronological order of the preceding volumes. The fifth volume, *In Search of Order*, was posthumously published in 1987. His works influenced various thinkers, including Russell Kirk, who some call the father of American conservatism.

Despite his vast production of nonfiction work, Voegelin defined himself as a "non-original author," because he thought philosophy should resume that which has already been transmitted by authors in the past. It is only through the reading and understanding of these authors, he thought, that one can elevate himself, enriching his own spirit and intellect.

Arnold Gehlen (1904–1976)

After studying in Cologne and Leipzig, Gehlen received his first teaching position in philosophy in 1930. Four years later, he became a professor at the University of Leipzig, going on to teach until 1943, when he joined the army.

In 1940, he published *Man: His Nature and Place in the World*, in which he considers man as an organic whole, made up of a body and soul (or spirit). This organic nature is not only revealed in the single individual, but also in the community, understood as a social system of belonging with the natural environment. He outlined a perfectly interconnected system in which every structure forms a single piece of a larger puzzle, creating a correlation between parts rather than contrast. Gehlen studied the relationship between man and the environment, in which the collective life plays an important role. If man becomes familiar with the world through action, Gehlen argued, this only happens thanks to the life of the community.

In 1969, he published *Moral und Hypermoral*, an essential book for understanding post-1945 German conservatism. In modern society, he argued, the institutions that govern the relationships between individuals suffer rapid decline. In 1956, he published *Urmensch und Spätkultur* (*Prehistoric Man and Late Culture*), in which he develops his "theory of institutions," which he considered necessary to avoid the disintegration already underway in modern society. Unlike thinkers such as Ortega y Gasset, a Spanish philosopher who considered technology a danger to man, Gehlen was convinced of the need for technology in human life:

Technology is as old as Man.... And the rough wedge of the fire striker conceals the same ambiguity that today is the same of atomic energy: it was simultaneously a work utensil and a deadly weapon. In Man, any transformation of the original aspects of nature to the service of his own ends is intertwined with the struggles of his fellow men from the beginning....[75]

Gerd-Klaus Kaltenbrunner (1939–2011)

The author of various writings dedicated to the analysis of conservatism, Kaltenbrunner's most well-known book is *Der schwierige Konservatismus*, published in Germany in 1974. Passing away in 2011, Kaltenbrunner was a fervent Catholic who dedicated his life to studying conservative and traditionalist thought, quickly becoming a point of reference for all German conservatives. Unfortunately, his work is not well-known in English-speaking countries.

Standing out among Kaltenbrunner's books published in German are his studies on Dionysius the Areopagite, Prester John, and Anne Catherine Emmerich. His book about Prester John, *Johannes ist sein Name* (*John Is His Name*), written in 1989 and published in 1993, is an ode to mysticism and spiritualism. The figure of Prester John, who probably never existed, is such a symbol of mystical thought that, in the second part of the book, Kaltenbrunner also dedicates space to the relationship between Prester John and the Holy Grail. The more than one-thousand-page text on Dionysius the Areopagite, titled *Dionysius vom Areopag. Das Unergrundliche, die Engel und das Eine* (*Dionysius of Areopagus, The Unfathomable, the Angel and the One*), published in 1996, examines the figure of Dionysius over the course of the Greek and Christian spiritual tradition. Kaltenbrunner's emphases on the spiritual was integral to all his work, and there were four chief principles of Kaltenbrunner's religious philosophy: 1) the invisible is real; 2) history is full of symbolic meaning; 3) legends, myths, and tradition are important keys for understanding eternity; and 4) the esoteric heart of each religion is convergent.

Despite his Catholicism, Kaltenbrunner's studies are not limited to Christianity. They embrace every scope of tradition, referencing the neopagan world and the work of Ludwig Klages, Julius Evola, and the traditionalist school founded by René Guenon. He also wrote about the hundreds of thinkers, philosophers, and writers of Europe's past millennia who articulated its spiritual sources in six volumes; the first three were published between 1981 and 1985, and the last three were published between 1987 and 1992.

Kaltenbrunner considered culture to be an infinite dialogue between the thinkers and poets of every era. He did not limit himself to a modern and enlightened approach to culture and was attracted to removed authors, heretics of modernity, and those who were not as well known to the general public. However, he was also a reader of Goethe, Novalis, and Angelus Silesius.

Kaltenbrunner was convinced that the elite members of society played an important role in preventing the spiritual and social disintegration of the world. He therefore attributed "elite" status to the hermits, mystics, ascetics, monks, thinkers, and writers of society. At the same time, he was interested in ecology and believed in the importance of living harmoniously with nature by making precise choices, such as growing a personal vegetable garden or not owning a car. Kaltenbrunner himself was an aristocrat who, while skeptical of a restoration of traditional nobility, was aware of the need for an elite government. He therefore frequently criticized the mediocrity of democratic governments, which remained a constant theme throughout his work. While in his initial writings he favored aristocratic republics like Venice's, he grew increasingly convinced in the 1980s of the universal Christian monarchy being the best system of government, as had occurred in the medieval period with Frederick I or Emperor Charles IV. The sphere of Kaltenbrunner's work that interests us most, however, is his study of conservatism:

> The conservative position interprets man as incomplete, being limited by nature, yet made better through discipline, and sustained by bonds and support; the emancipatory position, by contrast, presupposes man's perfectibility, and in him sees a call to the liberation of self, his corruption only occurring by exterior circumstances. These two poles can be identified under most

different names: classicism and Romanticism, Left and Right, realism and utopia, authoritarianism and anarchy, conservative and revolutionary.[76]

The contemporary conservative, Kaltenbrunner believed, must oppose the technocratic trends of society by guaranteeing essential individual liberties and encouraging the individual to ask himself how he can guarantee the meaning of the state and its structure in the contemporary era. He also must realize that:

> Recovery of the spiritual substance of our tradition is part of the great mission of conservatives, along with the fight against the nihilistic destruction of the culture's historical continuity. Conservatives will honor an idea that is on its way to exile, in the catacombs: the idea of culture. And they will lead it to salvation.[77]

Kaltenbrunner also calls for conservatives to look beyond national borders, with a vision that goes beyond their own country. He concludes the introduction to his book with a warning: "The conservative has stayed true to his calling if he does not interpret his achievements as a mere conservation of fragile remnants of past systems, but rather as an original contribution to a new order that not only is not destroyed, but connected with life."[78]

CHAPTER FOUR

French Conservatism

In his pamphlet *What Is the Third Estate?*, the abbot Emmanuel Joseph Sieyès outlines the revolutionary spirit and its battle against the nobility and traditional clergy. According to Sieyès, the third estate consists of every productive class of the nation and therefore constitutes the nation itself. Sieyès wrote the pamphlet shortly before the French Revolution began, but to fundamentally understand the French Revolution, one must note that Sieyès actually stood in favor of small landowners, traders, and professionals, rather than the masses without property.

Between 1789, the year the pamphlet was first published, and 1792, France saw ancient orders abolished, equal taxation for all, and equality before the law. In 1791, the property of the Catholic Church was nationalized through the Civil Constitution of the Clergy. In response, the pope condemned the Revolution and the king also aligned himself with the counterrevolutionaries. The church therefore developed a counteroffensive movement against secular, egalitarian sentiments. This movement considered religious tolerance and the separation of church and state to be an attack on the foundations of Christianity. The most radical revolutionaries regarded the pope as a foreign prince and the clergy as a rank that only defended its own interests and privileges rather than those of religion. The philosophers of the revolution identified the medieval past as an era dominated by tyrannies and superstitious priests.

While much has been written about the role of aristocrats and the clergy's opposition to the revolution, sufficient emphasis has not been placed on the counterrevolutionaries of the working class throughout France: peasants and artisans from more remote areas of the country who remained faithful to ancient religions. In these small communities, priests were the only figures capable of transmitting ideas and innovations coming from the outside. When revolutionaries arrested and deported the priests, accusing them of being traitors when in fact they were integral to the community, there were many uprisings to the cry of "long live the king and our dear priests." In the end, what advantages did the revolution bring to these people? Certainly not the right to vote, which was extended to the middle class, not to the working class.

Napoleon's rise to power led to a new drive of revolutionary reforms and principles. Many positions of power were given to Jacobins or French bureaucrats; aristocratic privileges were abolished and equality before the law was once again established. Furthermore, Napoleon conquered the church state by attacking the privileged position of the church in conquered territories through the seizure of property, the suppression of monasteries and convents, and the legalization of religious tolerance. Napoleon's policies instead favored merchant and industrial families—families that had already dominated the country before the revolution began.

Louis XVIII's return disappointed the hopes of French conservatives, in part because of the delicate political situation. However, Charles X's election to the throne followed and he introduced policies based on markedly conservative stances. The king placed the relationship with the church at the center of his actions, a partnership that culminated with the ordinances promulgated in July 1830—which led to a new revolution. The new order abolished Catholicism as the religion of the state, introduced a constitutional monarchy, and sanctioned the withdrawal of many noblemen from political activity.

The uprisings of 1848 upset many European countries. In the immediate aftermath, especially in France, the rebels found themselves without expected popular support. Thus, conservative forces triumphed in the elections of April 1848, thanks especially to campaigns carried out by noblemen and clergy in small provinces, warning against the dangers of the Jacobins. Napoleon III

(1808–1873) rose to power and immediately restored the church's control of education and removed republicans from positions of power. In 1852, he declared himself emperor with full legislative and foreign policy control, along with the right to nominate his own successor. He knew how to relate to modern society and was capable of manipulating the needs and requirements of people around him. He thus carried out a populist campaign that encouraged nationalism and imperialism, but his main concern was in the economic sphere: he desired the growth and well-being of the people to reduce the potential of another revolution.

Napoleon III was defeated by Prussian forces, which opened the door for the return of monarchy in France. In February 1871, a government was elected to negotiate peace terms. These terms, the divestiture of Alsace and Lorraine and a huge payment of war tribute, immediately generated discontent among the people. This discontent, inspired by the eighteenth-century revolution, aligned the self-governing municipality again with revolutionary stances. There was no delay in the reaction of the regular army; many communards were shot or imprisoned. In 1875, France officially became a republic, and during the 1881 elections, loyalists suffered a difficult defeat that allowed republican factions to bring their men into key positions of power. Conservative forces therefore joined forces with General Boulanger (1837–1891), who triumphed in the elections of 1889 but failed to restore the monarchy. In the next election, conservatives were again defeated.

What restored strength to the French conservative faction was the "Dreyfus affair." After a Jewish official was accused of treason and espionage on behalf of the Germans, conservatives used the scandal to exploit anti-Semitism to gather popular support, all in the name of Catholic loyalty and nationalism. Even the church sided against Dreyfus, clamoring for a restoration to ancient unity between the Throne and the Altar. The secretary of the Vatican State even went so far as to invite all Catholics to denounce Dreyfus, and Pope Pius X punished all bishops who supported the republic. The French government's reaction was immediate: at first, diplomatic relations with the Vatican were suspended, and in 1905, the law of separation between church and state was enacted, confiscating the riches and privileges of the church. A true *de-Christianization* of society occurred, with a consequential increase in civil marriages and unbaptized children.

The French Right viewed the role of the army positively, hoping it would overcome the republic, declare war and defeat Germany, and bring France back to authoritarian positions recognizing the position of the church. A society founded on discipline and hierarchy, in service of the protection of the most ancient French values, was their goal. Indeed, throughout the 1890s, a counterrevolutionary way of thinking progressively developed, identifying the French Revolution as the event in which the most important French values were eliminated. At that time, the ideas of right-wing conservatives in France were fragmented into different currents and movements: on the one hand, they favored debate and plurality of ideas, and on the other, they generated an exasperated and counterproductive division:

> At the end of the nineteenth century, the French Right was broken up into various factions: republican nationalists, liberal conserva-tives, common patriots, Alsatian-Lorraine irredentist followers of General Boulanger, a failed coup leader, anti-Semitic militants (this group was also widespread among the Left, where there were perhaps more followers than on the Right), Orléanist monarchists, Bonapartists, and men of law enforcement. All of these factions were, in turn, divided into many other factions, which were par-ticularly litigious, with a contentiousness that at times tended to cross over into sectarianism. Essentially, this was a sign that this magmatic movement, which was not numerically insignificant, lacked ideological solidity.[1]

This unbalanced and confused scene needed well-defined guidance, and an occasion presented itself with the "Dreyfus affair," which was surrounded by international attention. Charles Maurras wrote an article on the event titled "Il primo sangue"—"The first blood"—in which he portrays Colonel Henry, Dreyfus's accuser who later committed suicide, as a martyr, and accuses Drey-fus's defenders of plotting against the interests of France. Maurras quickly became a well-known name in French right-wing circles.

In 1899, Action Française, the French right-wing political movement, officially emerged with its patriotic manifesto, promoted by Maurice Pujo and Henri Vaugeois. Other intellectuals, such as Jacques Bainville and Léon Daudet, also quickly rallied around the movement. Vaugeois was initially aligned with center-left stances, but he later embraced nationalist ideas. Maurice Pujo also took up anti-Dreyfus stances and endorsed the creation of the Ligue de la Patrie Française (French Homeland League), a nationalist organization from which Action Française originated. Pujo had a strategic role within the movement even in 1908 when, along with Maxime Real del Sarte, he created Camelots du Roi, "King's Camelots," the youth organization of Action Française.

Defining Action Française as a Fascist movement distorts its true identity, as it lacks the main traits of Fascism, such as the adoration of a leader or military hierarchy. This is not to say that certain aspects of Action Française, which predated Fascism by about twenty years, were not later taken up by Fascism. Perhaps the most striking example would be the organization's corporatism. Under the leadership of Maurras, "the unexpected activism of the anti-democratic movement tirelessly thwarted both Jacobin centralism and the pro-German stances of many French liberals under the guidance of writer Charles Maurras, who hailed from 'Provençal regionalism.' His monarchist spirit was not traditional, like that of the Legitimists, but rather tended more toward the direction of a dictatorial state that utilized military power against the firm will of violent repression of any subversive tendencies."[2]

The social policies of Action Française, however, were achieved by René de la Tour du Pin (1834–1924). As the descendant of a noble family affected by the revolution, he believed that societies based on liberal individualism and egalitarianism frustrate man's need to be in society, alienating and isolating him, leading to the collapse of the family and traditional communities. La Tour compared this individualism with the conservative vision of an organic society, in which every French citizen belongs to a specific corporation associated with his job, social status, or profession, and in which every corporation is self-regulated by internal laws. He also wished for a corporative rather than individual voting system, in which every corporation could cast a vote. He envisioned a system analogous to that of pre-revolutionary states, in which the Chamber of Deputies would be replaced with a Chamber of Corporations.

In the elections of November 1919, French conservatives obtained a landslide victory through a campaign based on aggressive foreign policy to defend the status quo. In 1923, when the German government announced its inability to uphold its war debt, Poincaré invaded the Ruhr, justifying the operation with Germany's failure to comply with the Treaty of Versailles. By the end of the 1920s, France was only marginally affected by the international economic crisis, whereas Germany was greatly weakened, in part due to its high levels of unemployment.

Time passed, and in 1936, Léon Blum became France's first socialist prime minister. By the end of the 1930s, France's extreme right-wing groups began to see Italian Fascism as an example to be followed, in response to the economic crisis during the years of the depression brought on by the socialist regime. A strong base of associations and groups began to emerge in France, all of whom hoped for the rise of a strong leader capable of repressing the republic through a revolution unbound by ultra-nationalism, a cult of virility, imperialism, anti-Communism, and war ethics. Together, this set of values recalled Mussolini's brand of Fascism.

During World War II, some fringe conservatives saw Vichy France—the government headed by Marshal Philippe Pétain—as the only solution to Nazi expansion throughout the French territory. Pétain was seen as an authoritative leader capable of holding power. Pétain defined Maurras as "the most French of the French" and viewed the ideology of Action Française, combined with the notions of the old conservative order, as the only hope for France's future. Under his rule, he abolished republican institutions and replaced them with corporative groups that represented regions and professions. He also partially restored power to the church in France by restoring its properties, favoring the catechism, and allowing religious ranks to return to teaching. He replaced the revolutionary slogan "freedom, equality, and fraternity" with three new words of order: "work, family, and homeland."

The Vichy administration, however, was also characterized by a pronounced anti-Semitic tone that derived not only from Nazi demands, but also from a strong aversion to the spread of Jews in France. With the British invasion, Pétain believed Europe and France's fate would be determined by Russian Bolshevism and the Jewish-influenced United States. Maurras also shared this fear, waiting for a new wave of the revolutionary spirit.

Counterrevolutionaries

Between 1793 and 1797, a series of counterrevolutionary books were published in response to the upheavals brought on by the French Revolution. Among these works, the most renowned is *Considerations on France* by Joseph de Maistre, published in 1796. However, other works, such as Mallet du Pan's *Considerations on the Nature of the French Revolution and on the Causes that Prolonged Its Duration*, François-René de Chateaubriand's *Essay on the Revolutions*, and *Theory of Political and Religious Power* by Louis de Bonald, are also important. Counterrevolutionary Antoine de Rivarol, who defended the monarchy even during the most difficult years of the revolution, deserves particular attention:

> In 1788, *The Little Almanac of Our Great Men*, with the inscription, "To the unknown Gods," was anonymously published. Two years later, it was followed by *The Little Dictionary of Great Men of the Revolution*, in which characters of the caliber of Robespierre, Danton, and Marat do not escape his virulent definitions.[3]

The Little Dictionary of Great Men of the Revolution, courageously or perhaps unconsciously published under his real name, was a risk to Rivarol's life. It was only thanks to an invitation from Louis XVI to leave France for his own safety that Rivarol was able to avoid Jacobin revenge. He developed an increasingly counterrevolutionary way of thinking, along with a growing admiration for Burke. He accused those who contributed to the disintegration of the social structure of allowing barbaric and abusive actions to become the norm.

Joseph de Maistre (1753–1821)

The most well-known and staunch opponent of the Revolution was undoubt-edly Joseph de Maistre. After reading *Reflections on the Revolution in France* by Edmund Burke, he agreed with the Irishman on the differences between the events in France and those in England in 1688, emphasizing how the French Revolution had combined absolutism and the uprooting of human and religious traditions in a subversive attack on the roots of French civilization. His reading of Burke's book convinced him that what was happening in France was not "a simple revolt, but rather the beginning of an epic movement, an overthrow of the basis of that which he considered indispensable to the foundation of European and Christian civilization. More than a political event, the revolution demanded to be seen as a true cultural and philosophical phenomenon."[4]

To the celebrated motto "freedom, equality, and fraternity" of the French Revolution, Maistre countered with a true "throne and altar" slogan, in an attempt to reestablish the hereditary monarchy based on religion. As a coun-terrevolutionary, he was forced to abandon Savoy, his native land. Serving as the ambassador of the Kingdom of Sardinia in Russia for fourteen years, his book *St. Petersburg Dialogues* asks how to restore a traditional society in a time of revolution. He proposes that the solution is a greater faith, and greater order, though he was more inclined to defend the clergy than political author-ity. Maistre believed order coincided with an angelic vision, and chaos with diabolical forces.

In his *Essay on the Generative Principle of Political Constitutions*, first published in 1810, he denounced the greatest error of our time: believing that a constitution can be written *a priori*. According to Maistre, a constitution has divine origin, and the most important laws of a country cannot be written. Any authority that writes the law can indeed decide to nullify it—whereas natural law, which is sacred and immutable, is not written. Maistre thus out-lines four "undeniable truths":

1. The fundamental principles of political constitutions exist before all written laws.

2. A constitutional law is the progress of a preexisting, unwritten law.
3. That which is truly important has never been and can never be written without putting the state in danger.
4. The weakness and fragility of the constitution is proportional to the number of laws written.

The book *St. Petersburg Dialogues* is divided into eleven interviews between three fictional characters who discuss the main problems of the meaning of life, death, and history: the Count (who is Piedmontese), the Senator (who is Russian), and the Knight (who is French). The prelates, the aristocrats, and other dignitaries of the state are the guardians of truth, and it is up to them to teach the nation about that which is true or false, the moral and spiritual order.

Maistre poses a question perhaps more relevant today than ever: "Why have we been so hasty to allow anyone to speak freely?" Carl Schmitt writes:

> Maistre talks about sovereignty with particular predilection. To him, the sovereign was the place of pure decision. The value of the state consists of making decisions, and the value of the church consists of making the ultimate, unquestionable decision. He believed infallibility to be the essence of the unquestionable decision: the infallibility of the spiritual order and sovereignty of the state system were bound together and essentially the same.[5]

After the Revolution, he began his peregrination around Europe, which led him to Switzerland, then to Venice, Sardinia, and to Russia for a long time. During his travels for diplomatic work, he developed his idea that the Revolution was the work of Satan, and he published various counterrevolutionary pamphlets that would prelude *Considerations on France*. In *Studies on Sovereignty*, he points a finger and shames those who attempt to justify revolutionary actions in the name of greater liberty for man. These themes are reiterated in *Essay on the Generative Principle of Political Constitutions*, in which Maistre examines the origins of sovereignty:

The hand of God originally founded the nations, peoples, and states. He is the only "legislator," not a man or group of men who cannot *establish* a people or a state but at the most encode *a posteriori* laws for them. Even here, Rousseau is mistaken: in *The Social Contract*, he writes about a "legislator" that can give shape to a people and their government, without reflecting on the idea that, for the people, government is like language: it is something that is born, develops, and is perfected by and according to its nature, and not something that *begins* at a certain point at the hands of men.[6]

In Maistre's opinion, men are supposed to be governed by a monarchy, which is the most natural form of government because *personal unity* and *essential unity* coincide in the sovereign figure. The aristocracy, however, is "a monarchy with a vacant throne." It is different from a monarchy because sovereignty is distributed in various forms. Even the aristocracy prefers a hereditary model that guarantees people order and stability. On the other hand, democracy, in its purest form, cannot truly exist: the idea of a sovereign people and legislature, according to Maistre, doesn't make sense.

Maistre analyzes the origin of laws and constitutions with particular attention. Man can neither create, nor improve, nor perfect that which already exists without divine help:

> One of the biggest mistakes of the century was the belief that a political constitution could be written and created *a priori*. Reason and experience work together to establish that a constitution is a divine work and, that which is precisely most fundamental and essentially constitutional in the laws of a nation cannot be written.[7]

During the eighteenth century, a revolt against God was underway. Maistre defined his century as "theophobic," because many of the contemporary writers treated Christianity like a crucial enemy to fight against. His greatest concern was the loss of unity in the Christian European world:

Enlightenment thinkers and the Revolution hurled the most striking blows against that unity... with the initial affirmation of the
pernicious principle of *individual reason* to be seen in the Protestant Reform, where all the seeds of division, revolt, and rejection
of sovereignty were present and operative.[8]

His attention to the church and Catholicism became a central point in
his book *The Pope*, published in 1819, in which he describes the authority of
the church as capable of combining spiritual infallibility and temporal sovereignty. Infallibility and authority are united within the pontiff, who holds
an authority similar but superior to temporal sovereignties, thanks to the
universal character of the faith. As the church is one and universal, the infallibility principle sits naturally within the Catholic faith. Maistre dreamed of
a union of every Christian sovereignty in a universal republic, under the
supremacy of a spiritual power in the pontiff: a society of Christian nations,
in which earthly solidity is guaranteed by a single, superior, and impartial
power. The same themes are recalled in *St. Petersburg Dialogues*, in which he
analyzes the fundamental themes of Christianity, dedicating ample space to
the critical review of modernity.

Maistre, compared to other counterrevolutionary theorists, lived out his
own principles, atoning for the consequences of his ideas firsthand. In 1815, he
did not approve of the decrees dictated by the Congress of Vienna and the Restoration—which, according to Maistre, was affected by the revolutionary threat:

It would be a big mistake to believe that Louis XVIII ascended the
throne of his ancestors. He ascended the throne of Bonaparte, and
it is already a great fortune for humanity; but we are still very far
from stability. The Revolution was initially democratic, then oligarchic, then tyrannical; today it is royal, but always continues on
its way.[9]

The role of Divine Providence is key to *Considerations on France* and to
understanding Maistre's thought. He held that man's salvation comes from

Christianity, personified in pontifical authority considered infallible and absolute, as guaranteed by God. There must be a natural right at the foundation of human law—which, because the Enlightenment and the French Revolution brought on liberalism and radicalism, is increasingly removed from today's society.

Antoine de Rivarol (1753–1801)

According to Jünger, Rivarol must be read by "anyone trying to separate within their conservative ideas that which is long-lasting from that which is redundant and damaging."[10] Rivarol dedicated much of his life to studying languages. In 1783, he won an award from the Academy of Science in Berlin, where he was asked to explain the universality of French and planned to write an encyclopedia of the language. His political thought was based on the idea that the laws governing politics and society have a divine origin that men cannot avoid. *The Little Almanac of Our Great Men* directs Rivarol's own precepts toward thinkers who did not share his politics. These writings created more than a few problems for Rivarol: many people who objected to his sharp criticism became powerful Jacobins. Thus, on June 10, 1792, a few days before the king's capture, he decided to leave Paris.

After arriving in Brussels, he began simultaneously working on two projects, a French dictionary and a work on the art of governing. He stayed in Brussels until 1794 and then moved successively to the Netherlands, London, Hamburg, and eventually Berlin, where he died in 1801. Conservatism is much indebted to his thought; Jünger rightly wrote:

> In many of the greatest minds, in many of responsible spirits, we can find, just as in Rivarol, the desire to conserve the link to the past and to continue building upon the plot of the old civilization. This desire became even more pronounced with the development of revolutionary forces and the sight of the events in Paris.... A constitutional yet strong monarchy, the aristocracy as the enlightened class, the church as a conservative power that the individual must respect.... Rivarol was certainly a result of these fundamental thoughts, but not original. He not only shared a spiritual elite with

them, but also with the mentality of vast circles, which are still alive. As a matter of fact, their influence can be noted in every constitution of the nineteenth century.[11]

Louis Gabriel Ambroise de Bonald (1754–1840)

While Maistre is certainly one of the most well-known counterrevolutionaries, Louis de Bonald also went down in history as one of the most important conservative thinkers, thanks to his three-volume *Theory of Political and Religious Power*, published in 1796. The opening words of the book best summarize his thought: "One cannot deal with society without speaking of man, nor speak of man without returning to God."

Just as Maistre did, Bonald identified the monarch as the figure capable of personifying conservative power, and he emphasized the importance of the *unity* of power. Undermining this unity, as happened in the French Revolution, divides power among many members of society, which causes the very concept of power itself to fail:

> It is therefore clear that every time societies have refused their own fundamental laws, especially the conservative principle of the unity of power, they were punished by the fury of conquests, by internal disorder, and at times by foreign oppressions.... This begins by casting doubt on the basic principles of religion, then expanding the "progressive" separation between the "intelligent side" and the "material side" of man.[12]

Bonald distanced himself from Montesquieu's theory of the division of power. According to him, a society made up of three powers (legislative, executive, judiciary) must be understood as the emanation of a single power. Every *positive* society, he believed, is composed of three main instances: power, will, and action. These make up the natural laws of order, whose overthrow leads to disorder and destruction.

As the editor of the magazine *Le Conservateur*, Bonald frequently highlighted humanity's inability to live without a government. His doctrine of providential law "consists of retaining power: as a constitutive and peremptory principle of human communities, it makes up the providential order of the world. Societies can choose, within a certain measure, *how* to be governed, but they cannot choose *not* to be governed."[13]

Bonald continued writing and publishing books consistent with his ultra-royalist thought. He refused Napoleon's offer to reprint *Theory of Power* with the omission of the dedication to the king and, during the Restoration, he sided with the monarchy and became deputy from 1815 to 1822. Society, according to Bonald, is born of a power of divine origins, reincarnated in the king; this is why monarchy is the best form of government.

François-René de Chateaubriand (1768–1848)

Originally from a long-standing aristocratic family, Chateaubriand's father wished for a military career for his son. After serving for a short period in the navy in 1788, Chateaubriand moved to Paris, where he became interested in the literary world. Struck by the events of the French Revolution, he decided to set sail toward the United States in 1791. Upon his return the following year, he joined the army of royalist *émigrés* (made up of noblemen and royalist anti-revolutionary troops). After being wounded, he decided to relocate to London. Chateaubriand was the first thinker to use the term "conservative" in 1818, during the Restoration. He used it to refer to "respectable people" who supported the values of religion.

Returning to France in the early months of the nineteenth century, he wrote the novel *René*, a reference for Romanticist writers, and in 1802 published his most well-known work, *The Genius of Christianity*. In the book, he calls on his contemporaries to draw closer to the Catholic Church and distance themselves from anti-Christian, revolutionary ideology. *The Genius of Christianity*, as Stenio Solinas writes in *Il Giornale*, is a

> collection of extraordinary scholarship, a work of talent by one
> who is not afraid to pillage another man's field; "the original writer
> is not the one who does not imitate others, but rather the one who
> no one can imitate." The *Genius* moves from a simple and winning

assumption: "Do not experience the excellence of Christianity because it comes from God, but know it comes from God because it is excellent." It is not an apology that has anything to do with dogmas, reason, and the truth of faith, but with the "beauty," or rather the "beauties" that are, the values associated with the senses, with taste, with feelings.[14]

After his diplomatic endeavors with Napoleon in Rome and Valais, Chateaubriand resigned his post and traveled to Greece, Egypt, and Palestine. Upon returning to France, he bought an estate in the countryside outside of Paris, where he wrote *The Martyrs, Or, the Triumph of the Christian Religion*, published in 1809.

During the Restoration, Chateaubriand reached maximum notoriety, first with a pamphlet criticizing Napoleon and subsequently for his nomination as a state minister and a peer of France. His stances against the dissolvement of the *Chambre introuvable*, elected after the fall of Napoleon, led him to join the ultra-royalist opposition and to become one of the writers for the paper *Le Conservateur*. He later held important positions in the French government, particularly in foreign policy, until he finally withdrew from politics and dedicated his time to writing *Memoirs from beyond the Tomb*, a monumental, two-volume autobiography published posthumously between 1849 and 1850. In recounting his life, Chateaubriand retraces the most eventful years of French history, from the *ancien régime* to the French Revolution, as well as the Napoleonic period, with portraits of the most important protagonists coming to light through his own eyes.

Hugues Félicité Robert de Lamennais (1782–1854)

Lamennais reacted strongly against the Protestant Reformation, Enlightenment ideas, and the lack of trust in individualism so prevalent in his time. Unlike Maistre and Bonald, he refused the idea of popular sovereignty, distinguishing himself from traditional royalists. Deeply Catholic, to the point of becoming a priest in 1814, Lamennais understood that with the end of the *ancien régime* comes the weakening of the link between the state and the church, creating a secular state and a church devoid of privilege.

His most important work, *Essay on Indifference in Matters of Religion*, filled four volumes and was published between 1817 and 1823. It became one of the most-read counterrevolutionary texts. In addition to writing books, Lamennais worked with the magazines *Le Conservateur* (led by Chateabriand) and *Defenseur* (led by Bonald) to carry on his Catholic counterrevolutionary commitment.

In 1826, he experienced a true metamorphosis that brought him closer to liberal and democratic Catholicism—to the point of suffering ecclesiastical condemnation in 1832 and, two years later, receiving an in-person condemnation from the pope for his book *Words of a Believer*.

Despite his break from the church, Lamennais remained Catholic his entire life and was among the first of the French thinkers to denounce the revolutionaries' destruction of the social order. In his opinion, the Revolution

> destroyed society to re-create it based on a new model, but this ideal model must not be thought of as the same for every revolutionary sect. Actually, every individual has his own ideal model. The agreement between Protestants and political revolutionaries (regarding the social order) is to overthrow that which exists and has always existed. If it continues over time, this condition against nature will produce the complete dissolution of society, which is made up of the union of spirits solidified by common beliefs.[15]

Like other counterrevolutionary thinkers, Lamennais distanced himself from the centralized state, which, in centralizing all power, caused the destruction of intermediary associations. His early stances fluctuated between those of a conservative Catholic and those of a royalist. He believed Catholicism was the foundation of society:

> His early, militant defense of the church against the state was predicated on a principle of authority that was, at bottom,

pluralist. In the beginning, he was united with Bonald and Chateaubriand, Balmes, and other Catholic conservatives, for he
saw their vision of the church's freedom in society as one containing by implication the freedom of other associations as well:
family, co-operative, labor union, and locality. Only when
Lamennais came to realize the disharmony between his purposes and those of certain Catholic conservatives did he break
with them and with the church, bringing on his head, eventually, excommunication. But his essential work had been done,
and with such others in the church as Montalembert and Lacor-
daire to lead the way, modern social Catholicism, with its pluralist orientation, was a reality. Lamennais became, after his
excommunication, a leading figure in the cause of co-operatives
and labor unions in France. His ideological emphasis remained
strongly de-centralist.[16]

His arguments against a centralized state were set apart from liberal ones
expressed by thinkers such as Guizot, Royer-Collard, Mill, and Spencer.
Lamennais believed individualism was guilty of supporting the rise of an
authoritative state. The societal man, not the individual, creates the unity of
society through his membership to guilds such as the family, the church, and
the community, which all represented protection from political power during
the *ancien régime*. He considered the family the most important social group,
as it is at the base of every value of order.

With the Revolution of 1848, he was elected to be a member of the Con-
stituent Assembly.

During meetings of this important body, Lamennais tried to elevate the importance of the principle of decentralization in the new
constitution of France to the highest degree possible. However, his
pluralist ideas, unfortunately, were not expressed in the works of
the *Commission*, which favored the idea of a centralized and omni-
competent state.[17]

In *Essay on Indifference in Matters of Religion*, Lamennais addresses the illnesses of modernity, contesting indifference in particular:

> The mistakes of the "century of Enlightenment" and atheism (which is both the culmination and common denominator of the Enlightenment) are pernicious and satanic. But these are still *doctrines*, which can be contradicted and even defeated. It is a much different situation, however, for their firstborn child, *the spirit of indifference*, which is typical of modernity and by no means a doctrine, but rather a voluntary surrender and ridicule of *any* doctrine. The indifferent does not deny, he does not affirm, and is not even, as the skeptic is, in a state of doubt, but instead abandons himself to a "voluntary slumber of the soul," to a "general dullness of moral faculties and an absolute lack of ideas about anything that is important for a man to know."[18]

Lamennais thought indifference causes fatal consequences for religion, including the abandonment of the search for truth. Religion must be protected not only because it conserves society, but because it is as *necessary* as the society itself. While it may change shape over the course of time, it invariably maintains its fundamental dogmas and moral laws. Mankind needs stable laws, as human actions free from order generate evil and dissolution. It is no coincidence that the most catastrophic events in history originated from arbitrary constitutions and religions in which mankind claimed to create God in his own image and affinity. For society to be united, every aspect must be in order. In Lamennais's opinion, the church represents the perfect society, a foundation of order and stability for civil society. The dogmas of supreme reason and individualism, on the other hand,

> take us away from the truth; *common sense* brings us back to it by means of *authority*: this is the "general means" that must be sought in order to avoid abandoning oneself to the weakness of individual judgment that leads, like every "philosophical" system, to absolute doubt and places mankind in a state against nature.[19]

Jules Barbey d'Aurevilly (1808–1889)

Born to a legitimist Catholic family, Barbey d'Aurevilly began his education with a tutor. His family was against the public school system that emerged after the French Revolution; he continued studying at a private school in Valognes in Normandy and at the Collège Stanislas de Paris. After studying law at Caen University, he began working with newspapers and magazines, becoming a literary critic. In 1832, he published his first book, *Léa*. The following year, he moved to Paris to become a full-time journalist.

His study of Joseph de Maistre's work caused him to stray from his early liberalism and agnosticism, leading him to embrace traditionalist ideas:

> Reflection on original sin and on the theology of the fall of man changed the optimistic anthropology that had been indoctrinated with the works of the masters of the Revolution. History therefore presents itself as a battlefield, where good and evil, God and Satan, compete for the divine fate of individual men. The myth of unstoppable progress, the advent of a productive society, which today would be consumerist, utilitarian, and forced into industrialization, became the subject of Barbey's controversy.[20]

In 1846, he founded the Société Catholique in order to produce religious content, and in 1847, he founded the magazine *Revue du Monde Catholique* (*Review of the Catholic World*), which ceased publication with the uprising of the following year. He obtained greater success with his books: in 1851, he published *The Prophets of the Past*, a political analysis linked to Catholicism, and in the same year began writing *The Bewitched*, a historical fiction novel about the adventures of the *chouan*, the counterrevolutionary fighters. The work was so strong, due to both its content, its philosophical grounding, its historical relevancy, and its innovative linguistic style, that many well-known progressive writers like Victor Hugo opposed it. In response, Barbey ripped apart Hugo's *Les Misérables*. Nevertheless, thanks to *The Bewitched*, he became a prominent member of the legitimists, Catholics, and anti-conformists. His literary and cultural journey continued with the publication of *The Knight of*

Touches in 1864, in which he concludes the narration of the events of the Norman counterrevolution:

> Even in this novel, the charm of the *chouannerie* is felt as a hopeless, and therefore all the more noble, partisan fight that an entire people led in the name of God and the king. It was fought against the Bleus, the soldiers of the revolution, who came to "pacify" an entire region in blood. The knight of Touches, the liaison between the royalist insurgents and the French noblemen who emigrated to England... becomes the symbol of an aesthetic existence in a world dominated by Enlightenment reason and the dullness of bourgeois ethics.[21]

His work is characterized by its condemnation of the methods, practices, and customs of society at the time. He assumed intensely Catholic stances, and his characters take up the dispositions of the author: they hold reactionary stances, with aristocratic traces of snobbery and dandyism.

Louis Veuillot (1813–1883)

Veuillot began working as a journalist at daily and weekly newspapers and later established himself at *Univers Religieux*, the reference newspaper for French Catholicism. Initially uninterested in religion, he drew closer to ultramontanism after being brought to Rome in 1838. Veuillot recounts his trip and his experiences with Catholicism in various works including *Pilgrimages to Switzerland*, published in 1839, and *Rome and Loreto*, published in 1841.

His work at *Univers Religieux* led the newspaper to take ultramontanist propaganda positions, creating various controversies against moderate Catholics, the second French Empire, and the Italian government, especially after 1843 when Veuillot was named editor of the newspaper. His stance toward Napoleon III also changed at the moment the military campaign in Italy threatened the power of Pope Pius IX in 1859. His dispute with the emperor eventually led to the closure of the newspaper from 1860 to 1867.

As the author of various religious works, he published a collection of his articles titled *Free Thinkers* in 1848, in which he upholds the infallibility of the pope and the necessity of temporal power exercised by the church. The collection openly reveals his contrasting stances from those of the liberal church, proposed by Charles de Montalembert. During the First Vatican Council, he moved to Rome to experience the success of the ultramontanist stances, thanks to the confirmation of papal infallibility sanctioned by the council.

Veuillot, with the support of Pope Pius IX and Donoso Cortés, criticized Catholics who supported liberal democracy. At this historical moment, Christian society was preserved only thanks to two powers: the first was the enlightened infallibility of the powers of the pope, and the second was the power in the hands of the representatives of society. Veuillot's ideas on this are collected in his *Complete Works*, published posthumously in 1927–28, with inside stories, poems, biographies, letters, and controversial writings demonstrating his hate for bourgeois institutions and the structures that emerged after the French Revolution.

While he was still alive, he published *Religious, Historical, Political and Literary Mixes* in twelve volumes, which includes articles, notes, and writings summarizing forty years of religious history. The main themes of his work can be classified into three categories: the decline of the empire, the European conspiracy against the temporal power of the pope, and the consequences of the Vatican Council. Veuillot's uncompromising positions on the church were opposed by more moderate members, to the point of pushing Pope Pius IX to declare himself in favor of the work by *Univers Religieux* to quell the controversy. Veuillot, however, was foreign to any political games, declaring in 1842: "Avoid factions of all kinds; we belong only to our Church and our country."[22]

Gustave Le Bon (1841–1931)

Leaving aside Le Bon's studies of anthropology and the measurement of the human skull, the sphere that interests us most is his analyses of the masses. Considered the founder of the psychology of the masses, the French anthropologist and psychologist owed his notoriety to his book *The Crowd: A Study of the Popular Mind*. Before Le Bon, the behavior of the masses was actually the study of Italian psychologist Scipio Sighele (1868–1913) in his 1891 book *The Criminal Crowd*, in which he tried to discover the laws that govern the behavior of large and small groups.

After achieving literary success, Le Bon began organizing a series of weekly lunches in 1902 to which he invited some of the most important figures of the day, such as Bergson, Valéry and Poincaré. In 1895, the success of his books *The Psychology of Peoples* and *The Crowd: A Study of* the *Popular Mind* influenced many key political leaders, particularly Mussolini, who reread *The Crowd* countless times. Even Hitler and Stalin were fascinated by him, to the point that the German dictator was said to have retraced some of the French anthropologist's theories during the drafting of *Mein Kampf.*

Le Bon owes the writing of his well-known book to three specific events in France: the Paris Commune, General Georges Ernst Boulanger's rapid notoriety, and the Dreyfus affair, all of which were characterized by involvement of the masses. The crowd is described as an object of political work and as an unconscious collective. The text analyzes the role of the masses in the society of the time, describing them as a negative force that leads to decline. He compares the masses to the minorities, which he considered proactive forces:

> Civilisations as yet have only been created and directed by a small intellectual aristocracy, never by crowds. Crowds are only powerful for destruction. Their rule is always tantamount to a barbarian phase. A civilisation involves fixed rules, discipline, a passing from the instinctive to the rational state, forethought for the future, an elevated degree of culture—all of them conditions that crowds, left to themselves, have invariably shown themselves incapable of realising. In consequence of the purely destructive nature of their power, crowds act like those microbes which hasten the dissolution of enfeebled or dead bodies. When the structure of a civilisation is rotten, it is always the masses that bring about its downfall.[23]

Le Bon's prominence foresaw what would happen in the twentieth century, namely, the development of the so-called "age of the masses." He identified the defining traits of and allures of these masses aptly: anonymity in a crowd, contagion, and suggestibility.

Georg Simmel (1858–1918)

In 1897, Georg Simmel wrote *How Social Forms Are Maintained*, in which he researches motivations that lead society to conserve itself:

> At every moment, aggravating forces, external or not, attack society. If it were subordinate to their sole action, these forces would not delay in dissolving society, that is, to regroup its elements. However, conservative forces oppose these principles of destruction and keep these elements together, ensuring their cohesion and guaranteeing the unity of everything.[24]

Conservation, according to Simmel, must begin with the understanding that, even if social groups remain equal over time, members of each group change. Therefore, a community of blood and territory, for older members to pass on to younger ones as a testament to community, is necessary. This principle of transmission at the base of all communities is even more evident at higher levels, in the transference of power between king and prince, which takes place on an inheritance basis, not on the qualities of the successor:

> As long as the constitution of the group is uncertain and unsteady, the executive function requires very determined personal qualities.... However, when the shape of the social organization is already solid and defined, personal considerations become secondary. The maintenance of this abstract shape is what is important, and the best government is the one that best expresses the continuity and eternity of the established group.[25]

The main tools for the conservation of groups and communities are social organs that not only serve to protect the needs of citizens but also create a common set of shared values: the religious community in the clergy and the political community in the administration. These organs are required to maintain the ideals of the groups, and if that does not happen, they remain a mere set of members, destined to unrelenting decline.

The conservation of a group is the manifestation of a need to maintain its social life by objecting to dangers that could disrupt established balances and by avoiding changes and transformations. It could happen, however, that a group, in order to guarantee its own survival, is forced to adapt to new elements in society. In this case, conservation would entail maintaining unity but changing form.

Maurice Barrès (1862–1923)

Barrès's work is characterized by its traditionalism, nationalism, and attachment to the native land, all topics summarized in his book *The Uprooted*, published in 1897. Revanchism against Germany, the victor of the French-Prussian war in 1871, also played a central role in his work.

Barrès was born in the small town of Lorraine. After studying at the *lyceé* of Nancy, he moved to the Latin Quarter of Paris in 1883, where he worked on the monthly publication *Le Jeune France* (*Young France*) and started his own magazine, *Les Taches d'Encre* (*Ink Stains*).

Barrès overcame his individualism by putting aside the ego, which he conceived as an ephemeral product of society. The individualistic spirit emerges and is explored in his trilogy of novels *The Cult of the Self* (1888), *A Free Man* (1889), and *The Garden of Bérénice* (1891). These early works belong to the Symbolism movement in literature, just as subsequent volumes are written with an elaborate and dark style. When he wasn't writing, Barrès engaged in politics, becoming a deputy at twenty-seven years old. Initially elected in the coalition to support General Boulanger in a party of "nationalism, protectionism and socialism," the Dreyfus affair drew him closer to right-wing parties. Despite socialist party leader Léon Blum's attempts to convince him to abandon anti-Dreyfus stances, Barrès wrote that Dreyfus was undoubtedly guilty, not based on the facts themselves but on his race.

A convinced nationalist, he joined Paul Déroulède's League of Patriots. *La Cocarde* (*The Cockade*), which he founded in 1894, included people of various schools of thought among its collaborators. The publication was born with the intention of reducing the distances between the extreme Right and the extreme Left.

Catholic, but not a fervent believer, Barrés drew closer to religion in the final years of his life, supporting *Echo de Paris*, a campaign to support the restoration of the church, which was in decline after the 1905 laws sanctioned the separation between church and state.

Barrés alternated writing with long trips in Europe. From April to May of 1900, he was in Greece, while at the end of 1907 and in January of 1908, he traveled along the Nile River. In the spring of 1914, he went to the Middle East to visit Alexandria, Damascus, Aleppo, Antakya, and other cities.

He was a convinced interventionist and promoted war against Imperial Germany. His nationalism was marked by revanchist stances (the desire to take back Alsace and Lorraine) against the German Empire and by opposition to Rousseau's social contract. He had a concept of a conservative nation based on the multiplicity of local instances, on the family, the village, the region, and the nation state; he believed in the organismic concept, as opposed to concepts of universalism. But the nation must be based, he thought, on the union of various local realities making up a single national ethnicity. His individualist stances, expressed strongly during his youth, matured into a vision of a society based on social relationships, according to which the individual is nothing compared to the community.

The experiences of Charles Maurras and Action Française had a strong influence over Barrés, but he did not come to embrace Maurras's royalist ideas. His own work influenced different writers and thinkers of the time, such as Georges Bernanos and Jacques Maritain. His influence on French culture during the twentieth century is indubitable and remembered by a vast collection of critical literature:

> In his trilogy titled *The Cult of the Self*, he describes the itinerary of the young explorer, who became a nationalist with the help of

a methodical self-analysis. For the young explorer, history is something living, a demanding power, that takes and claims the responsibility of the individual.[26]

Léon Daudet (1867–1942)

Brought up with liberal and republican views, Daudet began drawing closer to monarchist stances from a young age because of the Dreyfus affair. He helped found the 1907 newspaper *Action Française* with Charles Maurras and became a powerful critic of democracy and the republic. He was always surrounded by artists; his father, Alphonse, was a writer, and Léon married Jeanne Hugo, Victor Hugo's niece, in 1891. From 1919 to 1924, he served as a deputy of parliament, outlining his political work with stances that were hostile to those of Prime Minister Léon Blum, the leader of the socialist coalition.

Being the son of a well-known writer, he was precociously allowed access to the major intellectuals of his time, such as Flaubert, Zola, Renan, and Mistral. He recalls these meetings in his 1929 book, *Paris Lived*. He himself became a prolific writer, and his works touched on a variety of subjects, relevant to both his life and the politics of his time. He was deeply shaken by the murder of his son in 1923, and he began writing short investigative essays in which he repeatedly attacked the police. He lost a defamation lawsuit and was sentenced to five months in prison. After his condemnation, he managed to escape, seeking refuge in Belgium. He dedicated himself to literary writing and memoirs, as well as more controversial works such as *The Stupid Nineteenth Century*, published in 1921:

> Daudet left a collection of more than one hundred fifty titles in which his passionate reactionary politics burn with intellectual irreverence. All of his writings are rich with brilliant ideas, and his courageous campaign on behalf of modern literature contributed to the discovery and affirmation of writers such as Gide and Proust.[27]

Charles Maurras (1868–1952)

Born in a small town to a bourgeois family, Maurras had a Catholic education, but religion never gripped him like politics. Action Française was his life's work and legacy; it supported the restoration of the monarchy without the use of force, thanks to the widespread organization of *Camelots du Roi*, the "King's Camelots." Maurras publicized his own ideas mostly through newspapers rather than individual books, which, he believed, would have had a lesser impact on public opinion.

Maurras's legitimism originated from one observed conviction: when France was governed by the monarchy, the French government was powerful. When it was passed over to the Napoleonic and republican government, it experienced defeat and disaster. This, according to Maurras, was no coincidence.

In 1899, Maurras drew up the manifesto for French monarchist intellectuals, *Dictator and King*. He expresses his vision of the French nation as a kingdom dominated by order, in direct opposition to the reality of France at that time. It was therefore necessary to reconstruct the natural order, in which "authority is above and freedom is below" and where the monarchical constitution is natural and rational. The end of the national monarchy would, Maurras believed, undoubtedly lead to the decline of intermediary bodies, of companies, and of communality. On the contrary, parliamentary democracy suffocates general politics and ministries. The parliament lives thanks only to the resources of citizens; therefore, the state becomes a slave to the chambers and political parties. In a monarchy, ministries respond to the king, and every year the delegation of provincial assemblies must meet in Paris for financial check-ups, making the capital the meeting point between the court and the bodies of the state:

> We call all the bodies worthy of this name: industrial and commercial chambers, union of the corporations, association of the farmers of France, institute, etc.
>
> The king's advisors will be, naturally, recruited from these high technical chambers, authentic testimonies to the activity and

production of France, that has nothing to do with that reception
of filth, cheaters, and gossipers that, under the pretext of an electoral mandate, swarm at Bourbon Palace and the Luxembourg
Palace: foreign to the country, rescinded from the country, because
of its own sentiments.[28]

Royal power allows the state to reestablish its main values: independence
and authority. The king must be the apex of the state, Maurras thought,
becoming both arbiter and guarantor.

But Maurras's unwavering faith in the monarchy was mainly due to the
observation that the liberal and democratic revolution failed, along with all
of its ideas connected to progress. He felt the need to stabilize society by putting individuals within a just order:

> The nation lasts because of a phenomena independent from indi-
> vidual wills. It is not chosen, it does not want to be French; it is
> born. The nation rises from birth, as the very name says: *natio,
> natus.* As the ideas of the nation and the family are almost iden-
> tical, their movement is in agreement. Anyone who wants to
> perpetuate the nation must also want to perpetuate families,
> without which it would disintegrate and perish. A nation that
> wants to make its state national therefore begins with restoring
> the stable and continuous family, wherever it is, to which the
> individual, vagrant atom, usurped beyond the limits of his
> strength and well-being, can belong.[29]

In addition to the proposal for a monarchy, a critique of democracy was
also at the foundation of Maurras's thought. Men, he observed, are not equal
to each other, and creating a system of government based on this prerogative
can only lead to ill-fated results. He took up a text written by Cardinal Billot,
who was also against democracy, that, during the conflicts between Action
Française and Pope Pius XI, supported his own movement. It read: "The government of number tends to disorganize the country. It inevitably destroys

everything that tempers it, everything that differs from it: religion, family, traditions, classes, every type of organization."[30]

The work of Action Française progressively lost its edge, beginning in the 1920s. Its rupture with the church did not help:

> In 1927, Pope Pius XI solemnly condemned the ideology of Action Française, forbidding Catholics to stay in the league; it was not an unexpected blow, but was nevertheless difficult. All of Maurras's and his followers' careful efforts to stay aligned with the legitimist tradition, inseparable from Catholicism in France, were frustrated. One of the main reasons for this condemnation was Maurras's propaganda, which exalted Roman wisdom. Nevertheless, Maurras refused to temper his stance, and accepted the loss of the Catholics.[31]

Throughout the 1930s, the movement suffered a progressive loss of popularity; eventually, it was no longer capable of monopolizing the anti-democratic protest scene. In 1935, it crumbled.

During the war, Maurras supported Marshal Pétain, and he continued publishing the *Action Française* newspaper until 1944. With the return of democracy, he was tried and sentenced to life in prison, even though he worked with Pétain, not the Germans. While in prison, he wrote his final works and, after being pardoned, he died on November 16, 1952.

Many conservative ideas of today have emerged from his ideas. He believed in the power of political action, and that it promoted the development of an ordered society:

> Society feeds off its past and grows on itself; it has its own end, and the state is its most important organ, the coordinating organ. Maurras's ideal society is unchanging: neither democratic nor aristocratic; his politics involve maintaining the conditions and the forms found to be advantageous, and making them even more advantageous by accentuating their strengths and extending their

dominance.... France's contingent situation is to convert Maurras from *static* to *dynamic*, to persuade him to contrast the revolution with a formally similar movement, the counterrevolution.[32]

The main goal of Action Française was to reorganize France and restore it to its former strength of the days of the *ancien régime*. For Maurras, restoring the monarchy was one of—if not the main—goal of the movement:

> Under a monarchy, France was more powerful and respected, and the Revolution led France to decline and eventual ruin. Because of this, Maurras postulated the intrinsic ontological superiority of the monarchy compared to a republic. There was no metaphysical reasoning behind Maurras's traditionalist call, but rather a pure and simple historical consideration.[33]

Although he was an atheist, Maurras recognized Catholicism's primary role in society. He considered the church to be the guardian of the nation's order. His penchant for Catholicism rose from a virulent anti-Protestantism. According to Maurras, the Lutheran Reformation was nothing more than an anticipation of that which was to come during the French Revolution.

As he was intensely anti-Protestant, so he was also anti-German. He considered Germans to be the enemies of the French and Latin civilization and hoped for "an impulse toward the classical and Apollonian order, greatly needed in this chaotic world that, absorbed by a very profane and Dionysian intoxication, seems to be running toward nowhere."[34]

Maurras's final years were tragic. After being arrested in September 1944, along with Maurice Pujo, he was sentenced to life in prison for complicity with the enemy. He was released from prison shortly before his death. In his last days, the Catholic faith of his youth was revived, and he received last rites.

Maurice Pujo (1872–1955)

Born to a Catholic and loyalist family, Pujo began his literary career by founding the *Le Revue Jeune*, (*The Young Journal*) newspaper. Early in his youth he was interested in German culture. His first book, *The Reign of Grace*, published in 1894, was an essay inspired by the philosophy of Novalis. During a visit to Germany in the 1890s, he embraced French nationalist stances.

As it was for many other intellectuals of the time, the Dreyfus affair was a turning point in his life. Along with Henri Vaugeois and other nationalists, he decided to found the Comitè d'Action Française (French Action Committee), proposing a petition against Zola, who defended Dreyfus.

On December 19, 1890, Pujo published an article expressing Action Française's goal: to reestablish France as a state founded on order and foreign policy power, as it was during the *ancien régime*. In order to achieve these goals, the Ligue de la Patrie Française (League of the French Homeland) was created. Pujo agreed with Maurras, who pushed for restoring the Bourbon monarchy, even if it required the violent use of force. Pujo was arrested with Maurras in 1944 and imprisoned for three years. After his release, he served as the political director of *Aspects de la France* until he died in 1955.

Alexis Carrel (1873–1944)

Awarded the Nobel Prize in Physiology or Medicine in 1912, Alexis Carrel simultaneously advanced a science and spirituality, with exceptional results in his research on transplants and vascular suture. Coming from a family that steered him toward a Catholic education, he was educated by Jesuits for ten years and then enrolled at the University of Lyon in 1891 to study medicine.

His life changed forever when he substituted for a medical colleague who was too busy to accompany a group of sick pilgrims to Lourdes. It was then that he witnessed the miraculous cure of an extremely sick woman. This event, which he recounts in the posthumously published book *The Journey to Lourdes*, pushed Carrel closer and closer to religion with increasing conviction, creating problems between him and his colleagues at the hospital in Lyon, which did not look kindly on the comingling between science and religion. Thus, in 1904, he transferred to North America, and after a brief period in Canada, he arrived in Chicago, where he was called to the Rockefeller Institute in New York.

During the war, Carrel was called to serve his country as a doctor on the frontlines. He continued his experiments on blood, and after returning to New York, he remained greatly affected by his experience in the war. He thus began a personal and cultural journey that coincided with his encounter with Father Cornelius Clifford, who became a sort of spiritual guide for him. In 1935, Carrel published his best-selling book, *Man, The Unknown*, followed shortly after by *Reflections on Life*.

He embraced a Christian vision of unity between matter and spirit and critiqued modernity's understanding of science as a tool for omitting and overcoming the nature of mankind. Man is indeed the union of body and spirit, he thought, and neither of these elements can be lacking. In continuation of his analysis, he identified three laws that govern man's life: conservation of life, reproduction of the species, and finally, spiritual ascent. His entire body of work is permeated with a sharp criticism of modernity.

Jacques Maritain (1882–1973)

A student of chemistry, physics, and biology at the Sorbonne, Maritain could not find the answers to his existential questions in science and so began a course of study that led him to courses by Henri Bergson. In 1906, he converted to Catholicism. In 1912, he began teaching, working as a professor at Toronto, Columbia, Chicago, and Princeton. In the meantime, he drew closer to Action Française, despite pressures from the Vatican. Maritain defended his stances with his book *Primacy of the Spiritual*. A reading of Aristotle and St. Thomas Aquinas, as well as the principles of metaphysics, are essential to understanding Maritain's thought, as he considered philosophy to be the true science.

Maritain puts the study of metaphysics at the center of his philosophical vision, often at the expense of epistemology. His philosophical thought is revealed in *Integral Humanism*, published in 1936, in which he collects some of his university lessons from Santander University and proposes an updated Christianity and new humanism that goes beyond Marxism, liberalism, Fascism, and the legacies of medieval Christianity.

Maritain entertained the possibility of a society that was both liberal and democratic, yet inspired by Christianity, because he viewed liberalism and democracy as the results of tireless implementation, unthinkable without the influence of the Gospel. In his final years of life, he criticized the liberal trends of the Second Vatican Council, observing that if a progressive spirit prevailed in the church, one could expect nothing good from civil society. He believed liberal stances sanctioned the triumphs of "false reformers" such as Luther, Descartes, and Rousseau, the architects of the separation of the body and soul.

In 1913, he published his first book, *The Bergsonian Philosophy*, which collects contributions from a series of conferences with particular attention given to the relationship between God and man. Maritain's interests also embraced a broader cultural field, especially in his work *Art and Scholasticism*, which formulates a philosophy of art based on Thomism and originated from Maritain's encounter with paintings by Rouault.

An interest in Thomist philosophy can also be found in *The Angelic Doctor*, dedicated to the work and thought of St. Thomas. In the preface, Maritain explains the main characteristics of Thomism, a philosophy that aims to purify modern thought by clearly distinguishing good from evil. The spread of this philosophy occurred thanks to the Societies of Thomistic Studies, created by Maritain and his wife Raïssa. They intended to organize cultural debates and give life to a new school of spirituality.

His philosophical research was accompanied by political positions that aligned with Action Française, although he never formally joined the movement. He did distance himself after the condemnation from Pope Pius XI, convinced that political and spiritual power should be allied. Despite being publicly involved in some political matters, such as signing legislature against the Spanish War and the Italian invasion of Ethiopia, he never subscribed to any particular political party, in order to protect his independence as a philosopher.

He upheld this decision in *Letter on Independence*, and again in 1953 at a conference at the Graduate College of Princeton. Through *Integral Humanism*, he created a cultural base for political movements that aim to create a Christian testament in society and distinguish themselves from Marxism, which was based on the concept of class, and Fascism, which favored the nation over the people.

In addition to the Institut Catholique (Catholic University of Paris), Maritain also began teaching at the Pontifical Institute of Mediaeval Studies in 1932. But when he found himself in Meudon, near Paris, in 1940, the Nazis tried to arrest him. He was forced to stay in the United States and began teaching at Princeton, where he worked to promote Thomistic philosophy. Such a philosophy was, he considered, more than just the philosophy of a man, but rather a cultural tradition that began developing during antiquity, becoming the chosen philosophy of the church.

His conviction to spread this tradition and his studies overseas led him, along with other exiles, to establish a publishing house and a university institute. On February 14, 1942, in New York, he founded the École Libre des Hautes Études (Free School of Higher Studies), a university bookstore that immediately became a hub for all intellectuals and scholars persecuted in their homeland and forced to move to the United States.

Though far away, Maritain closely monitored events at home. He engaged firsthand against German occupation and the Vichy government by sending various radio messages to the French people. He also published *France, My Country Through the Disaster*, followed by a second small volume, *Through the Victory*, in which he expressed his hope for collaboration between Catholics and socialists, held together by a resistance that united men of the French Revolution and men of faith.

While the fate of Europeans was being decided in Europe, Maritain also dedicated his time to writing his most important books. In 1943, he published *Education at the Crossroads*, which includes some of his lectures at Yale. Pedagogy and the problem with education are also addressed in his classic *Man and the State*, published in 1949, which includes some of his lectures from the University of Chicago.

Maritain's influence on American culture was so extensive that in September 1958, the Jacques Maritain Center was founded at the University of Notre Dame in Indiana. At the end of the war, he was also named French ambassador to the Holy See—but held the position for only a few months, preferring to preserve his intellectual independence. Afterwards, he set up the Institut Français – Centre Saint-Louis to organize conferences and debates.

Much of his political efforts were devoted to drafting the United Nations' Universal Declaration of Human Rights and carrying out his work in Christian social education. These efforts earned him the Pope Leo XIII Award in 1948.

Despite having established himself in the United States, he often returned to France in the early years after the war to hold conferences and meet with his overseas editorial colleagues. In 1961, he went to Toulouse, France, where he lived with the Little Brothers of Jesus. This period was rich with cultural motivation for Maritain, who held seminars, conferences, wrote newspaper and magazine articles, and became an important point of reference for Catholicism. In 1969, he published a new edition of *A Philosophy of Education*, and criticized the technocratic power developing in Europe: "As long as our civilization orients itself toward technology at the service of the good of mankind, purified of any technocratic ambition, we must, it seems to me, first and foremost count on the resources of human nature."[35]

Many of Maritain's positions were embraced in the Second Vatican Council, and unlike many Catholic traditionalists, he did not condemn the council. In 1966, he published *The Peasant of the Garonne: An Old Layman Questions Himself about the Present Time*, in which he agreed with the positions of the church; in 1970, he published *On the Church of Christ: The Person of the Church and Her Personnel*, in which he expresses his positions during the post-Second Vatican Council crisis, with particular attention given to his reflection on the mystery of the church. His wife Raïssa's role was fundamental during this period, so much so that Maritain collected her diary writings.

His journey of spiritual reflection and prayer led Maritain to join the Little Brothers of Jesus community, where he had already been living for quite some time. On September 2–3, 1973, the newspaper *Le Monde* published a true testament to the author, who died on April 28 of the same year, with the emblematic title "*Les Deux Grandes Patries*" ("The Two Great Homelands").

Georges Bernanos (1888–1948)

Born in Paris in 1888, Georges Bernanos had a Catholic upbringing, imparted by a Jesuit boarding school. He was raised with the conviction that the world offered itself to Satan with the dominance of materials goods, and that it needed spiritual regeneration.

Growing up in a humble family, Bernanos was alarmed and scarred by the weakness of the French toward Hitler's Germany. With extraordinary foresight, he predicted the worst for France after the Munich Agreement and decided to escape to Brazil. During his active participation in Action Française, he became the director of the daily *L'Avant-Garde de Normandie*. After returning from his voluntary service in the war, he distanced himself from the movement, only to later join the group once again after Pope Pius IX's condemnation. His official split with Maurras occurred because of his collaboration with *Le Figaro*.

Bernanos was a monarchist and fervent Catholic. But when the Church condemned certain stances take up by Action Française and Charles Maurras's attitude toward Christianity grew more wary, Bernanos distanced himself from the movement.

His first book, *Under the Sun of Satan*, was published in 1926 and received immediate critical and public success. But his true acclaim came ten years later with *The Diary of a Country Priest*. The protagonist of his spiritual and supernatural novel is a priest, the main reference point for the community made up of nobles, bourgeois, and commoners.

Daniele Zappalà highlights the importance of the spiritual aspect of Bernanos's work:

> As François Mauriac wrote, Bernanos had the gift of "making the supernatural seem natural": a writing force that, according to literary critics such as Claire Daudin, continues to grab contemporary readers by the neck and knock them out, especially those who have felt today's pitfall of a certain spiritual desertification.[36]

He was left disappointed by the developments of Franco's movement, and realized that the Spanish Civil War was a precursor to a radically different conflict, destined to upset European equilibriums and cause the end of Europe. He found himself in the Balearics at the outbreak of the war and aligned himself with Franco, but quickly changed his mind and published *The Great Cemeteries Under the Moon*. Francesco Perfetti wrote, "His famous pamphlet, passionate and indignant, raised the veil on the horrors of the civil war, making him a true icon of militant political literature."[37]

Gabriel Marcel (1889–1973)

Gabriel Marcel, originally Jewish, converted to Christianity in 1929 after in-depth spiritual study that led him to putting the relationship between man and God at the center of his work. In his analysis of human nature, he examined the dualism between "being" and "having": anyone who relies on having possessions therefore relies on the objectification of science, and is mistaken. On the other hand, those who rely on the experience of being accept the mystery and transcendence of existence, and live rightly.

This dualism can also be applied to different conceptions of knowledge, understood as objective-scientific and existential-philosophical. The ends and also the means of each are important aspects of the philosophical journey for Marcel—but the ends are the only things that count for the objective-scientific worldview.

Upon receiving a degree from the Sorbonne and becoming a lyceum teacher, he grew closer to ideas from Heidegger and Jaspers and to existentialism. In 1935, he published *Being and Having*, and in 1951 he published *The Mystery of Being*.

His reflections on the irrational nature of reality surfaced after the tragic events of the First World War. He was opposed to any idea or person reducing man and reality to mere abstract conceptions. He also dedicated much attention to the subject of technology and its relationship with man, inquiring about the effects of technology on human life—which, according to him, was overused in modern society. In *The Decline of Wisdom*, Marcel writes that our society is based on technology rather than what is sacred, and at this point the degradation of every sacred aspect of life is routine. This, according to Marcel, is how apathy toward life begins.

Marcel de Corte (1905–1994)

De Corte took a clear stance against the ideology of the protests of 1968, an architect of a "protest of the protest." In his book *Intelligence at Risk*, he calls for the protection of schools and family structures that transmit principles of tradition and education to future generations. His work also highlights how the growing distance between humans and nature would eventually lead to anarchy and nihilism. Like his inspirations, he was associated with Action Française:

> Just as a young Maritain, de Corte was also influenced by Maurras and was associated with Action Française. Maritain then abruptly broke away from the movement, arriving at a progressivism that tied him to liberal-Catholic and modernist fronts. However, de Corte made an opposite decision, radicalizing the anti-modern critique betrayed by his friend and contributing his counterrevolutionary stances in the wake of de Maistre. In fact, while he engaged in philosophy, poetry, and mysticism in his youth, starting in 1942, he devoted himself to the diagnosis of modern crises, denouncing their anti-Christian orientation.[38]

His attack of modernity was also launched on the church, which he accused of being dominated by progressivism. By becoming secularized, Christian thought became a tool of the Communist revolution, transforming the faith into a disintegrating factor for society. His work compared the laws of God to those of mankind in an attempt to defend the first from the demands of the second: "Belief in the divine Providence is being secularized, envisioning happiness for man that is no longer supernatural, celestial, or eternal, but rather natural, earthly, and futurist."[39]

De Corte recognized four causes of spiritual abuse in modern thought: subjectivism, immanentism, evolutionism, and relativism. While rationalism rejects reality, progressivism destroys it through radical revolution. De Corte also knew that in the modern world, technology plays a primary role in creating a new man whose freedom is dependent on technocracy. In the past, man relied on God for happiness; in modern times, that happiness is connected to technology.

De Corte also criticized democracy, which he believed offers man temporal redemption as opposed to divine and eternal redemption. A new religion is therefore created—man's religion—which aims to be a substitute for Christianity, and whose main architects are liberalism and social Communism.

Revolutions, whether they generate a liberal democracy or a socialist one, are characterized by the mass-man: that is, an individual who has neither a temporal dependency (tradition) nor a spatial one (community). The failure of the revolutionary's utopia is manifested by the crisis of modern civilization. It fails by an attempt to construct a society without, if not directly opposed to, God.

However, de Corte had certain conditions he laid out for rediscovering traditional civilization:

- recuperating tradition for the restoration of consciences
- returning to the search for common good by accepting the same fate for every member of society, elevating love, respect, and sacrifice
- reinstating legitimate authorities and rediscovering the importance of authority as a tool for spiritually and materialistically expanding the community
- reintroducing the social elites and the role of small communities and groups
- putting family at the center of society as the focal point of civic life

And finally, the most important condition: the return to God. The grounding of religion and the understanding of man's incarnation in society are the solutions to the problems of the contemporary man.

Nicolás Gómez Dávila (1913–1994)

Gómez Dávila was born on May 18, 1913, in Columbia, but he spent his youth in Paris before returning to his country of origin in the 1930s. He lived a self-taught life, never enrolling in university and building up a library of thousands of books. He preferred to stay out of politics, and in 1959, he refused the position of chief advisor to the Columbian president. In 1974, he refused the position of ambassador to England. Instead, he dedicated his time to his studies, forming a conservative and reactionary philosophy.

His most celebrated work is the collection of aphorisms, annotations, and notes, published between 1977 and 1992, titled *Scholia to an Implicit Text*. In the second volume, Dávila highlights the need for constructing "refuges against the inclemency of time," in our era and in future eras. He himself built such a refuge in his home in Bogotà, where he lived as a recluse for thirty years due to an accident while he was playing polo. Giovanni Cantoni writes:

> "Situated on a crowded street in Bogotà, in the middle of the traffic and noise of the street, like a prehistoric monument that the routine seems to condemn to forgetfulness despite its isolated beauty": Óscar Torres Duque, one of Davila's few critics, used these words to evocatively describe the Tudor style residence. Gómez Dávila lived in seclusion like this for almost thirty years, like a "Carthusian monk of the Altiplano"... [with] his monumental library of more than forty thousand volumes, all in original languages (he refused translations) of Greek, Latin, German, English, Portuguese, French, Italian and, naturally, Spanish.[40]

His targets of critique were rationalism and agnosticism, which he believed generated the divinization of man and egalitarianism. As Marcello Veneziani wrote, the South American philosopher was angry with the reformers in the church: "Idiots used to attack the Church, now they reform it."[41]

CHAPTER FIVE

Spanish Conservatism

Analyzing Iberian conservative thought first requires an understanding of Spanish civilization. Spain differs from other European nations in that it was immune to Cartesian-rationalist influences and maintained the values of *hispanidad* against Enlightenment and reformist tendencies.

In Spain, the Enlightenment was confined to a limited number of intellectuals. They were not able to make inroads with people who remained connected to Catholic values. This generated a division between the *hispanidad* and Cartesian rationalism, which meanwhile prevailed in France and Germany, and which gave rise to idealism and Romanticism:

> In other words, while other European nations threw away their spiritual and political traditions, Spain conserved them. In other places religious skepticism dominated, but in Spain wise people continued believing in the dogmas of the church. In France and Prussia, absolutism and "Enlightened despotism" triumphed, but in Spain the traditional monarchy persisted, respectful of the autonomy of municipalities, feuds, guilds, and regions.[1]

The attempt to embed the Enlightenment in Spain occurred with the French invasion, but in the name of traditional, Catholic, and royalist values, the anti-Napoleonic War of Independence ensued.

If one were to attempt to identify the precise moment in which the Iberian decline began, along with the resulting attempt to undermine traditional values, it would have to be October 24, 1648, the day the treaties of Westphalia were ratified. The Peace of Westphalia established the *cuius regio, eius religio* principle (the obligation to practice the king's religion), determining the triumph of Protestantism. While from a territorial perspective Spain did not undergo huge losses, the treaties gave way to an ideological defeat that accelerated Iberian decline.

In Gabriele Fergola's book *History of the Spanish Right*, the situation of Spanish conservatives is made apparent:

> Some of them, such as Vázquez de Mella, were active in the Carlist Party, while others such as Donoso Cortés served the Isabellist dynasty that had triumphed, and still others preferred to disengage from political disputes and throw themselves, heart and soul, into past history and extract their own ideal world from it. There are some commonalities among them, but also some diverging aspects: they were all convinced Catholics and royalists; they all rejected liberal and transalpine revolutionary ideologies with disdain. However, while Donoso Cortés accepted only implicitly certain principles of the absolute French monarchy, almost all the others considered absolutism the prelude to liberalism and democracy, and fought for a traditional, feudal, and corporate monarchy that respected local autonomy.[2]

In the nineteenth century, a bitter controversy between traditionalists and liberal-progressives developed in Spain, having emerged in 1812 with the Cádiz Cortes. The masses considered the anti-French War of Independence as a defense of Catholic tradition, while the ruling classes were in favor of the French invasion. A useful analysis of Spanish conservatism requires a look into the Spanish Civil War that occurred between 1936 and 1939, the fight between the two souls of Spain:

> For traditionalist writers like Menéndez y Pelayo and Maeztu there is no "other Spain," as the only true Spain is the traditional one that arose from the "Reconquista," from the uncompromising spirit of Castile, understood as the legitimate continuation of the Roman-Visigoth tradition. For them, the other Spain is nothing but the anti-Spain.[3]

The "Generation of '98" in particular tried to liquidate the traditional past of Spain by forming the so-called *otra España*, in which subversive influences that disowned the past emerged.

Carlism was a leading movement in the creation of Spanish conservative thought, even though, with Francisco's rise to power, Carlist ideas became common heritage and were established. But the Carlists, who should have had leadership positions in the movement, lost their superiority to the Falange party, in part due to the influence of the Axis powers.

Carlist Thinkers

Carlism played a significant role in Spanish conservatism. The movement began in 1833 and continued until the death of Francisco Cea Bermúdez, the moderate royalist. The Spanish throne then awaited Carlo Maria Isidoro of Bourbon Spain and his descendants.

The antecedents of the Carlist movement can be traced back to 1713, when King Phillip V changed the rules of succession of the throne by applying the *Lex salica* (Salic law), which limited succession to only the sons of the king. However, in 1789, Charles IV approved a reversion to previous laws, which provoked protests. In 1830, King Ferdinand VII, devoid of male descendants, crowned his daughter as the new queen on September 29, 1833, with the name Isabella II. Her coronation unleashed protests by Carlo of Spain, Ferdinand's brother, who, according to *Lex salica*, should have become king. In reality, it was not only a question of succession, but rather a dispute between two different visions of Spanish society: on one side, there were the absolutists who identified with the principles of the *ancien régime*, and on the other side were liberals of the Enlightenment who held revolutionary stances.

The divisions were exacerbated by Ferdinand VII's liberal viewpoints, creating a profound moment of political crisis during the so-called "ominous decade" between 1823 and 1833. At this time, the absolutists, whose radical faction was called Apostolicos, increasingly identified with Carlo, and in 1827, during the revolt of the *agraviados* in Catalonia, the rebels recognized him as their leader.

These proved to be turbulent years for Spain, not only from a political point of view but also from an economic point of view. The internal crisis and the loss of continental American colonies led to worsening fiscal pressure, especially for small and medium-sized landowners.

The Carlist movement was marked by three phases: the first, from 1833 to 1876, characterized by the Carlist Wars and the attempt to assume power through use of force; the second, from 1868 to 1936, was more passive; and the third began in 1936, when the movement supported Franco during the Spanish Civil War.

Without delving too deeply into the historical analysis of the events that characterize the wars and Carlist politics, it is important to understand the foundations of Carlist thought, which can be summarized in four words: *Dios, Patria, Fueros,* and *Rey*:

1. *Dios,* for belief in the Catholic Church as the foundation of Spain;
2. *Patria,* understood as the union of local communities united in a single ethnicity;
3. *Fueros,* the limit of royal and state power thanks to the protection of local and regional governments;
4. And finally, *Rey.* Carlists believed national sovereignty does not exist because sovereignty is represented by the king and is limited by both the doctrine of the church and intermediary bodies.

The tension between the Carlists and Isabella II's supporters was immediately characterized by its ideological element: on one hand, there were those who were faithful to traditional monarchy, and on the other hand, there were those who made up the liberal and constitutionalist party. This dualism remained unchanged in the years following, despite certain conservative figures such as Donoso Cortés, who remained loyal to Queen Isabella:

> The once purely dynastic dispute transformed to a dispute of politics and ideology. The Carlists became proponents of a traditional and representative monarchy, channeling feudal monarchies of the medieval period, while liberals surrounding Isabella hoped for a constitutional monarchy that could perhaps be inclined toward a parliamentary system.[4]

Ironically, due precisely to the Carlist Wars, Spain became a liberal country open to anti-traditional reforms. The queen, being supported by liberal forces, was forced to yield to the increasingly frequent pressures of an intellectual minority that managed to impose ideas and structures foreign to the traditions of the Spanish people. A constitutional monarchy was thus introduced, along with a secular culture that declared the state's religious neutrality. In response, Carlists clung to the defense of the *hispanidad*: "If European society born in the West during the medieval period...had to crumble under the blows of the Renaissance, of the Enlightenment, of Romanticism, and finally of Marxism, the *hispanidad*, thanks to Carlism, proved more resistant to such attacks."[5]

Juan Donoso Cortés (1809–1853)

From the moment it opposed the Napoleonic invasion, Spain became the most anti-liberal, anti-modern, and anti-democratic force in Europe. The biggest exponent of these tendencies was Juan Donoso Cortés. If John Stuart Mill is considered the child prodigy of liberalism, then Donoso Cortés is the child prodigy for conservatism.

The interior minister of Spain under King Ferdinand VII, Cortés was elected to the Spanish parliament in 1837. From 1850 until his death in 1853, he was the ambassador to Spain in France. During this time, he was close to the Russian ambassador, Baron Meyendorff, who wanted to preserve the alliance between Austria and Prussia with counterrevolutionary policy.

Donoso Cortés was against the creation of a strong Prussian-led German state. The birth of a strong state in central Europe could signal the beginning of a European war. In his opinion, Germany was made up of two separate nations: a southern Catholic one and a northern Protestant one. He negatively judged Prussian conservatism:

> He believed that he found himself in a dangerous situation: as a reactionary party distanced from the liberal middle class, which was then convinced to form a coalition with democrats; had his party been less reactionary and a bit more tolerant, forming an alliance with the wealthy middle classes, a somewhat lasting, but well-ordered government in Prussia could have been created; had he been openly reactionary and less dependent on the king... (that always seems like the misfortune of Prussian conservatism), and had he been freer and active, he could have promoted a restoration... capable of annihilating the absurd hopes of the revolutionaries.[6]

Donoso Cortés condemned both Jacobinism and Carlism, and in his work *Ensayo sobre el catolicismo, el liberalismo, y el socialismo* (*Essay on Catholicism, Liberalism, and Socialism*), he expressed the same anti-liberal stances that Pope Pius XI did in *Syllabus of Errors*. According to Cortés, the mistake made by liberals and socialists is seeing the devil in political institutions rather than in the hearts of men. If evil were inherent in external institutions, it would be easily eliminated; however, it is rooted in man. Therefore, no political or economic change can eliminate it. That is something only God can do.

The Spanish thinker believed that the best system of government, unlike what was theorized by the Carlists and Maistre, was a constitutional monarchy. His political philosophy could be defined as a kind of "socialist conservatism." He predicted social revolutions until Christian European monarchies could come together, beginning a new era based on helping the poor and new social policies.

In the destruction of order—political order for liberals, social order for socialists—both groups see fulfillment of the highest good for society. Catholicism and rationalism are not just incompatible but are antagonistic toward each other.

According to Donoso Cortés, evil exists and originates in man—not, as socialists believe, in political and social institutions. Man free from evil would be a creature comparable to God, and would therefore have no need for the divine in his life. Catholics believe evil derives from man and redemption from God, while socialists believe evil is born from society and redemption from man. Evil, disorder, rebellion, and disobedience are all comparable to each other in the Catholic view. The first rebellion in history was that of the angels, and, from that moment on, revolutions and rebellions against the established order followed.

Donoso Cortés compared the socialist and liberal schools of thought to the Catholic school of thought, stating that it would be better if socialists prevail over liberals because of their theological (but flawed) doctrine. But Catholic thought is superior because it is both theological and of divine origin, and therefore always true.

Adelphi published a book by Carl Schmitt titled *Donoso Cortés* (1950). In the essays dedicated to Donoso Cortés, Schmitt focuses on the influence of modernity on Spanish thinking. In the modern era, the masses have become indifferent to God, no longer searching for theology or morality. According to Schmitt, Donoso Cortés is at his best when dealing with this history, describing eras, civilizations, people, and kingdoms. He provoked hate from many of his contemporaries because of his stances:

> This hatred is tightly linked to the rationality of his nature. It
> would have been more appropriate of the time if the shocking
> things that the Spaniard had to say would have come from the
> mouth of a Romantic or irrationalist. His enemies would have

preferred that he were not a cold-blooded politician upsetting their claims of monopoly on rationality.[7]

Schmitt focuses on the idealization of the medieval era by "Catholic philosophers of the state," especially on Donoso Cortés's philosophy of history. The Spanish philosopher despised man and considered him a miserable creature. If God had not become man, he thought, a reptile crushed under the foot would be less despicable than man: *el reptil que piso con mis pies, seria a mis ojos menos despreciable que el hombre.*[8] Evil's earthly victory is obvious, and only a divine miracle can amend it.

He also points the finger at the bourgeoisie, which he defines as a *clase discutidora*, not up to the level of the age in which it exists, characterized by uncertainty and social struggle:

> Its liberal constitutionalism tries to paralyze the king through the parliament, while leaving him on the throne: it is the same incoherence, which stumbles upon deism when it banishes God from the world, continuing all the same to believe in his existence.... The liberal bourgeoisie therefore wants a God, but he must not be able to act; they want a monarchy, but it must be powerless; they ask for freedom and equality, and yet limit the right to vote to wealthy classes, to guarantee culture and property the power to condition legislations, as if culture and property ensure the right to oppress the poor and uneducated; he abolishes the dynastic aristocracy and blood, but recognizes the unworthy dominance of the aristocracy of money, the stupidest and most vulgar form of aristocracy; he wants neither sovereignty of the king nor of the people.[9]

As a fervent Catholic, he did not look kindly upon liberals who hoped to complete the path started by the French Revolution—but his criticism of moderates is even more biting, judging them as "the cause of universal ruin and perdition." Cortés believed the solutions to the problems of society lied in the restoration of Catholic principles. He was convinced that the new world that arose after the revolution was characterized only by injustice, blood, and disorder, and that it was therefore necessary to create a decisive return to Catholic values by perceiving "with extreme clarity, the incompatibility between European Christianity, with its political forms, and the new ideological and social forces whose affirmation appeared to him to be one with the elimination of the sacred and with universal secularization."[10]

Cortés studied philosophy at the University of Salamanca and the University of Seville. In 1828, he began teaching at the University of Cáceres and later moved to Madrid to become a lawyer, alongside his father Pedro, and to cultivate his literary passion by writing poetry. Around the same time, he dedicated one of his works to Ferdinand VII of Spain, defending the king from Don Carlos and the Carlists' pretensions to the throne. This act led to him becoming the secretary of the minister of justice.

In 1837, he was elected a member of parliament and then secretary of the Council of Ministers, but he resigned shortly after due to disagreements with Mendizábal, who chaired the council. He founded his own newspaper, *El Porvenir*, which served as a direct medium of his ideas.

Due to political events, he was forced to leave Spain for a time and only returned to the Iberian country by participating in the draft of the constitution of 1845. In 1847, he was marked by his brother Pedro's death, who had belonged to the Carlist army. The following year, he was named Spanish ambassador to Prussia and moved to Berlin.

The events of the French Revolution in February led him to withdraw from his juvenile stances, which were more closely aligned with liberalism. He moved closer to conservative and traditional thought, as theorized by Maistre and Bonald, emphasizing the veracity of the Catholic doctrine and the errors generated by the modern world: "I represent tradition, with which the nations remain in the whole dimension of the centuries. If my voice has any kind of authority, gentlemen, it is not because it is mine, but because it is the voice of our fathers."[11]

His diplomatic career eventually led him to Paris, where he established a close relationship with Napoleon III, who was the best man at his wedding. In that same year, 1851, he published his *Essay on Catholicism, Liberalism, and*

Socialism, which appeared in two languages (French and Spanish). The book—his most important work—gave rise to wide debate, especially in the Catholic Church, and was even attacked by some Catholics. However, it was positively reviewed by Louis Veuillot in *L'Univers* and by Pope Pius IX in a letter.

His philosophy put the concept of the "divine order" at the center of his reflection, a concept around which the laws governing life are based, and whose subversion causes the evils of the world. Donoso recognized God as the origin of political authority, and he condemned "every form of pride and rebellion, placing an insurmountable barrier toward revolutions and despotism. The principle of freedom of speech, affirmed by Enlightenment intellectuals, is absurd in so much as it is founded on two assumptions, the first being true and the second being false: the non-infallibility of governments and '*la infalibilidad de la discussion*.'"[12]

He envisioned the state organically and hierarchically, as an entity capable of respecting local and corporative autonomies. He also harshly criticized liberalism and socialism, which he considered negations of both divine and natural order. Finally, his conception of the economy is important for understanding his philosophy: "Donoso denied that economics, which liberals and socialists obsessively aid, is dominant in history and politics. Out of every founder of civilization or government, from Moses to Napoleon, no one 'founded his glory on economic truth.'"[13]

Jaime Luciano Balmes (1810–1848)

Balmes dedicated most of his life to the study of Catholicism and religion. His most important work is *European Civilization: Protestantism and Catholicity Compared in their Effects on the Civilization of Europe* (1844), but his other works *El Criterio* (1845) and *Fundamental Philosophy* (1846) are also worth noting. Balmes rejected the theory, expressed by Américo Castro, of an *hispanidad* born from the union between Islam and Kabbhalic Judaism, and he warned Christian Europe against the dangers of the East and the Slavic worlds that would attack the West as soon as it became aware of its demographic strength.

In his books, he studied the origins of authority and—in opposition to Rousseau and Enlightenment thinkers, who believed authority originates from a pact or contract between individuals—he asserted that true authority derived from God. He theorized about a state in which three elements merge: monarchy, aristocracy, and democracy. Monarchy was necessary for Europe to realize the unity of power; the aristocracy, the intermediary body, would be the glue between the supreme and the people. He understood democracy as a popular government *for* the people rather than *by* the people. Furthermore, his reflection was focused on the analysis of Protestantism:

> All of Balmes's thoughts can be summarized in "Protestantism"....
> The [Protestant] reform disrupted the unity of Europe and the West; with the reform, it was Europe that separated itself from Spain and from its own tradition, not Spain that separated itself from Europe. The very idea of liberty changed and, detached from the concept of order and authority, it took on a negative, almost demonic, devilish meaning. Balmes denied the Enlightenment and modern dogma, according to which progress would happen in Europe due largely to Protestantism: "Before Protestantism, European civilization was already as developed as possible; Protestantism diverted its course and caused immense evils in modern societies: the progress made since the existence of Protestantism was not made by it but rather in spite of it."[14]

In Protestantism and in the Lutheran Reformation, Balmes glimpsed the principle of process destined to lead to the French Revolution, to absolutism and to the dissolution of Christianity. Balmes underlined the superiority of *hispanidad* as a civilization founded on the Counter-Reformation, as compared to the rest of Protestant Europe.

Marcelino Menéndez y Pelayo (1856–1912)

Marcelino Menéndez y Pelayo was an eclectic character and a scholar, dedicated to the critique and history of Spanish and Spanish-American literature, as well as to the study of philosophy, the history of ideas, and dabbling in writing poetry. Educated at the University of Barcelona and the University of Madrid, he moved to Valladolid in 1874 where he developed his conservative ideas, resembling neo-Catholic stances. After traveling to various parts of Europe to perfect his training, he returned to Spain in 1878 at the age of twenty-two, where he became a university professor. From that moment, he began a career that led him to play a leading role in the Spanish cultural landscape, becoming a member of the Real Academia in 1880, a member of parliament, and director of the National Spanish Library from 1898 to 1912, the year of his death.

The author of a remarkable collection of nonfiction work, he achieved true success with his book *Spanish Science*, a collection of essays defending national Spanish tradition from the attacks of political and religious reformers. He continues this theme in *A History of the Spanish Heterodox* (1880–1886), making him one of the top representatives of Spain's Ultramontane Party. In addition to his book on Catholic thought, he dedicated particular attention to literary criticism and Spanish literature, publishing *History of Aesthetic Ideas in Spain* and an *Anthology of Castilian Lyric Poets*, as well as teaching Spanish literature at the University of Madrid from 1878 to 1898.

Pelayo dedicated his life to Spanish tradition, working to restore the pride of his country's past to his fellow countrymen. He believed the origin of Spanish decline could be found "in the introduction and supine acceptance of European encyclopedist thought at the end of the eighteenth century, and in the abandonment of Catholic and national tradition. In fact, the national unity of Spain was essentially due to Catholicism, and rejecting the Catholic ideal meant rejecting national ideals."[15]

George Santayana (1863–1952)

Born in Madrid, Santayana spent his childhood in Avila before moving to Boston in 1869. He initially attended the Boston Latin School and later Harvard University, where he was cofounder of the *Harvard Monthly*. He completed and refined his studies in Berlin and Cambridge.

Returning to Harvard with the intention of writing on Hermann Lotze, he worked as a professor of philosophy from 1898 until 1912, when he moved to Europe. He remained there for the rest of his life, spending nearly forty years dedicating his time to philosophical writing and reflection, refusing prestigious assignments and proposals. Despite his Spanish origins, all his books—nineteen in total—are written in English. His first considerable philosophical work, *The Sense of Beauty* (1896), was about aesthetic theory, highlighting human dependency on beauty in a psychological and biological context. Santayana believed a good society is characterized by beauty and imagination, and that religion is the best way to reorganize one's moral experience:

> Santayana's Catholicism had a strong influence on his social doctrine, which emphasized the institutions that form social allegiances: tradition, family, church, chivalry, community, and country. Not surprisingly, Santayana championed the role of hierarchy and authority in social life. The rational and beautiful society is always dominated by an aristocracy, he said, because any alternative collapses into sameness and arbitrary rule. A vociferous opponent of democracy, he viewed it as crushing to the most imaginative and interesting aspect of society, the diversity of its individuals and groups, in favor of rule by the majority, the "most cruel and unprogressive of masters."[16]

As evidenced in his biography, he connected democracy to liberalism and a Protestant form of social dissolution, in which the technocratic state becomes the architect of false equality. Instead, he supported a natural society where citizens can find a role most suitable to their abilities and characteristics. With much style and lucidity, he brilliantly criticizes utilitarianism, pragmatism, atomism, and positivism in his books.

One of his most relevant books is a five-volume work titled *The Life of Reason*. The first volume, *Reason in Common Sense*, contains one of Santayana's most well-known quotes: "those who cannot remember the past are condemned to repeat it." Influence from Hegel's *The Phenomenology of the Spirit* is also apparent in the structure of *The Life of Reason*; the work develops as a story of the evolution of human reason in different spheres of knowledge, with a deep look at its metaphysical applications.

Much of his reflections focused on the relationship between nature and reason, existence and essence. His critical realism distinguishes existence, considered in a special-temporal sense, from the atemporal essence:

> Politically and culturally, he was always of aristocratic stances, faithful to his original Catholic inspiration, tenaciously opposed to both Romantic individualism and democratic egalitarianism, to liberalism and pragmatism, which were typical expressions of the American ideological climate of his time.[17]

Despite being an atheist, Santayana defends the importance of religion in society in *Reason in Religion*, *The Idea of Christ in the Gospels*, and *Interpretations of Poetry and Religion*, which influenced well-known thinkers and writers like Bertrand Russell, T.S. Eliot, Walter Lippman, and Wallace Stevens.

Ramiro de Maeztu (1875–1936)

Of Basque origins, Maeztu lived in Madrid from a young age, writing for the magazine *El Socialista*. Shaken by the events of 1898, the Spanish-American War, and Spain's loss of its last colonial domains in Cuba, Puerto Rico, and the Philippines, he published *Towards Another Spain*, in which he worries about the country's future and the need for informed political decisions.

Although he was initially one of the leading thinkers of the Generation of '98, he quickly became one of the strongest supporters of Menéndez y Pelayo's traditionalism:

> He saw a continuous struggle in the world between truth and lies: on one hand, tradition, hierarchy, order, and religion, and on the other, the demonic and destructive progressive spirit. Spain's decline was not due to a lack of Europeanization, but rather to the abandonment of its traditions and the acceptance of foreign ideological influence, especially from France; Spain could only rediscover its greatness by returning to the spirit of the "Reconquista."[18]

After living in London for more than ten years, collaborating with the magazine the *New Age*, he returned to Spain, where he sympathized with Miguel Primo de Rivera. In 1928 he became an ambassador to Argentina, and the following year he published *Don Quixote, Don Juan, and La Celestina*, an in-depth analysis of Cervantes's work.

In his final years of life Maeztu grew closer to traditional stances, adhering to the National Monarchist Union and declaring his opposition to the republic proclaimed in 1931. Maeztu emphasized the importance of the *hispanidad*, conceiving it as a supranational civilization that unites different peoples and races by the traditional monarchy and Catholic religion. In the separation between the king and the people that occurred in the eighteenth century, in the infiltration of Enlightenment appeals, in the extinction of the Habsburg dynasty, and in the Bourbons' rise to power, he identified the main causes that led to the ruin of the Spanish Empire.

After being arrested and imprisoned by Republican forces during the Spanish Civil War, he was shot alongside Ramiro Ledesma Ramos.

José Ortega y Gasset (1883–1955)

Ortega y Gasset believed that the conservation of memory is the best way to live in the present and be projected toward the future. In his *La mentalità tradizionalista*, he emphasizes the important difference between the peasant revolts in the medieval period and modern revolutions: during the medieval period, the peasant rebellions occurred in opposition to the abuses of the nobles; modern revolutions were against societal practices.

Ortega defended the collectivity against individuality. He acknowledged that when society is dominated by tradition, individuals do not consistently make decisions outside of their social group; but on the other hand, when modernity is the ruler, individuality triumphs. With the spread of modernity in the human spirit, in addition to tradition, a new force takes effect: reason. The emergence of individual reason causes the denial of tradition and all the values connected to it. And so the individual, who no longer identifies with these values, must create a new universe based on reason. Such a task, Ortega felt, would not lead to anything good.

The crisis in Europe that plagued people and nations can be identified as a series of *rebellions of the masses*. The masses invaded every aspect of social life. Society was the combination of two components: the minorities and the masses. While the minorities identified themselves as a group of qualified individuals, non-qualified people represented the masses. Today, there has been a reversal of roles: the masses play a vital role in society, and they have stopped obeying and respecting the minorities. Mass man dominates, because we live in an era of leveling. Wealth is leveled, the culture's social classes are leveled, even the sexes are leveled.

Ortega y Gasset regarded the role of liberty as primary in the lives of people. But he criticized the liberalist understanding of liberty—which, due to the power of the masses in everyday life, denatures the concept of liberty for single individuals. Mass democracy is a product of modernity; it is therefore necessary to create an elite that governs the people, to allow for overcoming the problems of modernity with a plan that acts as glue between the nation and its citizens. Starting from this assumption, Ortega criticized both capitalist society and the utilitarian mentality.

In *The Revolt of the Masses*, his most important book, he supports nationalization that could lead to a new Spanish citizen capable of rediscovering an ideal continuity from the past, from which he could take a cue for the future, creating a new balance in which to reenact traditional principles.

Ortega based his reflection on certain topics like "the fragility of democracies, the feeble balance on which national particularism moves, the central vision of Europe," and he warned nations that did not develop a supranational or ultra-national unity of the risk of decline.[19]

Salvator de Madariaga (1886–1978)

Salvator de Madariaga represented the liberal-conservative opposition to Franco's regime. Despite his exile from Spain, he never renounced his country, nor the *hispanidad* that represented true pride for him.

His philosophy is characterized by strong anti-Marxism. Madariaga can be defined as a liberal-conservative aristocrat, as is evident in his main work *From Anguish to Freedom*, in which he expresses his anti-egalitarian and anti-feminist ideas. He did believe in the subordination of the economy to moral needs, a stance that separated him from capitalist ideologies; he was in favor of protecting the identity and traditions of the country.

While Madariaga received no respect from Franco, he was appreciated by Ortega y Gasset and Miguel de Unamuno, who wrote the preface to one of his books of poetry. His most evocative work, *Portrait of Europe*, is a true journey into European identity and tradition.

Ramiro Ledesma Ramos (1905–1936)

Ledesma Ramos's stances are more similar to Fascist doctrine than to the conservative tradition. Nevertheless, a conservative revolutionary spirit can still be found in his philosophy, making him an important Spanish exponent of the conservative revolution.

Born in a small town in Castile, he moved to Madrid where, while working at a post office, he began his journey in philosophy, leading him to identify with Nietzsche's "superhuman theory" and to refuse positivism and rationalism. Graduating with a degree in literature and philosophy in 1930, he collaborated with the *Revista de Occidente* (*Magazine of the West*) during his time at university, beginning to set the groundwork for his political career. His thoughts convey the influence of the master Ortega y Gasset; Ledesma not only shared his theory of the masses, but also became a supporter of the collaboration among social classes for the development of the nation, openly opposing the very concept of class. In 1931, he gave life to the "Conquest of the State" movement, which proclaimed revolutionary stances but opposed Marxism.

The "Conquest of the State" program, expressed in seventeen points, was diffused throughout Madrid and Barcelona through massive distribution of leaflets. Each one espoused the values of national community in opposition to individualism and irredentism—and the demand of a hierarchy in society emerged. The activities of the movement quickly made headlines, thanks to Ledesma's publicizing work that anticipated the symbols and slogan used by Franco in the following years.

He believed a revolution, led by an elite capable of leading masses, was necessary. While these premises aligned with conservative revolutionaries,

Ledesma thought the desired revolution should lead to the creation of an all-encompassing state, based on corporatism and national unionism. These demands more closely aligned him with the Fascist state than with a nation founded on conservative principles.

Following such precepts, the movement transformed into a political group, National Offensive-Syndicalist Boards, and in February 1934 the group united with Josè Antonio Primo de Rivera's (son of Miguel Primo) Spanish Falange party. This fusion was short-lived, due to Primo de Rivera's personality and the wide influence of his father's supporters, and the new movement was immediately organized around Falangist stances. A common purpose with Italian Fascism soon emerged, of which Ledesma did not approve. His exit from the movement coincided with the foundation of a new newspaper, *La Patria Libre* (*The Free Country*), in which he accused Rivera of abandoning the course of the social revolution. That same year, in 1935, he published his *Speech to the Youth of Spain* and *Fascism in Spain*. Before being captured and imprisoned by the Republicans in 1936, he founded his last newspaper, *Our Revolution*.

He was executed on October 29, 1936. Throughout his life, Ledesma tried to overcome the polemics between traditional, imperial Spain and the progressive renewal.

Juan Vázquez de Mella (1861–1928)

A prominent representative of Carlism, Mella began collaborating with the traditionalist newspapers the *Galactic Thought* and *The Restoration*, and in 1889 he began working with *Spanish Mail*, the main Carlist newspaper. In 1919, after distancing himself from Carlist stances, he founded his own newspaper, *Spanish Thought*.

An elected member of parliament, he refused to become a minister until his break with Carlism, due to Don Jaime I's support of France during the First World War. Mella tried to provide an ideological foundation for the Carlist movement, beginning with a criticism of liberalism, rationalism, and the French Revolution. The revolution resulted in the destruction of intermediary groups such as the family, worker associations, local entities, and the church, which were the links between the individual and the state. All of this led to the destruction of traditional society, which could only be restored by national unity and the resolution of social conflict through a monarchic, Catholic, and corporative order. Mella was in favor of a government made up of a monarchy supported by a parliament elected on a corporative basis, in which parliamentary members are not appointed through universal elections, but rather by and through the social groups to which they belong.

His ideas gave way to the so-called "Melisma," a political practice based on his own theories. Mellism spread after its break with Carlism and consisted of the desire to give life to an ultra-right party, one that disassociated itself from the ideas of liberal democracy in favor of a traditionalist and corporative monarchy.

The institutions of Franco's future state were inspired by Mella's thoughts: Spain's refusal to renounce Catholic doctrine was based on the assumption that the monarchy itself had a divine origin. Therefore, according to Mella, national Spanish history could not split from the history of the local church.

His traditional and conservative theories were based on the need for the decentralization of powers and on an *omnia potens* state rather than *omnia faciens*. This concept, which was later taken up by Evola, can be summarized by the expression, "without tradition there is no progress." Starting from the Catholic tradition and the doctrine of the church, it was therefore necessary to push back on Enlightenment and revolutionary ideologies.

Víctor Pradera Larumbe (1872–1936)

From a young age, Pradera Larumbe was drawn toward Carlist stances. He was elected a member of parliament, and in 1935 he published *The New State*, summarizing his political theory, in which Mella's ideas are evident. The main themes of his book are man, society, the nation, monarchy, political representation, legislation, administration, and a variety of social themes.

Larumbe knew that man depends on God, and he considered the liberal concept theorized by Rousseau to be wrong. The rights of man only exist, he wrote, if they are united with divine rights. Larumbe thought of society as an entity made up of different groups that interact with each other, and of the nation not as a set of individuals who share the same identity but rather a "society of societies," which differ from one another but share a common structure.

A nation is a political expression of society that can be governed by a republic or a monarchy. It is formed beginning with traditional values and a divine order, Larumbe thought—it is not possible for it to be formed without these principles. The hereditary monarchy does not depend on an oligarchy or referendum, but only a monarchy that respects the tradition of an organic and Catholic society can best govern its own citizens. Larumbe did not think political parties were the best representation for citizens. A nation is made up of six dependent classes, he thought, and the state in turn is—or rather, ought to be—represented by six structures. These classes are agricultural, industrial, commercial, property, free professions, and manual labor, whereas the state structures are diplomacy, judiciary, the army, the aristocracy, regions, and the clergy. Every class should elect fifty representatives, and the state structures should do the same (with the exception of the regions) so that parliament would be made up of 450 truly representative deputies.

According to his system of government, legislation is composed of three organs: the king, the parliament, and the council. Every legislative proposal, after being approved by the king, is debated by the parliament and, if accepted, passed to the council that analyzes it from a legal and constitutional point of view. The king has the last word and can either accept or reject the law.

Francisco Eías de Tejada y Spínola (1917–1978)

A professor of the philosophy of law and of natural law, Spinola was dedicated to writing academic books about both his own field of study and the analysis of contemporary society. Throughout his career, he became one of the biggest representatives of traditionalist Spanish thought and Carlist legitimism.

Carlism was rooted in Spain as a Catholic and counterrevolutionary school of thought, based on "historical-religious continuity of 'Catholic and missionary' Spain, the legal-political one of traditionalism and the dynastic-legitimist one."[20] In particular:

> Tejada was a follower of the counter-reformist Spanish school, a defender of national rights, and an adversary of legal positivism; as a political scientist, he supported the social doctrine of the church and was an enemy of both liberalism and socialism; as a philosopher, he followed Thomism and was an enemy of rationalism and irrationalism; as a Spanish citizen, he was a monarchist and Carlist; as a practicing Catholic, he was a convinced traditionalist, heir of the counterrevolutionary school, enemy of the anti-Christian revolution and neo-modernist progress.[21]

Within the social fabric, religion cannot be considered an accessory but rather, along with loyalty to the king and a tradition that unites all citizens, must be considered as one of the three elements that determine unity of the political body.

Tejada believed that a traditional nation must be established as an organic society in which the social organism represents the metaphysical order created by God. He supported community, and he imagined society as a "community of communities," consisting of groups of families opposed to the centralism theorized by liberals and socialists. He placed particular attention on the autonomy of these intermediary bodies.

Furthermore, he also retraces the causes of the revolutionary crisis to events that occurred centuries before the French Revolution:

> At the beginning of the modern era, the link with Christian tradition was compromised by five progressive breakups: the religious one with Luther, the ethical one with Machiavelli, the political one with Bodin, the legal one with Grozio and Hobbes, and finally, the diplomatic one with the Westphalia treaties (1648), which marked

the end of Christianity as an international public system. Since the ruin of the Christian Empire, and despite resistance of the *Christianitas minor* that became the Spanish Empire, modern Europe arose: a Europe that Tejada did not mean in a geographical sense but rather in a historical-political sense, identifying it with the Masonic, secularized, and basically anti-Christian revolution. Quickly, this Europe sanctioned the French Revolution, and subsequent liberal and socialist revolutions: the refusal of the sovereignty of God, the regality of Christ, and the jurisdiction of the church (which opposed the autonomy of man), the idolatry of "popular sovereignty," and the construction of a "universal Republic."[22]

His traditionalist thought was opposed to the ideas of nationalist movements such as the Falange party, which looked down on religious influence on the state, and he therefore clashed with Francisco Franco's dictatorship. The Spanish thinker had a rigorous vision of religion. He criticized certain decisions of the church after the Second Vatican Council, which favored modernizing and secularizing ideologies in ways that he believed betrayed traditional principles.

In addition to being a careful scholar, he was also an extremely versatile character: a tireless traveler; a polyglot who spoke Japanese, Greek, Bantu, Icelandic; and a book collector (his library contained more than fifty-thousand volumes).

CHAPTER SIX

Britain's Heir: American Conservatism

A merican conservatism differentiates from its European counterpart:

> From a European perspective, there are two opposing objectives of American conservatism. The first is that it does not reflect conservatism, but rather an erroneously labeled liberalism, and the second is that it is a purely American phenomenon that cannot be transferred to other countries.[1]

Understanding American conservatism actually requires an understanding of its two cores: "a traditionalist (critical of modern culture, moderately statist, philosophical, and literary) and a libertarian (individualistic, reductive of the range of government tasks)."[2]

Libertarians were the first to criticize the central "super state" by advocating for *laissez-faire* policy and a reduced state. Friedrich von Hayek, author of *The Road to Serfdom*, which denounces socialism and blames it for leading mankind to political and economic slavery, was a prominent exponent of this school of thought. Albert Jay Nock, founder of the magazine *The Freeman* and author of *Memoirs of a Superfluous Man*, also maintained that the state became an enemy when interfering in the social and economic lives of its citizens. He must also be counted among libertarians.

However, the main representatives for American conservatives are Robert A. Nisbet, Russell A. Kirk, and Richard Weaver—who, unlike Hayek, identified themselves as pure conservatives. In *The Constitution of Liberty*, Hayek criticizes every type of conservatism:

> By its very nature it cannot offer an alternative to the direction in which we are moving. It may succeed in its resistance to current tendencies by slowing down undesirable developments, but, since it does not indicate another direction, it cannot prevent their continuance. It has, for this reason, invariably been the fate of conservatism to be dragged along a path it did not choose.[3]

The best text to more deeply understand his life is *Hayek on Hayek: An Autobiographical Dialogue*, in which his contributions to economics, theoretical psychology, the theory of knowledge, political philosophy, law, and the history of ideas are revealed. The book also recounts his theoretical dispute with Keynes, from which he began his journey of reformulating classical liberalism, winning him the Nobel Prize in Economics in 1974.

Hayek's studies of liberalism are collected in *The Fortunes of Liberalism*. He traces an overview of liberalism's main foundations as well as the historical journey that led to the birth of the liberal movement. The book also reveals the differences between two types of liberalism: British and continental. British liberalism identifies individual liberty as a supreme value, whereas continental liberalism identifies with democratic movements, in hopes of securing greater social cooperation.

American conservatism is unquestionably different than the conservatism of Europe. Nevertheless, it has always stood as a witness to its European inheritance. A comprehensive analysis of European conservative though would therefore be incomplete without an analysis of its heir, the United States.

Between 1948 and 1954, a few important works on American conservatism were published: *Ideas Have Consequences* by Richard M. Weaver, *God and Man at Yale* by William F. Buckley Jr., *Witness* by Whittaker Chambers, and *The Conservative Mind* by Russell Kirk. Robert Nisbet defined this period as "the freshet of 1950–53."

Kirk believed conservatism represented not just a political program but a precise "mentality," based on the understanding that change cannot be imposed by a system of studied rules or by centralized bureaucracy.

Frank Straus Meyer, author of *What is Conservatism?*, introduced what is known as "fusionism," the union between conservatives and libertarians which places individual liberty at the center of society. In post-war American conservative thought, anti-Communism also took on a primary role in society, especially in Eric Voegelin's work. In his book *The New Science of Politics*, published in 1949, Voegelin maintains:

> There were two substantially meaningful features of modernity: the growing mistrust of transcendent thought and the consequent vision of politics as a pursuit of secular salvation. Modernity, in other words, is nothing more than the heir of ancient gnosis. And Communism is, among modern ideologies, that which is most similar to ancient gnostic heresy, which pledged happiness, peace, and well-being in this world, not in an improbable heavenly paradise.[4]

The conservative current that inspired most thinkers was the one led by traditionalists, among which we can name Richard M. Weaver, Peter Viereck, Russell Kirk, John Hallowell, and Robert Nisbet. Traditional conservatives criticized the moral relativism of society. They are against change, but, if change were to occur, they believe it must be reconciled with history and the traditions of the people. And before change occurs, the social order must be protected; it can be conserved with gradual reforms, rather than violent and radical revolutions. Traditional conservatives are not aprioristically against change, but they can be when the said change eliminates the basic principles and values of a society.

In his 1948 book *Ideas Have Consequences*, Richard M. Weaver outlines a clear philosophical path of conservatism, identifying moral relativism as the main enemy of society—by denying any type of transcendental

experience, it consequentially denies truth. Weaver traces the birth of relativism back to William of Ockham's work and to the nominalist disputes of
the fourteenth century, whereas in the modern world, relativism spread
from Communism.

The year after the publication of Weaver's book, Peter Viereck published
his book *Conservatism Revisited*, in which he demonstrates the need for an
alliance between conservatives and liberals to combat the radicalism of Communism and Fascism. But the most important work on conservatism published in post-war America is undoubtedly Russell Kirk's *The Conservative
Mind*, which expresses his opposition to libertarian theories and marks him
as the creator of a new form of individualism that minimizes intermediary
social institutions. Nine years after the publication of *The Conservative Mind*,
in 1962, Kirk published *A Program for Conservatives*, which studies the first
principles of conservatism. These include:

- the existence of a transcendental order that regulates societal
  trends
- opposition of utilitarianism and egalitarianism in favor of
  diversity, expressed by the concept of social class
- the link between liberty and private property, and its foundation of civilization

Another major critic of liberalism and its ties to capitalism was John H.
Hallowell (1913–1991), author of *The Decline of Liberalism as an Ideology*
and *Main Currents in Modern Political Thought*. In 1953, the same year *The
Conservative Mind* was published, Robert Nisbet published *The Quest for
Community*, which explored the importance of communities that served as
intermediary bodies between the state and the individual, and as the antidote to individualism.

In *The Social Philosophers*, Nisbet sharply criticizes Rousseau for having
theorized about the elimination of community relationships and traditional
social ties, which he considered "chains of existence." Rousseau contributed
to the absolutism of reason in society and believed the social community,

understood as a *community of communities*, had no reason to exist. The state, he thought, is the only tool for human development. In a passage from *The Social Contract*, Rousseau writes, "in order to have a clear declaration of the general will…there should be no factions in the State, and…every citizen should express only his own opinion."[5]

Rousseau wanted to eliminate all associations other than the state in his hostility toward social connections that bind individuals. An independent church was considered by him to be an interference in the "general will" of the people; he also thought the education of younger generations should be passed from the family—a similar interfering force—to the state.

John Adams (1735–1826)

John Adams, the second president of the United States, played an important role in the development of American conservatism, especially with his book *A Defense of the Constitutions*. He thought the elite were essential in preserving a democracy; they were a balance between the people and the king. Benefiting middle-class merchants (to the detriment of aristocratic landowners), the conservative impulse to defend property was transformed into the defense of the ideals of class (honor, tradition, self-discipline), all of which were based on the concept of *noblesse oblige*. But since the nobility had more privileges compared to other social classes, it had more ethical obligations to society.

Throughout the evolution of conservatism, nationalism and internationalism have adopted different meanings. From 1789 to 1848, most conservatives were internationalist and opposed nationalism. But after 1870, the roles switched. For example, Maistre's, Cortés's, and Metternich's internationalism was opposed to Barrès's and Treitschke's nationalism. Between 1815 and 1848, rebels used nationalism to destroy the status quo, especially in the Austrian Empire. Beginning in 1870 and continuing until the outbreak of the First World War, governments used nationalism to prevent social changes and to stabilize the status quo. While conservatives now believe the pride of belonging to a nation is just one of many values, for nationalists it is the most important one. When religion, loyalty, and ethics are sacrificed for the sake of the nation, the result becomes fanaticism.

Frank S. Meyer (1909–1972)

Born in Newark, New Jersey, in 1909, Meyer joined the Communist Party in 1931. But in 1945, he broke with the party due to changes in his beliefs. Meyer was deeply influenced by conservative literature and quickly became a fervent anti-Communist, both in opposition to its past and in opposition to the developments of the Cold War between the United States and Russia. In 1956, he began collaborating with Buckley's *National Review* editors and was immediately entrusted with curating the book section, as well as a column titled "Principles and Heresies."

His influence on conservative thought emerged with his book *In Defense of Freedom*, published in 1962. The book expresses his theory of fusionism, in which Meyer divided conservatism into two categories: the libertarian and the traditionalist. Despite the differences between the two types of conservatism, neither the libertarian nor the conservative holds mutually exclusive beliefs; each has certain commonalities with the other. Libertarians, while hoping to achieve limited influence of the state in the lives of citizens, revere freedom to the point of secularism and skepticism. They ignore the organic, moral order of society, and in their opposition to authoritarianism, do not recognize the authority of God.

Meyer worked on his study of conservatism in two main books: *The Conservative Mainstream* and *What is Conservatism?*, a collection of essays of various thinkers who present points in common between the different cores of conservatism, including F.A. Hayek, William F. Buckley Jr., Russell Kirk, and M. Stanton Evans.

Thomas Stearns Eliot (1888–1965)

Part of a bourgeois family in Saint Louis, Missouri, Eliot received a degree from Harvard and continued his studies at the Sorbonne and Oxford before he moved permanently to London in 1915. His first poems came out in 1917;

two years later, he published *Poems*, but he received true notoriety in 1922 with his poem *The Waste Land*. The poem, imbued with Christian humanity, is a critique of scientism and utilitarianism, describing the decline of Europe. Eliot saw a return to religion as the only solution for modern society.

While *The Waste Land* led him to worldwide fame, the legitimizing moment of his career came with the award of the Nobel Prize in Literature in 1948, following the publication of a series of philosophical poems titled *Four Quartets*. Through his literary work, Eliot opposed secularization and desacralization, a peculiarity of modernity:

> He denounced the hypocrisy of a historical philosophy that insists on interpreting the barely finished century according to the opposing pairs of democracy/dictatorship, liberty/totalitarianism, and Fascism/anti-Fascism. Actually, the great poet and essayist affirmed that the only true vision of society is a society founded on natural rights (to him accomplished by the Christian Revelation).[6]

As Roger Scruton writes, Eliot "perceived that it is precisely in modern conditions—conditions of fragmentation, heresy, and unbelief—that the conservative project acquires its sense."[7]

Eliot expressed his ideas in the literary quarterly *The Criterion*, which he founded in 1922 with the goal of collecting contributions from the best writers and thinkers of the day. The first edition contained his famous poem *The Waste Land*, while subsequent editions included writings by Pound, Yeats, Forster, Huxley, Chesterton, Dawson, and translations of Dostoevsky, Mann, and Pirandello. Particular attention to the religious vision emerges in all his work: *Murder in the Cathedral* is about Christian martyrdom and the conflict between church and state.

Eliot also distanced himself from humanism and attacked many of the fallacies of his contemporaries. In *After Strange Gods* and two other books published in 1940 and 1948, Eliot expresses perplexity and fear for the situation in Europe. His analysis hits on socialist and democratic ideas, starting with a critique of neo-Romantics, as well as liberal and "scientific humanism": "This liberalism seemed to him to be the avatar of moral chaos, since it permits any sentiment to flourish, and deadens all critical judgement with the idea of a democratic right to speak, which becomes insensibly a democratic right to feel."[8] In *The Idea of a Christian Society*, he writes:

> By destroying traditional social habits of the people, by dissolving their natural collective consciousness into individual constituents, by licensing the opinions of the most foolish, by substituting instruction for education, by encouraging cleverness rather than wisdom, the upstart rather than the qualified, by fostering a notion of *getting on* to which the alternative is hopeless apathy, Liberalism can prepare the way for that which is its own negation: the artificial, mechanized, or brutalized control which is a desperate remedy for its chaos.[9]

Richard Malcom Weaver (1910–1963)

Weaver's vision of independence for the American colonies from the English empire was not one that looked toward the future but rather a reaction to the revolutionary innovations introduced by King George III (not the colonists). The demands of American revolutionaries, he thought, were actually in line with the traditional conceptions of society; the revolution was intended as an institutional break, with the goal of maintaining a historical-cultural continuity.

Weaver's main book, *Ideas Have Consequences*, published in 1948, was crucial to the development of the ideas of the Republican Party after the war:

> Without going into a detailed account of the differences between conservative traditionalists, pre- and post-war "Old Right," new conservatives, "New Right," neoconservatives, libertarians, paleolibertarians, and paleoconservatives, it is necessary to take a historiographical note of the paternity of post-war conservative thought, often defined in terms of the true "rebirth," attributed to the "six canons" of the conservative *forma mentis* with which Kirk began his *magnum opus* of 1953 (that is, *The Conservative Mind: From Burke to Santayana*).[10]

In *Ideas Have Consequences*, Weaver describes the societal results of the rejection of the Christian philosophy that made the West great, and identifies three main solutions to thwart modernity:

- the restoration of private property understood correctly, not as abstract property of modern financial capitalism, but as personal property
- a rediscovery of respect for words and language
- a rediscovery of compassion understood through nature, the past, and other people

Weaver's influence on Russell Kirk's work is clear, demonstrated by the points in common between their ideas and those of Robert Nisbet and Peter Viereck, who represent the soul of the new conservative. Kirk also takes the concept of internal order from Weaver, sustaining the fragility of every social-political order that is not based on moral order. This idea is presented in *Visions of Order: The Cultural Crisis of Our Time*, published in 1964.

Henry Regnery (1912–1996)

Editor Henry Regnery was a main advocate of American conservative thought after the war until his death in 1996. His publishing house, Regnery Publishing, continues spreading conservative thought today, with the slogan, "Great Conservative Books. Great Conservative Authors."

On September 9, 1947, Regnery founded the Henry Regnery Company, which immediately became the main independent organ of the historical revisionism of the Second World War. With the publication of *God and Man at Yale* in 1951 and *The Conservative Mind* in 1953, American conservatism took on its own literary identity.

The publishing house is also known for its translations, including *Man against Mass Society* by Gabriel Marcel in 1962, *The World of Silence* by Max Picard in 1952, and *The Lord* by Romano Guardini in 1954.

Regnery collected his memories and the main events of his work as an editor in *Memoirs of a Dissident Publisher*, a book which recounts the history of American conservatism during the second half of the twentieth century through his own professional experience.

Robert Alexander Nisbet (1913–1996)

Besides being known for his studies of sociology, Robert Nisbet deepened the bond between sociology and conservatism, dedicating a valuable book to the topic titled *Conservatism: Dream and Reality*, in which he retraces the lines of conservative thought. Nisbet acknowledges the value of community as a traditional reality. This is a primary value of conservative society, destroyed in totalitarian regimes and mass societies in favor of a strong central state, whose creation was also favored by the French Revolutionists and proved unquestionably detrimental to traditional structures of the community.

Conservatism formed in two key historical periods: the first between 1770 and 1810, with the development of counterrevolutionary thought originating in Burke's work, and the second from the 1950s to 1960s, especially in the United States.

Nisbet identifies continuities between the ideological foundations of the French Revolution and totalitarianism. The first commonality is the political use of fear; then, the elimination of autonomous social relationships that impede the establishment of a strong central government.

With Burke, Nisbet supports the defense of "small patriotisms," such as churches and guilds. In *Twilight of Authority* (1975), he identifies the values that make up these true communities: functionality, dogma, authority, hierarchy, solidarity, a sense of superiority, and honor. It is lamentable that these values are disappearing in contemporary society.

In his book *Robert Nisbet e il conservatorism sociale*, Spartaco Pupo analyzes every facet of the American sociologist's ideas, dedicating particular attention to the concept of community that

> inherits the tragic vision of history from counterrevolutionary conservatism. Instead of seeing the evolutionary process—Reform, Enlightenment, capitalism, nationalism, democracy—as the work

of modern history, he sees these things as encompassing forces that man, as a finite being, is incapable of controlling, and that with the passing of time, demoralize cultures. Like conservatives such as Burke, Bonald, Maistre, etc., Nisbet saw new and more atrocious forms of power developing and being centralized, being made bureaucratic and popular in modern society on the ruins of ancient class authorities, of lineage, of the church and the monarchy. He also saw the "new order" as a displacement, social disorganization, and anarchy, all produced by the forces of modernity such as Romantic individualism and the penetration of political power in the social and technological structure.[11]

Nisbet traces the differences between conservatives and libertarians, placing particular emphasis on the different conceptions of freedom, which libertarians understand as *the* supreme value and conservatives understand as *an* important value belonging to a broader whole.

Conservatives view the nation as a "community of communities" based on "small patriotisms." Unlike libertarians, conservatives are able to see the weaknesses of the nation system just as we understand it today. The people are seen as "natural groups within which individuals invariably live: family, locality, church, region, social class, nation, and so on," rather than an aggregation of single individuals.[12] The existence of individuals cannot be separated from identities of the groups and associations.

While the differences between conservatives and libertarians are connected to individual aspects, the differences between conservatives and progressives are structural, beginning with the concept of change with which progressives try to alter the historical reality in favor of new visions of the world. A conservative, by contrast, is not one who aprioristically opposes change or innovation, but rather one who adheres to a defined system of ideals and values of social order which must be conserved over time.

Nisbet considered intellectuals to be true "fighting men" who protect the values of traditional order against modernists, and he highlighted "the need of appreciation of traditional communities and intermediary bodies" by favoring the constitution of a de-centralized state. In 1980, Nisbet published an essay in the *Modern Age* titled "Conservatives and Libertarians: Uneasy Cousins," in which he definitively eliminates the possibility of agreement between conservatism and libertarianism, rejecting the fusionist vision.

Nisbet studied guilds and intermediary classes beginning with the Roman Empire, in which the "laws of guilds" prevailed. He was inspired by the texts of German jurist Otto von Gierke (1841–1921). In von Gierke's main book, *Political Theories of the Middle Ages*, human communities are studied and considered to be made up of aggregations of groups (families, religious communities, etc.) that lead to the formation of the state. Thanks to the German jurist, Nisbet focused his attention on the medieval society, made up of feudal values and guilds.

In his work, Nisbet describes the typical prerogatives of conservative thought: the importance of a strong central government for defense, that does not need to be a *centralizer* but rather a *promoter* of natural communities. His form of conservatism does not refuse a dialogue with social democracy. It also stands at a distance from the extremism of pure *laissez-faire* policy, from capitalism, and from liberal individualism. Nisbet is not too shy to highlight the benefits of the welfare state.

According to Nisbet, conservative tenets can be summarized in seven main propositions:

1. Society is an organic entity governed by laws and made up of personal, institutional relationships.
2. Conservatives think society comes before the individual, from an ethical, historical, and logical point of view; it is only thanks to his associative manifestations that man becomes an individual.
3. It is futile to reduce society to basic individuals.
4. The existence of the principle of interdependence within social phenomena makes society an organic system made up of inter-relationships, of belief and of routine.
5. The needs and wants of man play a leading role in society.
6. The "principle of function," according to which every person and institution has an essential role in human life, contributes to and shapes the lives of other people.

7. The importance of small social groups, considered "irreducible units" of society such as religious groups, family and the association of workers, should never be underestimated.

Finally, Nisbet identifies two moments considered the "renascence" of conservatism: the first between 1770 and 1810 in Western Europe, the second between 1950 and 1970 in the United States:

> Let me repeat, and conclude here, that a conservative party (or any other group) has a double task confronting it. The first is to work tirelessly toward the diminution of the centralized, omnicompetent, and unitary state with its ever-soaring debt and deficit. The second and equally important task is that of protecting, reinforcing, nurturing where necessary the varied groups and associations which form the true building blocks of the social order.[13]

Peter Viereck (1916–2006)

Born in New York in 1916, Viereck finished his studies at Harvard in the early years after the war and began teaching history at Smith College and later at Mount Holyoke in 1948, where he spent nearly fifty years. He dedicated much of his time to the study of conservatism, publishing *Conservatism Revisited* in 1949, which "opened people's minds to the idea that being conservative does not mean being satanic."

Upon finishing his doctorate at Harvard, he published his research book in 1941 titled *Metapolitics: The Roots of the Nazi Mind*, and in 1949, he won the Pulitzer Prize for Poetry. Other notable books of his include *Shame and Glory of the Intellectuals* and *The Unadjusted Man*. He subscribed to a more humanistic, literary, moral, and aristocratic conservatism, distancing himself from Senator Joseph McCarthy's stances, and did not endorse Barry Goldwater for president.

Viereck's book *Conservatism: From John Adams to Churchill* is important for an in-depth study of conservatism. Published in 1956, it expounds upon the ideas and works of conservatives from the American Revolution to

Viereck's day. He distinguishes between two types of conservatism: the moderate conservatism, inspired by Burke, and the more extreme conservatism that draws upon the ideas of Joseph de Maistre. While both were opposed to the innovations introduced by the French Revolution, their end goals set them apart. Moderates oppose the loss of traditional liberties, whereas extremists fight against the loss of authority.

These two schools of thought are both opposed to Rousseau's theories, especially the societal triumph of rationalism. *The Social Contract* and *Émile*, both published in 1762, provided the foundation of progressivism and rationalism, theories which are the opposite of that which is expressed by conservatives.

In the first chapter of his book *Historical and Philosophical Origins of Conservatism*, Viereck traces some of the central points of the analysis of conservatism in history. Defense of private property is considered an indispensable element of society, as it guarantees order. Some conservatives, such as Disraeli and John Adams, only defend the materialistic concept of property if it is linked to a moral basis and therefore to a service of the community.

But Viereck knew that conservatism cannot be discussed without dedicating necessary attention to its birthplace, Great Britain. As stated by Chancellor Metternich of the Austrian Empire, British conservatism concerns every social class and renders England the freest nation on earth because it is the most disciplined. According to Tocqueville, England was the only protected nation during the riots of 1848, which plagued most European nations. This, Viereck wrote, was thanks to the rigor of its ancient customs.

Viereck identified three principal dualisms that distinguish conservatism from radicalism: apriorism versus experience, organicism versus atomism, and liberty versus equality. Rationalist and Enlightenment societies are based on *apriorism*, a term deriving from the Latin expression *a priori*, which refers to ideas not linked to historical experience that oppose the organic vision of society, so central to conservative thought.

Organic societies are such thanks to common religions and historical experiences, which give birth to nationalism, derived from monarchies and articulated within the constitution and values of loyalty and cooperation. On the other hand, atomist societies are united by materialism, class warfare, and by excessive economic *laissez-faire*.

Do liberty and equality necessarily have to be divided or linked to each other? According to the French Revolution, they must be linked (*libertè, égalité, fraternité*), but not according to conservatives, who believe that the diversity that characterizes every human being should be valued, even though it may preclude ideas of equality.

Charles Wright Mills (1916–1962)

Before becoming a professor at Columbia University, Mills was an associate professor of sociology at the University of Maryland from 1941 to 1945. While he has been accused of being left-leaning, his congruency with conservative thought is undeniable. In his books *The New Men of Power: American's Labor Leaders, White Collar: The American Middle Classes, The Power Elite and Power*, and *Politics and People*, he expresses the contradictions of American society by questioning the very concept of democracy.

Mills analyzed an important part of American conservative thought, observing that "in the historical, political, and social reality of the United States, a classical type of conservatism founded on the sanctity of a tradition transmitted by pre-industrial societies would be unthinkable today. In America, there is no conspicuous legacy of this kind."[14]

In his essay "The Conservative Mood," published in *The Power Elite*, Mills resumes Russell Kirk's ideas, stating that a conservative believes in a society governed by a divine plan. This, he believed, is because of man's ultimate inability to understand society's guiding forces. He believed in the need of a leader for society, someone connected to the nation's traditional life. For a conservative, tradition is sacred and guides his behavior. He must understand that events take place according to a divine plan, which seems irrational but becomes linked to tradition, in opposition to the supreme rationality of human reason. Mills highlights the importance of the elite and of conservatives who accept the guidance of a group of enlightened.

Russell Kirk (1918–1994)

Kirk spent most of his life in the small town of Mecosta, Michigan, in his family home called Piety Hill, which he shared with his wife Annette and his four children until his death on April 29, 1994. The two main biographies of Kirk's life are *Russell Kirk and the Age of Ideology* by W. Wesley McDonald and *Russell Kirk: A Critical Biography of a Conservative Mind* by James E. Person.

After receiving his bachelor's degree in history at Michigan State College in 1940, he received his MA the following year from Duke University, where he studied John Randolph of Roanoke's politics and made a collection of his work in *Randolph of Roanoke: A Study in Conservative Thought* (1951). While he was working on that book, he deepened his understanding of Burke and conservative thought, which set the foundation for his masterpiece, *The Conservative Mind*.

The Conservative Mind, originally titled *The Conservatives' Rout*, was published in 1953 with the subheading *from Burke to Santayana*. Later, because of Kirk's appreciation for T. S. Eliot, he changed it to *from Burke to Eliot*. With this book, the American political scientist and philosopher demonstrated that conservative thought is an integral part of Western political tradition. Although his is a history of conservatism, the book is intended to be both didactic and polemical, condemning rationalism, Rousseau's Romantic idealism, positivism, Marxism, socialism, and Darwinism. Achieving wide success, *Time* magazine dedicated its entire book section to it, and it received glowing reviews from a number of newspapers, including the *New York Times*.

Russell Kirk was a prolific writer. He wrote twenty-six essays; three novels; three collections of short stories; about 2,000 articles, between essays and reviews; and 2,687 short articles for the column To the Point (1962–75), published in various national newspapers. His main works include *The Roots of American Order*, *The Portable Conservative Reader*, and *The Conservative Constitution*. The 1995 posthumous autobiography *The Sword of Imagination: Memoirs of a Half-Century of Literary Conflict* is also crucial to understanding his work.

His task, as has already been mentioned, was not limited to publishing books, but also included spreading conservative ideas through articles and magazines. In 1957, he founded the academic journal *Modern Age*, edited at the time by Henry Regnery. In the first edition, Kirk identified the purpose of the journal: "to stimulate the discussion of the great moral and social and political and economic and literary questions of the hour, and to search for means by which the legacy of our civilization may be kept safe." In the mid-1960s, distribution dropped to 6,500 copies; the journal underwent a severe time of crisis until ISI (Intercollegiate Studies Institute) intervened in 1967, bringing circulation up to more than 10,000 copies.

The journal lives on today, focusing on the analysis of conservative theories with a series of articles on the relationship between libertarians and traditionalists, as well as contemporary texts of American conservatism. Over the years, there has been a continuous flow of numerous and noteworthy collaborations between Nisbet, Voegelin, Gottfried, and Mayer. In memory of twenty-five years of publication, George Panichas published the book *Modern Age: The First 25 Years*.

In *The Conservative Mind*, Kirk analyzes the path that led to the American colonies' independence from England and the birth of the United States of America. The action of the settlers was a response to the British Crown's attempt to impose a despotic deviation from European tradition. It was not *truly* a revolution; if anything, it was an attempt to *avoid* the occurrence of a revolution, especially of the kind that had happened in France. The United States of America was therefore born in opposition to the ideology of the French Revolution:

> Substantially animated by veneration for the past, shaped by an awareness of Christian customs, resistant to the ambiguous abstractions of philosophy and utopias that reject the concrete historical reality, Kirk's United States shaped the historical theater with a conservative mentality, described as the true soul of the country, the true "spirit of 1776." This spirit and the tendency toward liberalism and socialism, considered foreign and unwanted

to the body of national culture, are set against each other. The fight against the denial of classic and Christian tradition, against moral and cultural decline, against the world of ideologies, against the nationalization of society, and against the annihilation of intermediary social structures between the individual and the state...is the patrimony of the conservatism that Kirk has handed over to new generations.[15]

Kirk generated the diffusion of Burke's work in American society; reference to Burke and his *Reflections on the Revolution in France* is essential to understanding Kirk's philosophy. Nevertheless, in *The Politics of Prudence*, he indicates the ten main figures that influenced his conservative philosophy: Marcus Tullius Cicero, Marcus Aurelius Antoninus, Samuel Johnson, Sir Walter Scott, John Randolph of Roanoke, Nathaniel Hawthorne, Theodore Roosevelt, Joseph Conrad, Richard Malcolm Weaver, and Freya Stark. Today, Kirk's cultural legacy, along with his prestigious and monumental library, is preserved by the Russell Kirk Center for Cultural Renewal, founded after his death as a research center on Piety Hill and curated by his wife. The institute continues to spread the American philosopher's ideas by hosting meetings and seminars.

The *Imaginative Conservative* is an American online journal dedicated to expanding conservatism and Russell Kirk's ideas. In 2015, it reprinted *Prospects for Conservatives*, in which Kirk, after asking himself who conservatives are, deals with the various problems of modern society, from justice to order and community, from problems of the heart to those of the mind. The introduction of the book, written by Dr. Bradley J. Birzer, cofounder of the *Imaginative Conservative*, explains how Kirk's book, originally published by Regnery in 1954, can be defined as a "Christian humanistic manifesto."

Thomas Molnar (1921–2010)

Born in Budapest on June 26, 1921, Molnar studied in France, where he was accused of anti-German activity under Nazi occupation. He was placed in the Dachau concentration camp.

After the war, he came to the United States and became a teacher at Brooklyn College of New York. There, he drew inspiration from Russell Kirk's philosophy, and published more than forty books, debuting with a biography of Georges Bernanos titled *Bernanos: His Political Thought and Prophecy*. Molnar was an independent, nonconformist author and an adversary of the modern economic and political system, which he thought denies human nature.

In 1967, he published *Utopia: The Perennial Heresy*, in which he criticizes the transformations that arose from Communism and Western technologies. He also criticizes the Gnosticism taken from Eric Voegelin's philosophical work.

Molnar was interested in the counterrevolutionary movements of the twentieth century, such as Action française and Spanish Falangism. He examines them in-depth in *The Counter-Revolution*, and in the early 1960s this examination led him to rediscover the Catholic faith. In his books *Twin Powers: Politics and the Sacred* and *The Church: Pilgrim of Centuries*, he deals with the relationship between church and state in medieval and modern history by identifying two devastating tendencies: Erastianism (the superiority of the state over the church in religious matters) and Puritanism.

In *The Counter-Revolution*, Molnar describes the counterrevolutionary way of life after 1945. Although society obtained ideological neutrality at the end of the Second World War, the revolutionary spirit remained unchanged:

> This is shown by the fact that each time a category of people reaches a higher standard of living, the revolutionaries at once denounce their "rigid conservative-bourgeois mentality" and launch new "missionaries" against them in the name of progress, justice, and generally, movement.[16]

The revolutionary spirit, which began to spread in 1789, continued to hide behind the dynamics that controlled industrial society, and Molnar denounced how "in two hundred years, the revolutionaries will have succeeded in covering the world with a blanket of false concepts." The post-1945 world was divided into two philosophical camps: liberal and collectivist, both originating from the spirit of 1789. The Revolution, Molnar believed, was founded on terror, made graphically clear with Louis XVI's execution.

Today, the conflict between revolutionary and counterrevolutionary movements has moved from the political to the spiritual arena. The strength of the Revolution managed to weaken the most important Western institutions, from the church to the state, from universities to the magistracy—and, the state having lost its authority, the revolutionary spirit was free to gain every kind of power.

What is left of the counterrevolutionary spirit in modern society? According to Molnar, only the Catholic Church and Anglo-Saxon tradition preserve a pre-revolutionary worldview. Nevertheless, the revolutionary virus is even infecting the church: "Secularization of faith, dissolution of discipline, and denial of the magisterium follow from each other with the reversed logic of supernatural life. This is undoubtedly the work of the revolution and its immanentist ideology."[47]

Today, counterrevolutionaries must defend society and the principles on which community is built—an unspectacular role that requires constant and essential commitment.

William Frank Buckley Jr. (1925–2008)

After studying political science, history, and economics at Yale University, William Buckley graduated with honors in 1950 and became known for his first book, *God and Man at Yale*, published in 1951. In the book, he condemns liberalism along with his own university, where atheism and socialism prevailed.

Buckley considered the conservative movement to be an intellectual group that was fighting for the morality and freedom of the nation. In 1955, he founded the magazine *National Review*, which became the main outlet for his ideas. Originally a weekly publication, it became a bi-weekly publication in 1958 due to economic difficulties. The magazine had a well-defined editorial ethos:

> Preservation of freedom and the historic constitutional order, deference to traditional moral and cultural norms, rejection of the

New Deal legacy of highly centralized federal power (especially as embodied in the multiplication of regulatory agencies and in what came to be called the "nanny state"), adherence to free-market economic principles, support for a strong defense, and active opposition to Soviet global designs.[18]

Samuel P. Huntington (1927–2008)

Huntington considered conservative thought to be a historical reaction to the French Revolution, liberalism, and the emerging middle class. Conservatism presents a vision of an autonomous system characterized by order, balance, justice, and moderation. It is comprehensive in that it does not apply to a single social class and is used to defend institutions and established social order. Therefore, anyone who embraces conservative ideology must be ready to engage in the defense of order.

Huntington, recognizing Burke as the spiritual father of conservatism, summarized the main elements of his thought:

1. Religion is the foundation of civil society.
2. Society is the result of slow historical growth.
3. Man is a creature of instinct, emotion, and reason.
4. Community is superior to the individual.
5. Except in an ultimate moral sense, men are unequal.
6. There is an existing and rightful preference for forms of government already in place, and aversions are and should continue to be developed for new projects that have not yet been tested.

Conservatism sweepingly embraces all social classes. But if conservatives are not united by social class, they are united from a common status quo:

The characteristic elements of conservative thought—the "divine tactic" in history; prescription and tradition; the dislike of abstraction and metaphysics; the distrust of individual human reason; the organic conception of society; the stress on the evil man; the acceptance of social differentiation—all serve the overriding purpose of justifying the established order. The essence of conservatism is the rationalization of existing institutions in terms of history, God, nature, and man.[19]

Huntington, like many other thinkers, defined the difference between a conservative and a reactionary. A reactionary, he thought, is a defeated conservative who remains bound to a past idea of society. Huntington also deals with the main "hot topics" of the twenty-first century in his work: the proliferation of deadly weapons, demographic development, immigration, democracy, and human rights.

The Conscience of a Conservative *by Barry Goldwater*

In *American Conservatism: An Encyclopedia*, Lee Edwards writes, "It could be argued that no other book had a greater impact on the American politics of the second half of the twentieth century than did Barry Goldwater's *The Conscience of a Conservative* (1960)."[20] His 1964 candidacy for president of the United States—despite his electoral defeat—opened a political path that would lead to Ronald Reagan being elected president of the United States in 1980.

Goldwater's book begins with a call to demonstrate the relevancy of conservatism for the problems of contemporary society. While the book refers to the American situation and conservatism within the context of the United States, Goldwater's thoughts and proposals can also be attributed to European conservatism, helping to define conservative thought. Even though he identified the United States as a conservative nation and highlighted the citizens' desire to go back to conservative principles, he understood that these aspects do not always translate into the sphere of politics.

Conservatives, he observed, seem unable to apply their own principles to everyday life. Media commentators, presenting themselves as "enlightened" and "progressive," lead the masses to oblivion; conservatism is, according to these people, "out of date." Goldwater thought these charges were preposterous, and that conservatives ought to boldly declare them to be so.

Goldwater thus established the principles on which to base conservative thought:

> The principles on which the Conservative political position is based have been established by a process that has nothing to do with the social, economic, and political landscape that changes from decade to decade and from century to century. These principles are derived from the nature of man, and from the truths that God has revealed about His creation. Circumstances do change. So do the problems that are shaped by circumstances. But the principles that govern the solution of the problems do not. To suggest that the Conservative philosophy is out of date is akin to saying that the Golden Rule, or the Ten Commandments, or Aristotle's *Politics* are out of date. The Conservative approach is nothing more or less than an attempt to apply the wisdom and experience and the revealed truths of the past to the problems of today. The challenge is not to find new or different truths, but to learn how to apply established truths to the problems of the contemporary world.[21]

The main difference between conservatives and liberals is linked to the economy. While conservatives view man as a spiritual being with desires that must take precedence over materialistic ones, liberals believe that satisfying economic needs ought to be the main objective of society, and that it is necessary to do it as quickly as possible, through tools provided by progress. Conservatives think every individual represents a unique creature, and that to consider man as a mere part of a mass is akin to handing him over to slavery. At the same time, the economic and spiritual aspects of man are connected. Each person is the creator of his own destiny:

> Social and cultural change, however desirable, should not be effected by the engines of national power. Let us, through persuasion and

education, seek to improve institutions we deem defective. But let us, in doing so, respect the orderly processes of the law. Any other course enthrones tyrants and dooms freedom.[22]

This is why conservatives oppose totalitarianism and dictatorships that deny dignity and freedom to individuals. Obtaining freedom requires order; therefore, conservatives must not only conserve but also increase freedom in society. Doing this requires understanding the limits and dangers of state power—the state should not limit the freedom of citizens, even if it is done through laws and rules that act as an effective brake against the overwhelming power of a single authority. This is the task of the Constitution, which should not only limit the power of a single tyrant, but also the tyranny of the masses.

Toward the end of the Constitutional Convention, a woman asked Benjamin Franklin, "What have you given us?" He responded, "A Republic, if you can keep it!" The exercise of democracy and maintenance of freedom requires strong action of conservation: "We can be conquered by bombs or by subversions; but we can also be conquered by neglect—by ignoring the Constitution and disregarding the principles of limited government."[23]

Economically speaking, Goldwater's stances are associated with so-called "liberal conservatism." While in *The Conscience of a Conservative* he claims that the government is entitled to part of our wealth, he stresses that it is necessary to consider the individual's property rights before making such claims. Therefore, the government can demand an equal percentage of wealth from every citizen, and nothing more. He also condemns gradual taxation, defined as confiscatory, which aims to homologate all men to a common level: "We are all equal in the eyes of God but we are equal *in no other respect*. Artificial devices for enforcing equality among unequal men must be rejected if we would restore that charter and honor those laws."[24]

Another theme of *The Conscience of a Conservative* is the reduction of taxes. This can—and ought to—be realized with the management of government expenses, Goldwater wrote. Reducing taxes, of course, first requires reducing the expenses of the state:

The government must begin to *withdraw* from a whole series of programs that are outside its constitutional mandate—from social welfare programs, education, public power, agriculture, public housing, urban renewal, and all the other activities that can be better performed by lower levels of government or by private institutions or by individuals.[25]

The welfare state, Goldwater believed, is the opposite of a state that reduces its own expenses. He takes a strong stance against the welfare state, defining it as a tool for collectivization:

Socialism-through-Welfarism poses a far greater danger to freedom than Socialism-through-Nationalization precisely because it *is* more difficult to combat. The evils of Nationalization are self-evident and immediate. Those of Welfarism are veiled and tend to be postponed.[26]

Goldwater knew that this position is the toughest for conservatives to defend. In the eyes of citizens, such a position makes conservatives seem like men who are scornful toward those less fortunate. Actually, Goldwater wrote, conservatives take social problems to heart but do not believe that it is up to the state to solve them. "Welfarism" transforms man from a spiritual being with faith in himself and in his creator to a dependent creature at the mercy of the state.

Goldwater also dedicates a chapter of his book to education. He puts forward an education system based on conservative guidelines. As a first step, he differentiates the faulty *quantitative* criteria versus the correct *qualitative*; while most of public opinion proposes an increase in education spending as a solution to the problem, Goldwater suggests elevating the level of instruction. The main defect of American education (and European education), he writes, is having adopted so-called "progressive education":

Subscribing to the egalitarian notion that every child must have the same education, we have neglected to provide an education system which will tax the talents and stir the ambitions of our best students and which will thus insure us the kind of leaders we will need in the future. In our desire to make sure that our children learn to "adjust" to their environment, we have given them insufficient opportunity to acquire the knowledge that will enable them to *master* their environment. In our attempt to make education "fun," we have neglected the academic disciplines that develop sound minds and are conductive to sound characters.... Most important of all: in our anxiety to "improve" the world and insure "progress," we have permitted our schools to become laboratories for social and economic change according to predilections of the professional educators. We have forgotten that the proper function of the school is to transmit the cultural heritage of one generation to the next generation, and to so train the minds of the new generation as to make them capable of absorbing ancient learning and applying it to the problem of its own day.[27]

In other words, the progressive school has obscured the true scope of education. Even today, the cultural heritage of America is a mere generation away from being entirely lost.

CHAPTER SEVEN

Italian Conservatism

I n the early years after the unification of Italy, the tension between the political Right and Left created an alternating pattern between two ways of governance. The historical Right, however, does not fall into the category of the reactionary or conservative Right. As Prezzolini explains in *Intervista sulla destra*, "It is not conservative because nothing can be conserved from the 'old' Italy; there is nothing worth conserving. It is not reactionary because reactionaries are the *ultras*, connected to the Vatican, the House of Bourbon, or the 'old order' in general."[1]

Italian counterrevolutionaries of the Risorgimento, such as Monaldo Leopardi, Capece Minutolo, Solaro della Margarita, and Giacinto de' Sivo were all more reactionary than conservative. The historical Right is conservative by necessity, not by choice. Italy is a relatively new nation; its past was made up of many small autonomous states and the two encumbering presences of the church state and the Kingdom of Two Sicilies. Finding a historical reference point for the nation requires a closer look at Ancient Rome rather than the fragmented Italy of the late eighteenth century.

The ideological base of the historical Right is also reacting to ideas born from the French Revolution that, as we have seen, were refused by every conservative. Once again, Prezzolini gives us an explanation for this ideological point of reference:

> The Italian Right could not go back to the past. French conserva-
> tives wanted to return to the monarchy, but Italian conservatives
> did not want to return to Austrian monarchy or the Papal States.
> It is just like what we feel when we read Maurras. "We must to
> return to the king," Maurras always said. "What king?" we Italians
> responded. The Bourbons of Naples, the Lorraine of Tuscany, the
> Duke of Modena? No man of the Risorgimento, on the Right or
> the Left, dreamed of returning to that past. Therefore, the Italian
> Right had to inevitably be founded on the French Revolution.[2]

But understanding Italian conservatism must begin with this historical
fact: in Italy, there was never a revolution as in France. Rather, there was the
Risorgimento (meaning the resurgence or revival), which was a completely
different phenomenon.

As Armando Torno notes in *Il paradosso dei conservatori*, Italy has always
had an ambiguous relationship with conservatism because in Italy, unlike
other European countries, conservative thought did not naturally develop in
a way that would transform political action:

> The term was, and still is, as frightening as a contagious disease,
> so much so that in Italy it is easier to find someone who prefers
> to admit to all kinds of shameful relationships than define him-
> self as conservative. We do not have the same tradition that, by
> the seventeenth century in England... allowed members of par-
> liament to define themselves as "Tories" (conservatives) or
> "Whigs" (liberals).[3]

Italian history, in comparison to other European countries, presents certain characteristics and events that render it unique. There were no great
revolutions in Italy and consequentially no subsequent restorations. Though
there were revolts and changes, the moment that marks the birth of the Italian
State was the Risorgimento, which was an amalgamation between the French
Revolution and the Restoration: "[The Risorgimento], embracing the idea of

radical transformation and liberation from an authority, which it perceived as tyrannical; [and the Restoration], restoring Italian traditions."[4]

This marriage between revolutionary and traditional beliefs, which can be referred to as "revolutionary-restorer," embodies both the Risorgimento mentality and the Fascist mentality.

But even the Italian Republic, after the promulgation of the constitution, became a nation divided by conservative and progressive beliefs. The clearest example of this is the Christian Democratic party (DC), which, despite representing the conservative camp, has a progressive political program. Paradoxically, in analyzing certain positions taken up by the Italian Communist Party, certain stances similar to conservative thought can be found:

> The Communist Party has often fought against the outcomes of modernization or technology; it has defended social figures, examples of behavior, and ideal political types *overtaken* by technology and by progress: and it sustained some resistance to the very development of well-being, identified by the expansion of the bourgeoisie or dispelled as the danger of "mass gentrification."[5]

Just as certain thinkers in Italy drew closer to conservative revolutionary ideas, the same was true in France when figures from the cultural world—such as Drieu La Rochelle, Robert Brasillach, Bardèche, and Rebatet, to name some of the most well-known—shared some common philosophical traits with the conservative revolutionaries. This movement can therefore be defined as a "European conservative revolution." Though these commonalities among revolutionary European conservatism are worth noting, it must be said that the Italian situation

> has peculiar characteristics related to the development of its national history, to the intersecting effects of the Risorgimento and the anti-Risorgimento (of both reactionary and socialist mold), to its young unity, and to its recent national development, to which its ancient roots of civilization and culture act as a

contrast; to the plans of Italian supremacy and to the delays of its imperialism and colonialism, to the tensions between Neo-Guelphs and Neo-Ghibellines, between north and south, to the fluctuating Italian personalities between anarchism and statism.... All of these elements created a special "Italian situation" and drew a peculiar physiognomy of the Italian conservative revolution.[6]

Conservative revolutionary thought has a few marked differences from reactionary, traditionalist, and pure conservative thought. First of all, it does not refuse modernity by searching for a return to the past, but rather looks with traditional values toward the future. The Italian conservative revolution was the perfect synthesis of two principles: both the change and recovery of the historical and civil heritage of the nation.

Vincenzo Cuoco outlines the personality of the conservative revolution by first disassociating the Risorgimento revolution from the French Revolution and outlining a few substantial differences between the two historical events. The key concept is "innovation by conserving," which he expresses in his *Saggio storico sulla rivoluzione di Napoli*:

> Wanting to reform everything is the same as wanting to destroy everything. Conservatives call "strength of character" the boldness with which they attack ancient solemnity; I call it "foolishness" of a spirit that does not know how to reconcile with new things.[7]

Opposition to the French Revolution was born from the cultural legacies of work by Machiavelli, Gravina, and Vico, and in Cuoco's case, his ideas coincide with critiques made by Maistre and Bonald, who contested the top-heavy character of the revolutions. Cuoco, however, hoped for the creation of national and popular revolutions that would conserve the soul and traditions of the people. Francesco de Sanctis was of the same opinion, delineating the characteristics a revolution should have in order to respect conservative prerogatives:

not traumatic, but gradual, not humanitarian, but national, not "infinitely" libertarian but with a clear sense of limits, not exultant from history but operating in the wake of tradition and nature of the people, not abstractly created by the mind but cultivated by the reality of things; not unstoppable but capable of stopping itself.[8]

Alfredo Oriani, author of *La rivolta ideale*, drew closer to anarchist and revolutionary positions in his youth but developed a sense of rediscovery of his nation's traditions. He theorized about a spiritual revolution based on recuperating those traditions, and he understood that every revolution ends with conservation.

Italy's political fate has always been (and likely will always be) inseparable from the happenings of the Catholic Church. In 1848, Pope Pius IX was forced to leave Rome because of the revolts. The property of the church was distributed to the people, and the Inquisition ended. The following year, thanks to an intervention by the French army, Pope Pius IX returned to power, restoring pre-Enlightenment values and denouncing Catholic liberalism as heresy, receiving support from aristocratic elites and citizens. He responded to revolutionaries with conservative authoritarian policies, as expressed in the encyclical *Syllabus complectens praecipuos nostrae aetatis errors* (commonly referred to as the *Syllabus of Errors*) in 1864, which details eighty main errors of the time and condemns liberalism, rationalism, secularism, and scientific skepticism. Pope Pius IX highlighted how salvation outside of the church is nonexistent, a stance confirmed by the 1869–1870 Vatican Council, which declared the infallibility of the pope.

In 1891, Pope Leo XIII (1810–1903) published the encyclical *Rerum novarum*, in which he explains the need to return control of instruction and other aspects of society to the church. *Rerum novarum* was the first expression of the church's modern social doctrine: it recognized the need to change working conditions while simultaneously criticizing socialist and Marxist positions that aimed to abolish private property and encourage class struggle.

Nineteenth-century Italian literature presented a consistent number of books characterized by conservative subject matter and written by conservative authors. *The Leopard*, by Giuseppe Tomasi di Lampedusa (1896–1957), cannot be omitted from the most well-known novels of Italian literature. Its famous passage, "If we want things to stay as they are, things will have to change," summarizes the conservative vision of history. The decline of the aristocratic world along with its rituals and customs described by Tomasi di Lampedusa is a perfect representation of a "conservative" society. Lampedusa himself was born in Palermo in 1896, the eleventh prince of Lampedusa, baron of Torretta, and grandee of Spain of the first class.

Fascism and Conservative Thought

Defining Fascism as a conservative revolution is a complex philosophical choice. The restorative and revolutionary nature of the Fascist movement, especially at the beginning, was unquestionable. But identifying it in the Fascist government experience is more difficult. The definition of Fascism as a "conservative revolution" is owed to Sergio Panunzio (1886–1944), who identified the nature of "revolutionary conservation" in the books *Teoria generale dello stato fascista* and *Sentimento dello stato*.

The relationship between Fascism and conservatism is a delicate subject, difficult to analyze given the uniqueness and heterogeneous characteristics of Fascist thought. There are two books that are helpful in understanding how conservative thinkers contributed to Fascism: *Storia della culturea fascista* by Alessandra Tarquini and *Il Ventennio degli intellettuali* by Giovanni Belardelli.

According to Eugenio Garin, Fascist culture was essentially reactionary, with a Catholic and spiritualist mold.[9] And according to Marxist historiography, Fascism was a counterrevolutionary phenomenon, born as a bourgeoisie reaction to the working class. Mussolini's socialist education, combined with his belief that the government should be held by a minority, led to the creation of his revolutionary thought with conservative ideals.

The Fascist revolution hearkened back to the past, rediscovering spiritual and cultural Italian heritage and renovating it according to Fascist teachings.

Mussolini's acknowledgment of the role of intermediary bodies in society, structures that, beyond political parties, acted as intermediaries between the state and the citizens (unions, corporations, the church, the monarchy), was undoubtedly a conservative element of his Fascism. Mussolini also considered the nation to be a unifying force for the community. It is the state's duty, he thought, to train Italians and to lead a great intellectual reform. This is identified in Mussolini's plan to create a Fascist "New Man."

For Mussolini, conservative ideals and the need for modernization and economic development were antithetical. This tension between tendencies toward modernization and those tendencies towards recuperating the natural soul of the Italian province can be synthesized in the debate between the Strapaese and Stracittà movements, and in the journals *Il Selvaggio* and *900*. In *Il Pensiero conservatore*, Mongardini writes:

> A blend of foreigners and compatriot authors labeled Fascism as reactionary because of its authoritarian tendencies. However, this is absurd. While it is true that Fascism advocates for certain ideals of the past . . . as a whole it demonstrates a clear prevalence and predominance of futuristic incentives over old ones. Think about corporatism, which certainly does not seek to reestablish bygone and outdated economic conditions, but rather constitutes an attempt to introduce new, prospective elements to national life.[10]

In analyzing the Fascist revolution, Gramsci also highlighted the negative aspects and the nature of the revolution-restoration. It was such a full-scale conservative revolution that in 1921, Mussolini wrote in *Il Popolo d'Italia*, "We allow ourselves the luxury of being aristocrats and democrats, conservatives and progressives, revolutionaries and reactionaries; legal and illegal."[11]

Mussolini substituted the pluralism of political parties with social pluralism, thanks to the mediation of structures that arose between the individual and the state. In this way, he reaffirmed the need for every revolution destined to be remembered by history to also be a restoration:

Fascism experienced tension between freedom and authority, which has always been the fundamental tension between revolution and conservation. On one hand, Fascism was born from a voluntary and interventionist impulse, powerfully innovative and revolutionary, which is an impulse of creative freedom; on the other hand, it grew and was received by many Italians as a safe and stabilizing factor, a "conservative" request for order, certainty, and authority.[12]

It is difficult to say with certainty what dispositions of the conservative revolution can be found in Fascism and vice versa, and to what extent the thinkers of the Konservative Revolution in Germany were influenced by Fascism as a model to be adopted. They certainly followed the Fascist experience with extreme curiosity and particular attention to its developments:

Exactly one week before the March on Rome, Moeller had published an article with the eloquent title "Italia docet"; the following year, Carl Schmitt expressed his admiration to Mussolini. In 1925, Spengler sent his writings to "the Leader," after having already defined him as the embodiment of the Italian spirit. In 1927, Helmut Franke published a series of articles in *Arminius* in which he suggests Fascism as a modernized version of the Prussian model that was to be reimported. During the subsequent period, cross references to Fascism became so frequent that many spoke of a global affinity between Fascism and the conservative revolution.[13]

Fascism also speaks of strong ties to nationalism. In 1923, the Italian Nationalist Association of Luigi Federzoni and Alfredo Rocco merged with the National Fascist Party. The two men obtained positions in the Ministry of the Interior and the Ministry of Justice, working to create a strong, centralized state and to carry out the transition from a revolutionary phase to a conservative one.

There is no uniformity of thought toward Fascism among various conservative revolutionary authors. There are those who most identify with Fascism as a movement, those who identify with the policies of the regime, and those who identify with the figure of Mussolini: "Moeller and Zehrer positively judged the activist phase, but rejected the actual Fascist regime, whereas Spengler idolized Mussolini, and Schmitt bowed down to the regime."[14] Moeller confronted the theme of Fascism on two occasions. In October 1922, in an article directed at young Germans, he pointed to the Fascist model as a conservative countermovement to be exported to Germany; thereafter, he changed his position, judging Fascism as a strictly Italian phenomenon and a modern manifestation of a nationalism that could not be adapted to Germany. Spengler appreciated the structure of the regime more than the Fascist Party itself. He did praise Mussolini as someone who disciplined Italy and was preparing it for imperialism with strong statism. Carl Schmitt emphasized the nationalist nature of Fascism, paying particular attention to the relationship between Fascism and the state, which he analyzes in *Constitutional Theory*.

While Jünger also initially praised the heroic, vivacious aspect of Fascism, by August 1927 he agreed that Germany needed to go beyond the Fascist model. He considered Italian Fascism unsuitable for Germany, due to the differing situations in the two countries. His separation from Nazism in 1930 also constituted his break from Fascism, which he judged to be "just as bad as Bolshevism."

Edgar Jung, the most religious thinker of the Konservative Revolution, initially appreciated Fascism's novelty and its break from liberal tradition, particularly highlighting "the creation of a heroic idol; the defeat of political parties; the creation of a real personal authority; the salvation of the private economy from collectivist free will."[15] However, he complained about the lack of a decisive approach to Christianity, which led to his disavowal of the ideology.

In the chapter titled "Le due Italie" in Marcello Veneziani's book *La rivoluzione conservatrice in Italia*, he offers a way of understanding the spread of ideologies in Italy after its unification. Veneziani compares the Piedmontese ideology and Italian ideology; the Piedmontese ideology is characterized by its attempt to distance Italy from its own roots in favor of modernity and in opposition to the south (rendering it an anti-national ideology). On the contrary, Fascism became the architecture of Italian and Mediterranean ideology,

taking up the typical dispositions of Roman tradition and exalting spiritualistic realism. Giambattista Vico said of Italian ideology:

> The essential elements of the Mediterranean and Italian ideology
> can be found *in nuce* in the Neapolitan philosophy: a call back to
> the classical world, Romanism in particular, traditional and reli-
> gious heritage, the Roman sense of law and the state, the synthesis
> of the ideal with the real, and the cyclic and analogical vision of
> history that opposes the ideology of progress.[16]

A clear and well-defined comparison between the two ideologies would
inevitably be wrong; they are both characterized by their attempt to modern-
ize conservative ideals. Italian ideology combines the conservative spirit and
other modernized stances:

> Italian ideology is indeed born out of encounters with social and
> popular components. It is not Marxist and not internationalist, not
> positivist and not materialist; it has a traditionalist and spiritualistic
> component, but one not attached to the past, not counterrevolution-
> ary, not anti-social. It is this intersection between modern ideals and
> "traditional" themes that instills Italian ideology with a peculiar
> disposition of the "conservative revolution."[17]

Italian ideology is not to be understood as anti-European. Mediterranean
civilization actually coincides with the ideal, historical and cultural European
spirit. A summary of the divergence between the two ideologies helps in
understanding the opposing conceptions of the Piedmontese ideology and
Italian ideology:

> The major historical inspirations of the Italian ideology expressed
> in Fascism are the Roman spirit, Catholicism, and the Renais-
> sance.... The major historical inspirations of Piedmontese ideol-
> ogy, however, are the revolutions originating in the North: the

Protestant and Puritan Revolution, the Industrial Revolution, the French and American Revolutions.... Overall, it can be said that Italian ideology is a conception of a civilization that *mainly exports its values to Europe and the rest of the world*; the Piedmontese ideology is, on the contrary, a plan of a society that *mainly imports its values from Europe and the rest of the world*. If there is a common trait throughout Piedmontese ideology, it is expressed in the desire for a reform, like the one started by Luther, developed by Calvin, expressed in "individualism," and described by Weber in the transition from Protestant ethics to a capitalist spirit.... The entire Piedmontese ideology ... is united by this ideal of the intellectual and moral, secular and modernist, industrial and social Great Reform. In the eyes of Italian ideology, however, the reform appears as a foreign body, as a breaking from Italy's historical and religious roots, from its traditions, and indeed, its own "nature."[18]

It must be acknowledged that much of the criticism put forth by Piedmontese ideology was correct: Rome's ministerial stagnant politics, welfare, and flaws were nestled in Italian ideology. Piedmontese ideology identifies the primacy of the society in the economy; the Italian spirit views economic dynamics as subordinate to ethical and political demands. The true Italian ideology sees modernization as a way to introduce traditional values such as family, country, and honor to the era of the masses, in an attempt to avoid the secularization of society. But baked into Piedmontese ideology is a necessary acceleration toward the secularization process, and a favoring of the economy and technology.

Vincenzo Cuoco (1770–1823)

While philosophers in France analyzed the effects of the French Revolution and, alongside the official vulgate, created a space for counterrevolutionary thought, Italian philosophers referred these ideas to their own internal political events. This was the case for Vincenzo Cuoco, whose most well-known book,

Historical Essay on the Neapolitan Revolution of 1799, analyzes the Neapolitan revolution:

> Cuoco joined the Republic of '99, and was therefore a Jacobin; however, by 1800, and even more in the 1806 edition and his subsequent writings, he bitterly condemned the mistakes made by Jacobin Neapolitans and by Jacobinism itself, objecting to the utopian revolutionary-enlightenment abstractionism and advocating for the concreteness of popular traditions.[19]

Cuoco's ideas reveal "the unyielding condemnation of utopian Jacobin-Enlightenment abstractionism, which he opposed with the realism of Italian tradition (with clear influence from Machiavelli and Vico) and the political practicality of the Anglo-Saxon tradition (Burke's influence); though he had an elitist conception of society (but not according to the traditional vision of the aristocracy), he was open to social mobility structured on the solid defense of the prerogatives of private property."[20]

The failure of the Neapolitan revolution rose from its attempt to emulate the French Revolution and Enlightenment ideas.   Destroying the traditional and secular customs of the people and the subsequent loss of identity and collective memory also accounted for the Neapolitan revolution's failure. This was at the root of the French Revolution's failure too, of course, because doing so fomented the discontent of the people, resulting in counterrevolutionary movements.

Cuoco's work also pushes for the understanding that every people has its own nature and history, and that customs and forms of government cannot be imposed by force. The Neapolitan and Italian peoples' rejection of the revolution that, unlike what happened in France, never actually achieved *true* revolution, is a testimony to the lack of conviction in profound change. Cuoco was

> the first of our authors... to accuse the French Revolution (and therefore the Italian Jacobin revolution) of doing more harm than good, interrupting the reformist process started by sovereign

legitimists in the decades before the Revolution, deteriorating entire nations into anarchy and revolutionary violence. All in all, according to Cuoco, the French Revolution, as well as that of the Neapolitans, interrupted the true progress of the people that began and was implemented with much more consistency, intelligence, and coherence by the Bourbons of France than those of Naples.[21]

Cuoco insisted upon the protection of private property, the creation of an elite government (a constitutional monarchy), a meritocratic education of the people, and perhaps above all, the condemnation of Jacobinism. He ultimately separated the Italian transformation from the fierce Jacobinism that characterized the French Revolution, and he even took over the Neapolitan revolution that he had initially supported.

Vilfredo Pareto (1848–1923)

An engineer, economist, and sociologist, Pareto was widely known as "the sociologist of the elite." While he had a scientific background, his work also delved into economics, sociology, and classical studies without hesitation. In 1894, he became a political economics professor at the University of Lausanne, dedicating his study to the theory of economic equilibrium.

After abandoning teaching to dedicate more attention to writing *The Mind and Society* (1916), in 1910 he published *Il mito virtuista e la letteratura immorale* and positioned himself against the prevalence of rationality.

He met Benito Mussolini in Switzerland, and his works influenced the future building blocks of the Fascist doctrine. After encouraging Mussolini to carry out the March on Rome through telegram and being subsequently named the Italian representative on the committee for reducing arms at the League of Nations, he died on August 19, 1923, without ever becoming a senator in the "Kingdom." Without going into the technical analysis of his economic thought, attention must be given to his "theory of the elite."

According to Pareto, in every context and social activity, there are people who excel and elevate themselves from the masses, becoming part of the elite.

Social states, therefore, organize themselves into superior and inferior groups, particularly in the political sphere. This "theory of the elite" is coupled with a conservative perspective on government.

Two types of changes happen within the elite: horizontal changes, occurring within the same elite group, and vertical changes, such as the declassification and rise of the masses to the elites. Pareto's political confidence in the elites was expressed in his rejection of universal suffrage; he thought that in an ideal society, the dominant class would be made up of the elites who have a constant and dynamic turnover. When this does not happen, he thought, there is a risk of static equilibrium that leads to subversion—experienced as revolution—capable of generating an entirely new system of government. In other words, the circulation of the elite is essential for the prosperity of the state. Revolution, however, is judged negatively, understood as a setback:

> When Pareto moved into the political sphere, he concluded that the society had an elitist structure, that the masses are incapable of governing themselves, and that the elites (given the law of competition and the subsequent selection of the strongest) are destined to rise and fall ("circulation of the elites"). The people...are always guided by an aristocracy.[22]

Society is to be divided into two social groups: the rulers and the ruled. The rulers make up an elite group, divided between those who hold the power and those who would take it away.

Alfredo Oriani (1852–1909)

Oriani's works, especially *La lotta politica in Italia* and *La rivolta ideale*, offered valuable insights into the Fascist doctrine. In fact, they were so valuable that on April 27, 1924, Mussolini defined the writer as "a precursor" to his movement. Anti-parliamentarianism, nationalism, and anti-socialism, in part, were elements that Mussolini extracted from Oriani's work and made his own.

Today, Alfredo Oriani is remembered by the Fondazione Casa di Oriani that, other than promoting the publication of books and journals, manages the museum-house called the Cardello, where Oriani lived while he was putting together his writings. The Cardello is a historical building named in documents from the fifteenth century, and its construction dates back to the twelfth century. Purchased by his father Luigi in 1855, the building was the family's property until 1978, when it was donated to the Casa Oriani entity. Today, it still houses Oriani's office with more than six hundred volumes in his library.

Oriani did not obtain much success as a poet; in 1878, he declared "I am not and was not a poet, and the most disheartening proof lies in my deservingly forgotten book of verses." As a narrator, however, he left behind a series of publications of undoubted literary value. His first book was an autobiographical novel titled *Memorie inutili*, published by Sonzogno in 1876. The following year, he published *Al di là*, a love story about two women. The book's signed manuscript was found in Mussolini's bag during his escape from Italy. Oriani's third novel, *No*, is rich with literary references and features an anticonformist woman as its protagonist, who rejects the rules and conventions of society only to later become an integral part of its system.

Oriani was also devoted to writing collections of stories. In 1878, he published *Gramigne*, followed by *Quartetto* in 1883, which idealistically marked the end of his first literary season. His second narrative season, which established him as a truly successful author, began with the novel *Il nemico* in 1894, followed by *Gelosia* and *La disfatta* in 1896. However, his most successful narrative was without question *Vortice*, which reveals the pure conception of drama that characterizes much of his writing.

His philosophical ideas, however, are thoroughly articulated in his historical-political books, with the first published in 1886 by Barbera with the title *Matrimonio*, a project originating from a discussion about proposed legislation on divorce. In 1889, he published a collection of essays titled *Fino a Dogali*, and in 1892 in Turin, he financed the publication of *La Lotta politica in Italia. Origini della lotta attuale 476–1887* in nine different books, in which he recounts Italy's history from the fall of the Western Roman

Empire to 1887. The text is written without much research but is studded with thinkers and criticisms that give life to a revisionist history of the Italian political struggle.

Mario Missiroli (1886–1974), a writer, journalist, and editor of important Italian newspapers, described Oriani's most well-known book, *La rivolta ideale*, as one of the most clearly written analyses of modernity. The relationship between Missiroli and Oriani was that of pupil and master. Missiroli was deeply influenced by Oriani, and he often went to the Cardello to read *La rivolta ideale*. As Luciano Simonelli notes in *Mario Missiroli: il più rivoluzionario dei conservatori*:

> He [Missiroli] met, saw, and became a close friend to Alfredo Oriani. The writer and historian had a profound influence on Missiroli, especially pushing him on the road to a critical revision of the myth of the Risorgimento. According to Oriani, he too had done a lot for him, and managed to spread his work despite being rejected by many other editors. In 1909, after the death of Oriani, Missiroli wrote of his friend, "You know how much I loved him. It therefore will not seem like an exaggeration if I tell you that today something inside me died forever that I will never find again. I loved him with the devotion and affection of a spiritual child and I have the profound conviction to have penetrated, if only slightly, that complex soul."[23]

A rediscovery of Oriani during the second half of the twentieth century occurred thanks to Prezzolini, who reprinted *La lotta politica in Italia*, defining it as "the first big nationalist book" capable of defining the "conscience of a great nation." He was previously remembered only for his influence on Fascism; in 1924, Mussolini personally guided the "Cardello March" in honor of his death and worked to publish a collection of his work. Known as the "loner of the Cardello," Oriani was a free spirit, difficultly classified within a precise category.

Gaetano Mosca (1858–1941)

After receiving a law degree in Palermo in 1881, Mosca, Sicilian jurist and political expert, taught constitutional law in Palermo, Rome, Turin, and Milan. Elected deputy in 1909 and serving as a senator from 1919 until Salandra's administration, he was the secretary of state for the colonies and opposed the Fascist state during its rise to power.

In 1884, he published his first book, *Sulla teorica dei governi e sul governo parlamentare*, in which he outlines general guidelines for opposing a democratic government. He also began to develop his oligarchic conception and introduced his theory on the political class: essentially, he believed that a small number of powerful and organized elites govern a large number of powerless and unorganized masses. Mosca's own political participation was consistent with his ideas; he defended the ideals of the middle class, emphasizing the risks and mistakes of the proletariat classes.

In comparing the democratic innovative principle and the principles of the aristocratic conservative, Mosca identified the main dialectic in contemporary history. While the aristocratic principle tends to conserve power in the hands of the same people, the democratic principle is a force against the advantages set forth by inheritance. Mosca understood both principles deeply:

How much more difficult it is to destroy than rebuild... [but] how great is the resistance that is encountered when trying to remove preexisting traditional outlooks from the human mind, even when they no longer live up to the maturity of thought that was reached at one time. How the day comes when the habits and the needs of modern life prevail in such a way, in a city undergoing continuous development and progress, that it makes the existence of the streets, alleyways, and the little ancient houses intolerable and impose their own destruction, just as how in science the moment arrives in which it is necessary to free up the land from ancient doctrines that are no longer in harmony with the present.[24]

Mosca knew that in the past, governing men, owning land, and preserving property required military and political capabilities. But with the rise of modernity, it took (and still only takes) being rich to become powerful. The only consistency between the past and present is that those who get to the highest point in society create a wall to defend their status. In the medieval period, this defense occurred with the construction of a castle that became a bequest for heirs; today, this defense occurs through financial revenue.

The birth of new faiths and ideas and the decadence of old aristocracies allowed for this formation of a new ruling class. Once the rotation at the top of the social ladder was completed, the new classes promptly proceeded in building armor in defense of the acquired status quo.

If in the comparison it is fair to protect the democratic principle over the aristocratic one, the conservative principle must be fixed upon both—because "eliminating the aristocratic principle would bring on the fight for dominance to such a furor as to completely absorb every useful activity for the social body and thus prepare it for paralysis or decline."[25]

Enrico Corradini (1865–1931)

A prominent proponent of Italian nationalism, Enrico Corradini's work presents all the typical elements of conservative thought. After founding and assuming the supervision of the journal *Marzocco* in 1896, he continued his journalistic expertise with the creation of *Il Regno* in 1903 alongside Papini, Pareto, and Prezzolini.

Beginning in 1910, his nationalist stances grew stronger with the foundation of the Italian Nationalist Association, the essay "L'ora di Tripoli," and finally, with his writings in the weekly newspaper *L'idea nazionale*. An intense interventionist, he played a central role in creating nationalist propaganda during the First World War. After being named a senator, Corradini increasingly distanced himself from Fascist stances and became politically marginalized, while continuing to be a prominent member of the Grand Council of Fascism until 1929. His political speeches are collected in the book *Discorsi politici (1902–1923)*, which summarizes his nationalist thought. After passing away in 1931, Luigi Federzoni, president of the Senate of the Kingdom of Italy, remembered him with these words:

> The name Enrico Corradini will live on in history. His admirably unique personality as a writer is ingrained in his political prose, with the most incise characteristics of the best of the Tuscan tradition, with a pure dialectic profile and vivid expressive clarity. His prose will never perish. And, as it takes on more importance and beauty from a historical perspective, the Fascist revolution, elevated and pure, the man of thought and battle who was able to foresee and prepare the renewal of the nation from the distant eve, will shine.[26]

Corradini invoked Italy's need for a colonial policy, capable of thwarting plutocratic nations like France and Germany. In this context, the spiritual and material guidance of the aristocracy, made up of the best men, is indispensable.

Alfredo Rocco (1875–1935)

A conservative nationalist, Alfred Rocco played a primary role in the Fascist regime. Concerned with the disposition of the masses in Italy, he thought about a political plan with a modernized awareness. As a nationalist, he viewed liberalism disapprovingly, especially criticizing individualism and socialism—the biggest enemy of nationalism—which rejected moral and national values in favor of individualist selfishness, for the sole purpose of gaining economic and material wealth. Despite its goal, socialism, Rocco believed, does not necessarily lead to economic wealth; this is because a socialist economic revolution, while favoring a slight increase in wages for workers, inevitably leads to a worsening of conditions for small entrepreneurs and landowners.

Rocco perceived the nation as an "organic body." Unlike people, nations last for hundreds and thousands of years, and therefore must act as a glue and aggregate for citizens. The weakening of the state lies in the individualist and anti-statist spirit. Rocco wrote:

In perceiving society as a sum of equal individuals, like a shapeless and uniform grey mass, liberalism, since its appearance as a political practice, destroyed the extremely ancient professional organizations, the guilds of art and trade, that, arising separately from the state, were absorbed by it, disciplined and made their own.... The state must go back to its old tradition that was interrupted by the triumph of liberal ideology, and treat modern labor unions exactly as it treated medieval guilds. It must absorb them and make them its organs. In order to obtain this result, it is not enough to simply acknowledge it. It requires a much deeper transformation. It requires proclaiming the mandatory nature of trade unions on one hand, and on the other hand resolutely putting them under the control of the state.[27]

In 1925, Rocco became the minister of justice and worked to reform the Fascist state, identifying Fascism as the only sustainable alternative to democracy and liberalism. He compared the sovereignty of the people, as in a democracy, to that of organized sovereignty of the state. It would be the state's duty to carry out social justice to the social classes, with corporatism as the most suitable tool to this end.

Ardengo Soffici (1879–1964)

In *Autoritratto d'artista italiano nel quadro del suo tempo*, published in four volumes between 1951 and 1955 (*L'uva e la croce*, *Passi tra le rovine*, *Il salto vitale*, and *Fine di un mondo*), Soffici wrote his autobiography up to 1915, recounting the history of Italy at the time over his thirty-five years of life. He wanted to be the creator of a cultural and artistic renewal in support of Fascism. His cultural education was primarily oriented around the study of art and partly around literature. After moving to Paris in 1900, he began working as an illustrator for different magazines and met Picasso, Guillaume Apollinaire, and Max Jacob. Returning to Italy in 1907, he developed his profile as a writer, writing art critiques for *Leonardo*. In the same period, he became close friends with Prezzolini, and the following year, when Papini and Prezzolini founded *La Voce*, Soffici designed the front page and curated the art columns.

In 1911, after visiting a Futurist exhibit in Milan, he wrote a critical article about it in *La Voce*, which provoked a violent reaction from Futurists. In Florence, at the Caffè Giubbe Rosse, the Futurist painter Boccioni slapped Soffici, provoking a furious brawl that continued the following night at the Santa Maria Novella train station. Despite this violent confrontation, Soffici founded the literary magazine *Lacerba* with Papini in January 1913, thanks to Aldo Palazzeschi's mediation. It aligned with Futurist positions, and Soffici promoted the first Futurist exhibit in Florence. In 1914, with Papini's hand, he also published *L'almanacco purgativo*, which promoted the most noteworthy works of Futurism. His romance with Marinetti's Futurist movement, however, was short-lived, and at the end of the same year another breakup occurred, this time proving permanent.

Soffici's participation in the war was distinguishing, and he received military decoration. These experiences in battle, so disabling for so many, did not prevent him from continuing his editorial work. His political views also remained consistent. As a signatory of the Manifesto of the Fascist Intellectuals, he remained faithful to Mussolini for the entire duration of the regime, even adhering to the Republic of Salò. After the war, he withdrew from the public scene until his death in 1964.

Giovanni Papini (1881–1956)

Understanding Giovanni Papini's intellectual and cultural journey requires going back to his childhood, which he spent reading the books in his grandfather's library. After receiving a teaching degree, he became a librarian and deepened his study even further. Dedicating his time to writing, he initially collaborated with some literary Florentine magazines, and later engaged firsthand in the publication and design of Italian magazines. In 1903, he was one of the founders of *Leonardo* along with Prezzolini, Vailati, and Calderoni, and consequentially he became the editor in chief of *Il Regno*, directed by

Corradini. He simultaneously spent time writing books, and in 1906 he published *Il crepuscolo dei filosofi*, in which he declared the death of philosophy.
The following year, he published *Il tragico quotidiano* and closed *Leonardo*
due to differences between the different collaborators.

Papini proved to be an extraordinary entertainer and founder of literary
magazines destined to revolutionize the cultural panorama of the time. His
ideas were characterized by radical anti-conformism and a strong incitement
of anti-Christian sentiments. In the early years of the twentieth century he
published *The Memoirs of God*, which led to a trial for contempt of religion.
His polemical spirit brought him to support Futurism, and he justified this
choice in *L'esperienza futurista*, *1913–1914*. However, it was with his book
Stoncature in 1916 that his polemical spirit reached its peak, with his criticism
of the works of Boccaccio, Croce, Gentile, Goethe, and Shakespeare. Although
it was never completed, his 1923 publication *Dizionario dell'omo salvatico*,
written with Domenico Giulotti, also caused a stir due to Papini's stances
against Protestants, secularism, Jews, and democracy.

The year 1913 was important for Papini. In January, the first edition of
Lacerba was published, the same year in which he published *The Failure*, an
autobiography written at just thirty years of age, demonstrating his extraordinary maturity and ambition. In 1914, at the outbreak of the First World War,
he became a convinced interventionist, publishing an article in *Lacerba* on
October 1 with the provoking title "Amiamo la Guerra" ("We love war").
Afterwards, however, he changed his position and defined the war as "an
immense waste of blood and lives." On February 14, 1915, his article in *Lacerba* titled "Futurismo e Marinetti" marked his official split from the Futurists.

At various times in his life, Papini had second thoughts about his positions,
but his most radical change in opinion was his conversion to Christianity,
which coincided with his publication *The Story of Christ*. The book, which
achieved so much success that the Università del Sacro Cuore offered him the
professorship of Italian literature (which he refused), recounts the life of Jesus
based on what was told both in the canonical Gospels and in the Apocrypha.
In 1929 he published a biography on Saint Augustine. He became a Franciscan
tertiary in 1943. Many of his publications after the war are animated by

Catholic sentiments, expressed most poignantly in *Letters of Pope Celestine VI to All Mankind* and *The Devil*.

During his final years, Papini suffered a degenerative disease, losing the use of his legs, arms, and finally, his ability to speak. This, however, did not stop him from completing, with the help of his nephew, the posthumously published book *Giudizio universale. La seconda nascita* (1958), which traces his life, focusing on his conversion and expressing his regret for supporting interventionism during the war.

Giuseppe Prezzolini (1882–1982)

Born in Perugia in 1882 to a family from Siena, Prezzolini moved to Tuscany as a child and was shaped by his father's library. After abandoning his high school studies, he dedicated his time to cultural activities at a young age. Early on, he rejected the welfare state and centralized control due to his distrust of the state, placing his trust in the tried-and-true traditions of hierarchy, the time-tested values that govern society.

While Papini published his autobiography, *The Failure*, at just thirty years old, Prezzolini published his own autobiography early in 1954, at the invitation of Leo Longanesi, titled *L'italiano inutile*. It was not premature from a personal point of view, as Prezzolini was sixty-two years old, but rather from an experiential point of view, considering the events and the journey that had yet to unfold. But in 1954, Prezzolini already considered himself to be in a descending phase of life, and therefore decided to collect his thoughts, all of which were characterized by strong pessimism and a deep relationship with twentieth-century Italian culture.

Through his involvement with *La Voce*, he became one of the leading figures of Italian culture. He believed culture did not only belong to a purely spiritual sphere, but also must be used as a national tool. In order to cover the costs of the journal, he put his own paternal inheritance toward operating costs. The first edition was published on December 20, 1908; in the subsequent edition, published December 27, in an article titled "La nostra promessa," Prezzolini summarized the methodical intent of the journal:

We believe that Italy needs more character, sincerity, open-mindedness and seriousness than intelligence and spirit. A brain is not
lacking, but the sin lies in that it is used for frivolous, vulgar, and
low ends: for the love of fame and not honor, for the torment of
profit and luxury and not existence, for voluptuous fraud and not
to nourish the mind. We strongly feel the ethical code of intellectual life, and it sickens us to see the misery and distress and the
nauseating bustling that is done on behalf of the spirit.[28]

The ambition of *La Voce* was to carry out a plan for Italy's future by
affirming the rebirth of the country through a culture that would broaden
minds and be capable of giving life to a new ruling and political class. The
first issue of the journal was published when Prezzolini was twenty-six years
old; by then, he was already the author of several books, as well as studies on
modernism and unionism, and his name circulated in Italian cultural spheres
as one of the most promising young intellectuals. *La Voce* was destined to go
down in the history of journalism and Italian publishing as a cutting-edge
publication in both content and form:

For years, this journal meticulously analyzed the traits of Italian society (school, the south, public administration, localism, university,
political parties, the economy, etc.), and through these observations
it accumulated a wealth of ideas as well as a series of suggestions on
how to direct change. Its analyses delved into different spheres and
someone was assembling them into a more political project.[29]

"Our aspiration is to launch conservatives forward, to make them reformers, the authentic modernizers," Prezzolini wrote.[30] Prezzolini's main points
of reference for conservatism were Gaetano Mosca, Vilfredo Pareto, and
Alfredo Oriani:

The discovery of Oriani ended up becoming one of the dominant
themes of *La Voce*—indeed, this writer became the means through

which the so-called "myth of the Italian revolution" was defined. For young adults of *La Voce*, he was the prophet of the new Italy, "sacred to the new dawn," the attempt to connect the heroic Risorgimento to the expectations of the new century. In his greatest work, *La lotta politica in Italia* (1892), Oriani traces the "mission" of Italy: completing the unity between Trento and Trieste, the hegemony on the Adriatic coast in order to recover the dominion of Venice and participating in colonial expansion in competition with other countries.... This was the "first big nationalist book" for Prezzolini, and "Oriani was the most original source of the awaking of Italian nationalism." The spread of his writings was taken on as a mission of *La Voce*, and a year after his death in 1909, Prezzolini's spiritual testament was published, titled *La rivolta ideale*—the synthesis of his ideas, from the tracing of the myths of the nation to spiritualistic criticism of industrialism.[31]

The journal came to serve as a melting pot of heresies in which different schools of thought could have a space: "Prezzolini's aspiration for another Italy, a greater Italy, fueled by the living current of a *new culture*, enlivened and enriched both Fascism and anti-Fascism to its highest level."[32]

Prezzolini also had a precise vision of the role of the intellectual in society:

He collected the most fertile tensions that crossed his era and felt the moral and civil responsibility of his ideas.... Prezzolini outlined an intellectual who believed in the relationship of continuity between culture and politics; and thus rejected the absolute distinction of those who would like to relegate culture to the classrooms and libraries and leave politics to the opportunism of the day. He also rejected the stances of those who would like to overlap culture and politics to the point of flattening each other. In this sense, the Prezzolini intellectual is far from both the Croce intellectual and the Gramsci intellectual (and in many ways the

Gentile intellectual).... [Prezzolini] is perhaps the only important
Italian intellectual who openly and knowingly defined himself as
"conservative": and yet, his work and his presence in Italian culture and in civil society, especially in the living crucible of the
first twenty years of our century, had an undeniable revolutionary-conservative influence.[33]

Following his participation in the first world conflict, for which he was
awarded the War Merit Cross, he published *Codice della vita italiana* in 1921,
in which he exposes the vices and virtues of Italians, which emerged with particular vehemence during the war. In 1923, he made his first trip to the United
States, and subsequently moved to New York where he became an Italian professor at Columbia University and took over the direction of Casa Italiana:

For Prezzolini, America not only represented the place that best
welcomed him... but also gave a certain confirmation of his ideas.
The national and political affairs of the United States were a viat-
icum to his conservatism, based on intrinsic pessimism, on the
disillusioned understanding of the true essence of human nature.
He stood behind his conviction that only conservation, understood as a reference to the principles that exist in the history of
every people, could be the antidote to the false myths of utopias.[34]

During the years he spent in the United States, Prezzolini delved into and
studied American society and further developed his conservative ideas. The
central point of his observations was the middle class, the social class to which
conservatism usually addresses itself. He noted their abandonment of sound
conservative principles in favor of progressivism, thus creating a cultural concession before a political or electoral concession.

His opinions on Italy are expressed in *The Legacy of Italy*, in which he
compares the Italian State, made up of undefined structures initially linked
to a dictatorship and then to an unstable democracy, to the glorious history
of Italian civilization.

With all this in mind—the great history of European conservatism and the seeming aimlessness of the middle-class masses—Prezzolini decided to dedicate his time to writing *Manifesto dei conservatori*:

> During those years, in which leftist, Marxist cultural hegemony reached the maximum degree of penetration, it was unpopular to call yourself conservative—it was equivalent to being assimilated to a reactionary, if not a Fascist. In defiance of colloquial speech that made the term conservative a "disreputable" word, Giuseppe Prezzolini accepted an invitation from the publisher Rusconi to outline the theoretical principles of being conservative in an essay…. Defining himself and reassessing the term "conservative" was an anti-conformist challenge, which Prezzolini completed at almost ninety years old. The overwhelming majority of Italian intellectuals, meanwhile, had let themselves be disciplined by the PCI (Italian Communist Party). In publishing *Manifesto dei conservatori*, Prezzolini did not limit himself to writing an essay similar to many others he had written, but rather offered a tool to those who at the time were searching for a political, and especially cultural, identity.[35]

In order to create a right-wing culture, Prezzolini stressed the importance of keeping in contact with reality—he himself took to demolishing the paper castles of madmen and demagogues. He was deeply influenced by Machiavelli's work and considered *The Prince* essential to understanding modern society. He thus decided to write a biography dedicated to the Florentine writer, *Vita di Nicolò Machiavelli fiorentino*, which quickly became his most read and most popular book.

Manifesto dei conservatori *by Giuseppe Prezzolini*

From a linguistic point of view, the term "conservative" belongs to an Indo-European lineage. Prezzolini traces its first historical use back to when it referred to a servant who, observing the village and the flock, was sure that by safely conserving it, no enemy or thief could inflict damage upon it. In the introduction of *Manifesto dei conservatori*, Gennaro Sangiuliano defines Prezzolini as "the only prominent interpreter of modern conservatism, which, in Italy, contrary to the other great Western democracies, struggled to take root because of complex historical reasons."[36] According to Prezzolini, *conservation* is a state of mind that "goes beyond religions, society, and families. It can be found anywhere. It is common to many nations."[37]

The instinct of conservation originates from nature; this is because "the universal rule of life is therefore not evolution; it is conservation. Conservation is the rule; change is the exception; or rather, biologists consider it an error."[38] From a philosophical point of view, the foundation of conservatism is *being*, not *becoming*: "stability, permanence, continuity, are more important than the revolution, than interruption, than transformation."[39]

The "conservation of history" is central to Prezzolini's manifesto. He dedicates a whole chapter to this idea, which begins with the counterrevolutionaries during both the French Revolution and the revolution in Naples in 1799. The counterrevolutionaries were the first conservatives, he writes, because in the face of the upheavals in society, they defended the established order with the protection of secular institutions.

Although united by some universal ideas, conservatives change objectives according to the historical period. This, writes Prezzolini, is not a bad thing:

> Every county has conservatives who want to conserve different situations and properties and oppose different movements and revolutions. A French conservative gladly goes back in his mind to a time before the French Revolution; but how could an American conservative propose the United States subject to the domination of Her Majesty of England? No Italian conservative would propose the restitution of Lombardo-Veneto to Austria and the extension of Vatican City to the territory of the church states before 1860. There were those who called themselves Bourbon, like Salvatore Di Giacomo. But he did it to offend, as a joke, for melancholy and for aestheticism. The writer Acton defended the

Bourbon Kingdom, and he did it well; but I believe that no one, not even him, thought it possible for them to return to the throne.⁴⁰

The main difference between conservatives and liberals is their perception of change, which conservatives regard with suspicion and those on the Left—whom Prezzolini defined as "radicals"—regard with trust. Conservative thought is firmly established in history, originating from events that already happened—unlike radical thought that wants to change institutions with no traditional values for a foundation.

In the fifth chapter of Prezzolini's *Manifesto*, he lists the "fifty-three principles of conservative thought," a summation of the feelings of the "true conservative":

> The conservative looks to the tradition of the homeland. He wants to "maintain, slowly transform"; he is aware of duties and bases his claims on "expertise and experience"; he uses realism and the "value of facts" as a method. The differences are not just cultural— they are marked by the economy, between "individual recommended savings" and "mandatory state assistance," between "small property" and "big companies." In some cases, the differences are so clear they almost have an anthropological trait: conservatives like books more than television; conservatives like classical music instead of jazz, a selective school instead of mass schools, etc.⁴¹

The second part of the book, titled "How I became conservative (confessions of a child of the century)," is mostly autobiographical. Prezzolini retraces the main phases of his life, explaining to the reader how he grew closer to conservative thought:

> The book *The Origins of Contemporary France* by Hippolyte Taine was the first serious book that opened the door for me to criticize my society—corrupted by humanitarianism, the crudeness of the

masses, and the naivety of "positivists" (aligned with socialists), the worthy heirs of the abstractions of the Enlightenment.[42]

He believed conservatives have a pessimistic calling: "the fruitless efforts that mankind has made for centuries in order to remedy his struggling condition against nature, against his peers and against himself are fundamental reasons for distrusting innovation and risks of rapid and rationalistic upheavals," he wrote.[43] But it is also important to point out that conservatives do not want to conserve all that the society in which they live has to offer them; rather only a few prerogatives characterize their thought: "Always fighting for the defense of family, the state, the army, property, language, and all the institutions or customs that regard the reality, the stability, and the legacy of the fundamental traits of their own society."[44]

Conservatism's main goal is exasperating change. "The charm of innovation is powerful for men, especially when they are young or inexperienced.... Fighting against it is one of the most difficult tasks. It is a commitment. The merit of a conservative is just as great," Prezzolini believed.[45] Conservatives must be aware of the sacrifices and tragedies that renunciations and radical change can bring. So too must they understand the fragility of the order established after years of struggle and war. Therefore, before approving innovations, they must take the time to evaluate the pros and cons.

In order to avoid upheaval of the norms that govern society, a strong sovereign state that is not influenced by foreign powers and is not identified with the church is necessary. Concerning religion, Prezzolini's stance stands apart from other conservative thinkers much more in favor of the church's interference in state affairs:

> A conservative willingly recognizes the church's role in upholding the conscience of individuals at peace with themselves and thus in respecting the obligations that they take on; however, Prezzolini does not tolerate the church dictating law in the domain of the state, or even suggesting the law to part of its own citizens; and he

is increasingly suspect of any religious organization that would compete with or split the powers of the state.[46]

The *Manifesto dei conservatori* concludes with Prezzolini's assumption that "today is the time of conservation"; he explains the reasons to justify a conservative movement in the current moment. Prezzolini believed that, in a society such as that of the modern era, characterized by a "spread of foolishness," the best road was, as Machiavelli suggested, a "return to ancient principles":

> The government is powerless, religion uncertain of itself, bureaucracy corrupt and inefficient, the army a ghost, the youth rebellious, writers alienated, art faded, social classes divided, political parties atomized. Never has the world seen such a carefree, desperate, excited people. The radio and television encourage its manias.[47]

The solution must be a strong conservative movement, which, more than forty years after Prezzolini's words were written, is still lacking in Italy.

Panfilo Gentile (1889–1971)

An anti-Fascist pupil of Mosca and Pareto, Panfilo Gentile was refused by the anti-Fascist military because of his stances expressed in the books *Polemica contro il mio tempo*, *Opinioni sgradevoli*, and *Democrazie mafiose*. As a collaborator with the main Italian newspapers, he was a prolific author who denounced the distorted dynamics of democracy, including the selection of an unprepared ruling class. For this reason specifically, he supported the need of a presidential republic in Italy.

Under the pseudonym Averroè, he repeatedly wrote in favor of the free market with interventions similar to those affirmed by liberal thinkers such as Friedrich von Hayek and Luigi Einaudi. A complete analysis of his work, however, reveals a distinctly conservative tone. In the new edition of his most important book, *Democrazie mafiose*, published by Ponte alle Grazie, the editor Gianfranco De Turris underscores how Gentile was "completely disenchanted with the utopias of the modern and contemporary word, utopias which soon became untouchable taboos: democracy, the people, universal suffrage, peace, equality."[48]

Throughout his work, Gentile repeatedly attacked progressives for demolishing historicism. Paolo Granzotto, in an article titled "Panfilo Gentile. L'eresia liberale," wrote:

> [Gentile attacked] the belief that what comes later is always better than what came before and that over time we continuously move toward greater happiness and greater justice... There is no such thing as internal fate or an external mechanism that inevitably determines the historical course of humanity. Everything is conditioned by a network of natural, anthropological, ethnic, physiological, and cultural data that together represents environmental solicitation; there is always a plurality of possible replicas, and the replica depends exclusively on the deep nature of the subject and his intelligence, which always introduces an arbitrary and unpredictable element to human facts.[49]

His opposition to an electoral system with universal suffrage and his distaste for the birth of metropolises and large urban conglomerates marked his conservatism. These systems and metropolises, along with the loss of traditional values, led, he said, to the fall of healthy norms and the rise of a toxic moral relativism.

Panfilo Gentile accused the bourgeoisie of abandoning small towns for metropolises. They had become, he believed, an amorphous mass of people with petty interests. He even held the intellectuals of the time in contempt:

> Apart from a few exceptions, [the intellectuals] are almost all *ratés*, amateurs, or insider subordinates of culture. If they were truly intellectuals, they would not feel the need to show off their status

so insistently. No one wishes to pass as noble as much as someone who is not. Therefore, those who neither by right of nature nor by consecutive works of brilliance can legitimately carry this title greatly care about passing for intellectuals. However, every literary, journalistic, cinematographic nobody that interlopes in the cultural club petulantly claims this title.[50]

Giovanni Ansaldo (1895–1969)

Coming from one of the most important bourgeois families in Genoa, Giovanni Ansaldo began his journalistic endeavors with progressive and socialist publications, writing for *L'Unità* and, after serving on the battlefront, the Genoese newspaper *Il Lavoro*, for which he became the leading editor. During this time, he was among the contributors of the Manifesto of the Anti-Fascist Intellectuals and was distinguished for his anti-Fascist stances. He was arrested in Como and accused of anti-Fascism, for which he was sentenced to confinement in Lipari. Eventually he was granted pardon under the condition that he was prohibited from writing articles—he thus chose to write under the pseudonym "Stella nera."

In the early 1930s, his viewpoints began to change after his collaboration with Longanesi and *L'Italiano*. He drew closer to Fascism and obtained increasingly prestigious positions. Ansaldo's relationship with Longanesi played a central role in his life and led him to work with *Il Libraio* and with *Il Borghese* in 1950, the same year in which he was called to head the newspaper Il *Mattino*.

In an article with the self-explanatory title "Ansaldo, un eretico conservatore," taken from a depiction written by Henry Furst in the *New York Times* Book Review, Francesco Perfetti explains the conservative qualities of Ansaldo's writings:

> Ansaldo had no modern pretense. His writing was therefore filled with fairness, grace, tragedy, and curial robes, resembling the eighteenth century more than the nineteenth century. He believed in common sense, tradition, in the value of humanism, and all that is in great decline today.[51]

Ansaldo was a man of the nineteenth century not just in writing, but in behavior. It was not by chance that in 1947 he published, along with Longanesi under the pseudonym Willy Farnese, *The Real Gentleman: A Guide to Beautiful Manners*.

Leo Longanesi (1905–1957)

Labeling an eclectic, volcanic, independent figure like Leo Longanesi is a difficult task that risks resulting in error. But classifying the Romagnolo genius as a conservative is without a doubt a correct affirmation. Longanesi defined himself as such in one of his most famous aphorisms: "I am a conservative in a country with nothing left to conserve."

His entire cultural journey was characterized by a commonly conservative sentiment: from the nostalgia of youth, the longing for a past to which one cannot return, represented by nineteenth-century bourgeoisie regret, with which Longanesi had a love-hate relationship.

That feeling of nostalgia characterized Longanesi's life, especially after the war and in the years following. It is erroneously interpreted as nostalgia for Fascism; it was a nostalgia for his lost youth, the Bolognese outings, and, even before that, his childhood in Romagna. When he no longer recognized the city where he grew up, he wrote, "Every memory is gone: the streets and the colors, sounds and the voices did not recall those of the past.... 'Something happened here,' I tell myself, but I cannot understand what it is."[52]

Longanesi did not think highly of his bourgeois contemporaries, most of whom did not share his spiritual nostalgia. In 1933, Longanesi compared the contemporary bourgeois to the bourgeois of the nineteenth century:

> The myth of an economic, hardworking, honest, and conservative bourgeois is now in opposition to that of one who is romantic and confused, determined to make progress, in favor of ambiguous novelty, increasingly mediocre and false. Full of needs and lacking in ability, the new middle class insists on following the rhetoric of affluence and decorum that it did not earn: athletic and distracted,

politically zealous, skeptical and unscrupulous, renouncing more and more of its duties and merits.[53]

The book that most accurately represents his conservative sentiment is *The Old Aunts Will Save Us*. Published in 1953, he describes the disorder created by democracy and modernity in Italian homes. He writes:

> We thought we would find vestals of the great myths that govern the state in the old aunts: duty, honor, trust in the homeland, love of something done well, contempt for all that is improvised, fake, and artificial; we thought we would track down, in the stubborn instinct to save, a high moral sense of property, the abstract defense of a civil order to which an adequate economic strength no longer corresponded. We believed we would find the secular guardians of a decorum that one finds in the pride of his own sacrifice of historical tradition to contrast with the spiteful classes of the rich and proletariat. We identified the life of the state in those old spinsters, the last Amazonian ideals, in a corrupted and foolish society without ideals.[54]

The old aunts represented at last a stronghold of defense of the values of the nineteenth-century bourgeoisie that Longanesi held dear, the last opportunity to save Italy from its moral and social drifting. Two years after its publication, Longanesi asked the basic question of the book: "*Ci salveranno le vecchie zie dall'incalzante rovina che ci minaccia?*" ("Will the old aunts save us from the pressing ruin that threatens us? Will they allow pessimism or realism to take the upper hand?") He wrote:

> Two years went by quickly, and Communism did not conquer the state. Something worse, and possibly irreparable, happened; and that is that the aunts gave in, they led the way for the nephews, the radio, the TV, the refrigerator, Marlon Brando, canned milk, the temporary, for the easy, the futile, the subdued; even they fell into

288 THE HISTORY OF EUROPEAN CONSERVATIVE THOUGHT

the great misunderstanding of progressivism that swept through
the bourgeoisie: a broad misunderstanding, in which everything
blends together, everything gets confused, everything breaks down
in that old cowardice, the tired national habit of conformism.[55]

Giovanni Volpe (1906–1984)

Giovanni Volpe, the son of the historian Gioacchino Volpe, also publicized conservative thought through his work as an editor at his namesake
publishing house. Born in 1906 in Santarcangelo di Romagna, a picturesque
town, he graduated with a degree in engineering and began to cultivate his
cultural and philosophical studies, with a marked inclination toward right-
wing culture. In 1962, he founded the publishing house alongside the Fondazione Gioacchino Volpe to organize events, as well as two journals: *La Torre*
and *Intervento*. La Volpe quickly became a true point of reference in the conservative arena, publishing books by Ramiro de Maeztu, Francisco Elias de
Tejada, Panfilo Gentile, Ernst Jünger, Charles Maurras, Thomas Molnar, and
others. As Annalisa Terranova notes in *Il Secolo d'Italia*, the cultural blanket
of silence that fell over the public discourse of Volpe's time did not preclude
his extraordinary collection of cultural work:

> Volpe also understood how to appreciate young intellectual
> energy that revolved in the cultural setting of the time (recalling,
> among others, Maurizio Cabona, Gennaro Malgieri, Marcello
> Veneziani, Stenio Solinas, Gianfranco De Turris and Adriano
> Romualdo), playing a dual role, especially during the difficult
> and bleak years of the seventies, of distributing important texts
> of right-wing culture and discovering talents well-versed in cul-
> tural elaboration.
> [...] Especially with the *L'Architrave* series, Volpe offered a
> useful counter-information tool at a time when the young pan-
> theon was greatly influenced by Marxism. The series consisted of
> short essays that introduced an anthology of scholars worth

rediscovering: from Sombart to Ortega y Gasset, from de Maistre to Michels. "Not only was he the most important anti-conformist, right-wing editor in Italy after the war," Gennaro Malgieri emphasizes, "but he was also an extraordinary cultural organizer who focused on organizing seminars every summer in Monteleone in Romagna, especially for young intellectuals... the most important non-progressive scholars from around the world would meet every spring."[56]

Indro Montanelli (1909–2001)

The most important journalistic Italian writings of the twentieth century were characterized by an independence of opinion, which allowed Montanelli to be a free thinker with an undeniable conservative spirit. The anarchist-conservative label fits him perfectly. It is not surprising that the book of interviews accomplished with Marcello Staglieno is titled *The Passions of an Anarcho-Conservative*. Montanelli could also be defined as a "revolutionary conservative":

> Montanelli defined himself as "an anarchist in my own way": "I do not want to undermine the state, I believe in law and order" but "I am deeply and irresistibly allergic to power." A bourgeois anarchist or revolutionary conservative are the oxymorons that define the great Italian journalist.[57]

Sandro Gerbi and Raffaele Liucci published an attentive, two-volume biography, the second of which is titled *Montanelli, the Bourgeois Anarchist* and portrays Montanelli as "conservative, but also libertarian and anti-clerical." His many journalist "pupils" included Giancarlo Mazzuca, the ex-editor of *Il Resto del Carlino*, who dedicated a book of recollections to his mentor titled *Indro Montanelli: A Foreigner at Home*.

In response to a left-leaning reader who said that she found Montanelli's newspaper to be fanatical, he wrote:

In speaking about the "spirit of the times," you hit the nail on the head, as the times indeed have a spirit that changes with the times. And I believe I interpret our time correctly, that it is going into oblivion. I write without any resentment of all the insults (unfortunately, not only verbal ones) that I brought upon myself when the spirit of the times forced me to displease you and for you to despise me. Now, I know I fought for a dream. Just open your eyes and see how I accomplished my Right. But you as well, my dear, have fought for a dream. Do not regret it, just as I do not regret it. We are both on the right side of the issue: that of the losers.[58]

Montanelli expressed his conception of the political Right in relation to *La Voce*:

We wanted to create, as men of the Right, a right-wing daily news-paper that was truly free, anchored to its historical values: the spirit of service (real, silent and practiced), the sense of the state, the strict codes of conduct.... In other words, we want to be the organ of the Right that today is outraged by the abuse that the current plagiarists make of it. This faithful Right exists in Italy. However, it is an elite too small to cultivate a newspaper. And thus, the original flaw that the *Voce* made, as Michele Serra wrote, is that it was the wrong, or rather a "foreign," newspaper, even though it was by Italians for Italians.[59]

While Montanelli's views were those of a revolutionary and Jacobin Fascist, his young age being an accomplice to his extremism, the end of the regime brought out his conservative spirit, though the anarchist component of his personality remained unchanged. While a young Montanelli was shaped by the pages of Ricci's *L'Universale*, his work with *Omnibus*, *Il Borghese*, and Longanesi's influence prepared him for the big jump. In fact, his decision to detach from Fascism and distance himself from his philosophical past likened him to another major anarchist-conservative of the twentieth century, Ernst Jünger:

> As sons of the passions of the twentieth century, at a certain point, and at the right time, both writers managed to "distance themselves" from the storms in which they themselves had participated and helped shape. The German writer, coming to write the metaphorical novel against totalitarian degeneration, *On the Marble Cliffs*, participated in the failed *putsch* against Hitler and took refuge, through literature and entomology, in aristocratic isolation. The Italian writer, distancing himself from the passions of the epoch, entangled himself in "pessimism of reason" as a skeptic...and experienced journalism as detached narration. They both chose the "life of an anarchist," of one who is convinced that "carefully observing" is more important than "unwittingly participating."[60]

The will to create a space where irregular and anti-conformist thinkers could express themselves emerged in the editorial line of two newspapers founded by Montanelli: on June 25, 1974, he created *Il Giornale*, founded against historical compromise and political correctness. Twenty years later, on March 22, 1994, the first edition of *La Voce* was published.

Ennio Flaiano (1910–1972)

Ennio Flaiano was also an integral part of the conservative arena. He specialized in literary writings; his fulminant aphorisms—revealing Leo Longanesi's influence—are well-known. Flaiano worked with *Omnibus*, and later, after Fascists closed the magazine, he began working with *Oggi*, where he wrote about the cinema. He then became the editor of *Il Mondo*, where he wrote the Night Diary column (which would later be published in a book by Bompiani in 1956).

Pascal Schembri published a biography of Flaiano titled *A Martian in Italy* with a preface by Walter Pedulla—who, when interviewed by Adnkronos, stated:

> When I am asked to identify an exemplary text by Flaiano, I provide the example of *A Martian in Italy*, a long story (or short novel) that became a myth of our time, as well as a proverb. It tells of a people obsessed with the new at all costs, because the old is boring. The moral of the story is this: in Italy, extraordinary novelty is pleasing, but it does not last long, as with every toy.[61]

Although published posthumously, the book that most evidently reveals Flaiano's conservatism is *The Solitude of the Satyr*, in which the author walks through the streets of Rome while determining the deterioration of the city through a collection of stories, memories, and thoughts. Structured in three parts, the work is punctuated with references to a changing society with which Flaiano increasingly struggles to identify:

> Perhaps I was not from this era. I am not from this era, perhaps I belong to another world; I feel more at peace when I read Giovenale, Marziale, Catullo. It is likely that I am an ancient Roman who still lives here, forgotten by history, in order to write things that others have written much better than me.[62]

The conviction that one is not "from this era"; the longing for a world forgotten, a culture forsaken, a history lost; and the call to remind one's contemporaries of all that has been inherited: these are the spiritual markers of every true conservative.

Notes

Chapter One: Conservatism: Interpretations, Ideas, and Principles

1. *Oxford English Reference Dictionary*, 2nd ed. (New York: Oxford University Press, 1996).
2. Gennaro Malgieri, ed. *Conservatori: Da Edmund Burke a Russell Kirk* (Milan: Il Minotauro, 2006).
3. Malgieri, ed., *Conservatori*, 9. Trans. Rachel Stone.
4. Robert Nisbet, *Conservatism: Dream and Reality* (Soveria Mannelli: Rubbettino, 2012). Trans. Rachel Stone.
5. Giuseppe A. Balistreri, *Filosofia della Konservative Revolution: Arthur Moeller van den Bruck* (Milan: Lampi di Stampa, 2004), 351. Trans. Rachel Stone.
6. Carlo Mongardini and Maria Luisa Maniscalco, *Il pensiero conservatore. Interpretazioni, giustificazioni e critiche* (Milan: FrancoAngeli, 1999), 15. Trans. Rachel Stone.
7. Mongardini and Maniscalco, *Il pensiero conservatore*, 20. Trans. Rachel Stone.
8. Gennaro Malgieri, *Conservatori europei del Novecento. Un'antologia* (Rome: Pagine, 2014), 49. Trans. Rachel Stone.
9. Roger Scruton, *How to Be a Conservative* (London: Bloomsbury Publishing, 2014), e-book.
10. Scruton, *How to Be a Conservative*, 107.
11. Roger Scruton, *How to Be a Conservative*. Trans. from Italian edition by Rachel Stone.
12. Scruton, *How to Be a Conservative*, 235.
13. Gerd-Klaus Kaltenbrunner, *La sfida dei conservatori* (Rome: Volpe, 1977), 173. Trans. Rachel Stone.
14. Robert Nisbet, *Conservatism: Dream and Reality* (Minneapolis: University of Minnesota Press, 1986), 1–2.
15. Albrecht Jünger, *Rivarol. Massime di un conservatore* (Milan: Guanda, 1992), 53. Trans. Rachel Stone.
16. Junger, *Rivarol.*
17. A. Mohler, "Perchè non conservatore?" *La Destra* 3, 1972. Trans. Rachel Stone.
18. Robert Nisbet, "The Dilemma of Conservatives in a Populist Society," *Policy Review*, Spring 1978, 91–104.
19. Robert Nisbet, *Conservatism: Dream and Reality* (Minneapolis: University of Minnesota Press, 1986).
20. Nisbet, *Conservatism: Dream and Reality*, vii.
21. Ibid.

22. Marco Respinti and Russell Kirk, "Dove vanno gli Stati Uniti? La politica estera nordamericana e il 'Nuovo Ordine Mondiale,'" *Cristianità*, April 1991. Trans. Rachel Stone.

23. Russell Kirk, *A Program for Conservatives* (Chicago: Henry Regnery Company, 1954), 6.

24. Kirk, *A Program for Conservatives*. Trans. from the Italian edition by Rachel Stone.

25. Spartaco Pupo, *Robert Nisbet e il conservatorismo sociale* (Milan: Mimesis, 2012). Trans. Rachel Stone.

26. Robert Nisbet, *Conservatism: Dream and Reality* (Minneapolis, University of Minnesota Press), 1986.

27. Nisbet, *Conservatism: Dream and Reality*, 9.

28. Ibid., 11.

29. Benjamin Disraeli, "Letter to the Editor," *Morning Post*, August 11, 1843.

30. Nisbet, *Conservatism: Dream and Reality*, 25.

31. Ibid., 18.

32. Burke, *Reflections,* quoted in Nisbet, *Conservatism: Dream and Reality*, 23.

33. Nisbet, *Conservatism: Dream and Reality*, 34.

34. Alexis de Tocqueville, *Democracy in America*, quoted in Nisbet, *Conservatism: Dream and Reality*, 41.

35. Nisbet, *Conservatism: Dream and Reality*, 44.

36. Ibid., 46.

37. Ibid., 47.

38. Ibid., 57.

39. Ibid., 66.

40. Ibid., 68.

41. Kaltenbrunner, *La sfida dei conservatori*, 98. Trans. Rachel Stone.

42. Kaltenbrunner, La sfida dei conservatori, 103. Trans. Rachel Stone.

43. Ibid., 109. Trans. Rachel Stone.

44. Ibid., 150. Trans. Rachel Stone.

45. Ibid.

46. Scruton, *How to Be a Conservative*. Trans. from the Italian edition by Rachel Stone.

47. Adam Wolfson, "Conservatives and neoconservatives," *The Public Interest* 154 (2004), 32.

48. Wolfson, "Conservatives and neoconservatives," 34.

49. Ibid., 48.

50. Ibid., 37.

51. Paul Gottfried and Thomas Fleming, *The Conservative Movement*. Trans. from the Italian edition by Rachel Stone.

52. Giuseppe Prezzolini, *Manifesto dei conservatori* (Storia e Letteratura, 2014), 29. Trans. Rachel Stone.

53. Karl Mannheim, *Conservatism: A Contribution to the Sociology of Knowledge* (New York: Routledge and Kegan Paul, 1986), 76–77.

54. Prezzolini, *Manifesto dei conservatori*, 29. Trans. Rachel Stone.

55. Ibid., 79. Trans. Rachel Stone.
56. Kaltenbrunner, *La sfida dei conservatori*, Trans. Rachel Stone.
57. Giuseppe Prezzolini, *Intervista sulla destra* (Rome: Pagine, 2012), 203. Trans. Rachel Stone.
58. Prezzolini, *Intervista sulla destra*, 141. Trans. Rachel Stone.
59. Jacob L. Talmon, *The Origins of Totalitarian Democracy* (New York: Frederick A Praeger, Inc., 1960), 69.
60. Balistreri, *Filosofia della Konservative Revolution*, 325. Trans. Rachel Stone.
61. Mongardini and Maniscalco, *Il pensiero conservatore*, 11. Trans. Rachel Stone.
62. Prezzolini, *Intervista sulla destra*, 153. Trans. Rachel Stone.
63. Ibid., 154. Trans. Rachel Stone.
64. Ibid., 155. Trans. Rachel Stone.
65. Ibid., 159. Trans. Rachel Stone.
66. Giuseppe Bedeschi, *Storia del pensiero liberale* (Soveria Mannelli: Rubbettino, 2015), 9. Trans. Rachel Stone.
67. Giuseppe Bedeschi, *Storia del pensiero liberale*, 12. Trans. Rachel Stone.
68. Ibid., 30. Trans. Rachel Stone.
69. Anthony Louis Marasco, "Sono i liberali conservatori?" *Centro Einaudi*, November 12, 2014. Trans. Rachel Stone.
70. Quoted in Bedeschi, *Storia del pensiero liberale*, 50. Trans. Rachel Stone.
71. Alexis de Tocqueville, *Democracy in America* (Indianapolis: Liberty Fund Inc., 2012), ebook, 132.
72. Tocqueville, *Democracy in America*, 404.
73. Ibid., 418.
74. Ibid., 736.
75. Tocqueville, *Democracy in America*. Trans. Rachel Stone.
76. Robert Nisbet, "Conservatives and Libertarians: Uneasy Cousins," The Imaginative Conservative, July 15, 2012, https://theimaginativeconservative.org/2012/07/conservatives-and-libertarians-uneasy.html.
77. Nisbet, "Conservatives and Libertarians: Uneasy Cousins."
78. Ibid.
79. Nisbet, "The Dilemma of Conservatives in a Populist Society," 91–104.
80. Nisbet, "Conservatives and Libertarians: Uneasy Cousins."
81. Ibid.
82. Ibid.
83. Ibid.

Chapter Two: British Conservatism

1. Conservatore, partito, in *Treccani*. Trans. Rachel Stone.
2. Kenneth O. Morgan, *Lord Blake: Conservative Party historian and biographer of Disraeli*, The Independent, September 25, 2003, https://www.independent.co.uk/news/obituaries/lord-blake-755468.html.

3. Robert Blake, *Disraeli* (London: St. Martin's Press, 1966).
4. John Henry Newman, *Tract 90* (Cambridge: Cambridge Scholars Publishing, 2009).
5. John Henry Newman, *An Essay in Aid of a Grammar of Assent* (Oxford: Oxford University Press, 2004).
6. Edmund Burke, *Reflections on the Revolution in France* (New Haven: Yale University, 2003).
7. Burke, *Reflections on the Revolution in France*, xxix.
8. Edmund Burke, *Speech on American Taxation*, Leopold Classic Library, 2016; Edmund Burke, Speech on *Conciliation*, Leopold Classic Library, 2016; Edmund Burke, *A Letter to the Sheriffs of Bristol*, Leopold Classic Library, 2016.
9. Bruce Frohnen, ed., Jeremy Beer, ed., Jeffrey O. Nelson, ed., *American Conservatism: An Encyclopedia* (Wilmington, ISI Books, 2006), 106.
10. Gennaro Malgieri, ed., *Conservatori. Da Edmund Burke a Russell Kirk*, 29. Trans. Rachel Stone.
11. Malgieri, ed., *Conservatori. Da Edmund Burke a Russell Kirk*, 31. Trans. Rachel Stone.
12. Ibid., 32. Trans. Rachel Stone.
13. Ibid., 35. Trans. Rachel Stone.
14. Ibid., 386. Trans. Rachel Stone.
15. Burke, *Reflections on the Revolution in France*, 65.
16. Ibid., 168, 140.
17. Christopher Dawson, *The Formation of Christendom* (San Francisco: Ignatius Press, 2008), 14.
18. Dawson, *The Formation of Christendom*, 73.
19. Gerald J. Russello, "Christopher Dawson–Christ in History", Catholic Education Resource Center, https://www.catholiceducation.org/en/culture/history/christopher-dawson-christ-in-history.html.
20. Malgieri, ed., *Conservatori. Da Edmund Burke a Russell Kirk*, 237. Trans. Rachel Stone.
21. J.R.R. Tolkien, *The Letters of J.R.R. Tolkien* (Boston: Houghton Mifflin, 1981), 122 (e-book).
22. Tolkien, *The Letters of J.R.R. Tolkien*, 71.
23. Humphrey Carpenter, J.R.R. *Tolkien: A Biography* (Boston: Houghton Mifflin, 1977), 132.
24. Charles A. Coulombe, "Romantic Conservatives: The Inklings in Their Political Context," Tumblar House, May 7, 2018, https://www.tumblarhouse.com/blogs/news/romantic-conservatives-the-inklings-in-their-political-context.
25. Jesse Norman, "Michael Oakeshott, conservative thinker who went beyond politics," *New Statesman*, April 17, 2014, https://www.newstatesman.com/politics/2014/04/michael-oakeshott-conservative-thinker-who-went-beyond-politics.
26. Roger Scruton, *The Meaning of Conservatism* (Totowa, NJ: Barnes and Nobles Book, 1980), 11.
27. Roger Scruton, *The West and the Rest: Globalization and the Terrorist Threat* (Wilmington, DE: ISI Books, 2002), 159.

28. Roger Scruton, *How to Be a Conservative* (London: Bloomsbury Publishing, 2014), 6 (e-book).

29. Scruton, *How to Be a Conservative*, 7, e-book.

30. Ibid., 20.

31. Ibid., 24.

32. Ibid., 34.

33. Ibid., 44.

34. Ibid., 49.

35. Ibid., 53.

36. Ibid., 61.

37. Ibid., 68.

38. Ibid., 79.

39. Ibid., 81.

40. Ibid., 85.

41. Ibid., 95.

42. Ibid., 116.

43. Ibid., 120.

44. Ibid., 124.

45. Ibid., 139.

46. Ibid., 172.

47. Ibid., 178.

48. Ibid., 182.

49. Ibid., 184.

50. Ibid., 195.

51. Ibid., 207.

52. Ibid.

53. Ibid., 209.

54. Ibid., 221.

55. Ibid., 236.

56. Roger Scruton, *A Political Philosophy: Arguments for Conservatism* (London: Continuum International Publishing Group, 2006), 34.

57. Scruton, *A Political Philosophy: Arguments for Conservatism*, 2.

58. Ibid., 10.

59. Ibid., 24.

60. Ibid., 33.

61. Ibid., 45.

62. Ibid., 37.

63. Ibid., 38.

64. Ibid., 86.

65. Ibid., 95.

66. Ibid., 117.

67. Ibid., 150.

68. Ibid., 155.

69. Roger Scruton, *A Political Philosophy: Arguments for Conservatism*, trans. from the Italian edition by Rachel Stone.

Chapter Three: German, Austrian, and Prussian Conservatism

1. Heimo Schwilk, *Ernst Jünger. Una vita lunga un secolo* (Cantalupa: Effatà, 2013), 78.
2. Ernst Nolte, *La rivoluzione conservatrice nella Germania della Repubblica di Weimar*, ed. L. Iannore, 38. Trans. Rachel Stone.
3. Nolte, *La rivoluzione conservatrice nella Germania della Repubblica di Weimar*, 57. Trans. Rachel Stone.
4. Ibid., 39. Trans. Rachel Stone.
5. Gennaro Malgieri, ed., *Conservatori. Da Edmund Burke a Russell Kirk*, 63. Trans. Rachel Stone.
6. Malgieri, ed., *Conservatori. Da Edmund Burke a Russell Kirk*, 64. Trans. Rachel Stone.
7. Carl Jacob Burckhardt, *Gestalten und Machte* (Zurich, Manesse, 1961), 333. Trans. Rachel Stone.
8. Malgieri, ed., *Conservatori. Da Edmund Burke a Russell Kirk*, 105. Trans. Rachel Stone.
9. Ibid., 106. Trans. Rachel Stone.
10. "Thomas Mann" entry in *Treccani*. Trans. Rachel Stone.
11. Thomas Mann, *I Buddenbrook. Decadenza di una famiglia*. Trans. Rachel Stone.
12. Mann, *I Buddenbrook. Decadenza di una famiglia*. Trans. Rachel Stone.
13. Britta Böhler, *The Decision*. Trans Rachel Stone.
14. Böhler, *The Decision*. Trans. Rachel Stone.
15. Ezio Mauro, "Thomas Mann, nella notte d'Europa il dilemma tra silenzio e denuncia del male," *la Repubblica*, May 28, 2016. Trans. Rachel Stone.
16. Malgieri, ed., *Conservatori. Da Edmund Burke a Russell Kirk*, 161. Trans. Rachel Stone.
17. Nolte, *La rivoluzione conservatrice nella Germania della Repubblica di Weimar*, 22. Trans. Rachel Stone.
18. Malgieri, ed., *Conservatori. Da Edmund Burke a Russell Kirk*, 141. Trans. Rachel Stone.
19. Arthur Moeller van den Bruck, *Germany's Third Empire* (New York: Howard Fertig, 1971), 201.
20. Malgieri, ed., *Conservatori. Da Edmund Burke a Russell Kirk*, 144. Trans. Rachel Stone.
21. Ibid., 152, Trans. Rachel Stone.
22. Ibid., 153, Trans. Rachel Stone.
23. Ibid., 157, Trans. Rachel Stone.
24. Gennaro Malgieri, *Conservatori europei del Novecento. Un'antologia*, 133. Trans. Rachel Stone.

25. Carlo Mongardini and Maria Luisa Maniscalco, *Il pensiero conservatore. Interpretazioni, giustificazioni e critiche* (Milan: FrancoAngeli, 1999), 24. Trans. Rachel Stone.

26. Mongardini and Maniscalco, *Il pensiero conservatore*, 27. Trans. Rachel Stone.

27. Ibid., 107. Trans. Rachel Stone.

28. Ibid., 108. Trans. Rachel Stone.

29. Ibid., 111. Trans. Rachel Stone.

30. Corrado Malandrino, "Il pensiero di Roberto Michels sull'oligarchia, la classe politica e il capo carismatico from *Corso di sociologia politica* (1927) ai *Nuovi studi sulla classe politica* (1936)", in *POLIS Working Papers* n. 165, May 2010.

31. Malandrino, "Il pensiero di Roberto Michels," 183. Trans. Rachel Stone.

32. Malgieri, ed., *Conservatori. Da Edmund Burke a Russell Kirk*, 186. Trans. Rachel Stone.

33. Giovanni Franchi, "Critica dell'individualismo," in *Società italiana di filosofia politica*. Trans. Rachel Stone.

34. Giovanni Franchi, "Othmar Spann tra idealismo e filosofia cristiana," fondazionejuliusevola.it. Trans. Rachel Stone.

35. Oswald Spengler, *Il tramonto dell'Occidente* (Milan: Longanesi, 2015). Trans. Rachel Stone.

36. Nolte, *La rivoluzione conservatrice nella Germania della Repubblica di Weimar*, 28. Trans. Rachel Stone.

37. "Oswald Spengler" entry in *Treccani*. Trans. Rachel Stone.

38. Franco Cardini, "Spengler, profeta del XXI secolo," *Avvenire*, September 1, 2008. Trans. Rachel Stone.

39. Marcello Veneziani, "Il 'Tramonto' di Spengler. Alba del (neo) pessimism," *Il Giornale*, August 11, 2014. Trans. Rachel Stone.

40. Veneziani, "Il 'Tramonto' di Spengler. Alba del (neo) pessimism." Trans. Rachel Stone.

41. Marcello Veneziani, "Il Machiavelli del '900 contro il potere di tecnici e finanza. Spoliticizzazione e predominio dell'economia e del falso umanitarismo: ecco le profezie (avverate) di Carl Schmitt," in *Il Giornale*, November 26, 2012. Trans. Rachel Stone.

42. Antonio Gnoli, Franco Volpi, "L'imputato Carl Schmitt," in *la Repubblica*, February 28, 2013. Trans. Rachel Stone.

43. Marco Ravera, *Introduzione a il tradizionalismo francese*, 126. Trans. Rachel Stone.

44. Raymond Aron, *Memorie: 50 anni di riflessione politica* (Milan: Mondadori, 1985). Trans. Rachel Stone.

45. Nolte, *La rivoluzione conservatrice nella Germania della Repubblica di Weimar*. Trans. Rachel Stone.

46. Malgieri, *Conservatori europei del Novecento. Un'antologia*. Trans. Rachel Stone.

47. Carl Schmitt, *Political Romanticism,* (Cambridge: Massachusetts Institute of Technology, 1986), 109.

48. Carl Schmitt, *Donoso Cortés interpretato in una prospettiva paneuropea* (Milan: Adelphi, 1996). Trans. Rachel Stone.

49. Nolte, *La rivoluzione conservatrice nella Germania della Repubblica di Weimar*. Trans. Rachel Stone.

50. Karl Mannheim, *Ideologia e utopia*, xxvi. Trans. Rachel Stone.

51. Karl Mannheim, *Conservatism: A Contribution to the Sociology of Knowledge* (New York: Routledge and Kegan Paul, 1986), 73.

52. Karl Mannheim, *Conservatism: A Contribution to the Sociology of Knowledge*, 99.

53. Ibid., 100.

54. Carmelina Chiara Canta, *Ricostruire la società. Teoria del mutamento sociale in Karl Mannheim*, 14. Trans. Rachel Stone.

55. Nolte, *La rivoluzione conservatrice nella Germania della Repubblica di Weimar*, 39. Trans. Rachel Stone.

56. Ernst Jünger, *L'operaio* (Milan: Guanda, 1990).

57. Gerd-Klaus Kaltenbrunner, *La sfida dei conservatori* (Rome: Volpe, 1977), 185. Trans. Rachel Stone.

58. Ernst Jünger, *Nelle tempeste d'acciaio*, vii. Trans. Rachel Stone.

59. Heimo Schwilk, *Ernst Jünger. Una vita lunga un secolo*, 283. Trans. Rachel Stone.

60. Schwilk, *Ernst Jünger. Una vita lunga un secolo*, 40. Trans. Rachel Stone.

61. Ernst Jünger, "Rivoluzione e Idea," in *Volkischer Beobachter*, September 23–24, 1923. Trans. Rachel Stone.

62. Schwilk, *Ernst Jünger. Una vita lunga un secolo*, 314. Trans. Rachel Stone.

63. Ernst Jünger, "Il soldato del fronte e la politica interna," *Die Standarte*, November 29, 1925. Trans. Rachel Stone.

64. Schwilk, *Ernst Jünger. Una vita lunga un secolo*, 341. Trans. Rachel Stone.

65. Ernst Jünger, "Il nazionalismo," *Die Standarte*, April 1, 1926. Trans. Rachel Stone.

66. Schwilk, *Ernst Jünger. Una vita lunga un secolo*, 409. Trans. Rachel Stone.

67. Ibid., 528. Trans. Rachel Stone.

68. Ibid., 564. Trans. Rachel Stone.

69. Ibid., 181. Trans. Rachel Stone.

70. Letter to Hans Speidel on March 4, 1958. Trans. Rachel Stone.

71. Schwilk, *Ernst Jünger. Una vita lunga un secolo*, 672. Trans. Rachel Stone.

72. Diego Fusaro, *Presentazione del pensiero*, in Filosofico.net. Trans. Rachel Stone.

73. Leo Strauss, *Natural Right and History* (Chicago: University of Chicago Press, 1965), 5–6.

74. A. Sangalli, *Antichi e moderni*, Filosofico.net. Trans. Rachel Stone.

75. Arnold Gehlen, *L'uomo delle origini e la tarda cultura* (Milan: Mimesis, 2016). Trans. Rachel Stone.

76. Kaltenbrunner, *La sfida dei conservatori*, 10. Trans. Rachel Stone.

77. Ibid., 14. Trans. Rachel Stone.

78. Ibid., 15. Trans. Rachel Stone.

Chapter Four: French Conservatism

1. Gennaro Malgieri, ed., *Conservatori. Da Edmund Burke a Russell Kirk*, 132. Trans. Rachel Stone.
2. Ernst Nolte, *La rivoluzione conservatrice nella Germania della Repubblica di Weimar*, ed. L. Iannore, 6. Trans. Rachel Stone.
3. Nolte, *La rivoluzione conservatrice nella Germania della Repubblica di Weimar*, 13.
4. Ibid.
5. Carl Schmitt, *Donoso Cortés* (Milan: Adelphi, 1996). Trans. Rachel Stone.
6. Marco Ravera, *Introduzione al tradizionalismo francese*, 23. Trans. Rachel Stone.
7. Ravera, *Introduzione al tradizionalismo francese*, 29. Trans. Rachel Stone.
8. Ibid., 39. Trans. Rachel Stone.
9. Joseph de Maistre, *The Pope: Considered in His Relations with the Church, Temporal Sovereignties, Separated Churches, and the Cause of Civilization* (London: C. Dolman, 1850). Trans. Rachel Stone.
10. Ernst Jünger, *Rivarol. Massime di un conservatore*. Trans. Rachel Stone.
11. Jünger, *Rivarol. Massime di un conservatore*, 43. Trans. Rachel Stone.
12. Ibid., 60. Trans. Rachel Stone.
13. Malgieri, ed., *Conservatori. Da Edmund Burke a Russell Kirk*, 60. Trans. Rachel Stone.
14. Stenio Solinas, "Il cristianesimo è meglio. Parola di Chateaubriand," in *Il Giornale*, December 9, 2014. Trans. Rachel Stone.
15. Hugues Felicité Robert de Lamennais, *Oeuvres complètes* (Paris: Paul Daubree et Cailleux Editeurs, 1836), 130. Trans. Rachel Stone.
16. Robert Nisbet, *The Sociological Tradition* (New York: Basic Books, 1966), 114–15.
17. Spartaco Pupo, *Robert Nisbet e il conservatorismo sociale*, 117. Trans. Rachel Stone.
18. Ravera, *Introduzione al tradizionalismo francese*, 86. Trans. Rachel Stone.
19. Ibid., 93. Trans. Rachel Stone.
20. Alessandro Massobrio, "Jules Amédée Barbey d'Aurevilly," santibeati.it/dettaglio/95078. Trans. Rachel Stone.
21. Massobrio, "Jules Amédée Barbey d'Aurevilly." Trans. Rachel Stone.
22. Eugène Tavernier, "Louis Veuillot" entry in *The Catholic Encyclopedia*, Vol. 15 (New York: Robert Appleton Company, 1912), http://www.newadvent.org/cathen/15394b.htm.
23. Gustave Le Bon, *The Crowd: A Study of the Popular Mind* (London: T. Fisher Unwin, 1903), 19.
24. Carlo Mongardini and Maria Luisa Maniscalco, *Il pensiero conservatore. Interpretazioni, giustificazioni e critiche* (Milan: FrancoAngeli, 1999), 37. Trans. Rachel Stone.
25. Georg Simmel, "Comment les formes sociales se maintiennent", *L'Année Sociologique*, Première Année (1896–1897), (Paris: Félix Alcan, 1898), 71–107. Trans. Rachel Stone.
26. Henri Vaugeois, *L'Action française, conférence du 20 juin 1899* (Paris: Bureaux de l'Action française, 1899). Trans. Rachel Stone.
27. Barbara Carnevali, "Aura e Ambiance: Léon Daudet tra Proust e Benjamin," *Rivista de Estetica* 46 no. 3, (2006), 117–41. Trans. Rachel Stone.

28. Franco Pintore, *Maurras* (Rome: Volpe, 1965), 54. Trans. Rachel Stone.
29. Pintore, *Maurras*, 76. Trans. Rachel Stone.
30. Ibid. Trans. Rachel Stone.
31. Ibid., 16. Trans. Rachel Stone.
32. Ibid., 23. Trans. Rachel Stone.
33. Malgieri, ed., *Conservatori. Da Edmund Burke a Russell Kirk*, 133. Trans. Rachel Stone.
34. Ibid., 136. Trans. Rachel Stone.
35. Jacques Maritain, *Per una filosofia dell'educazione*. Trans. Rachel Stone.
36. Daniele Zappalà, "Giù le mani da Bernanos," *Avvenire*, December 17, 2015. Trans. Rachel Stone.
37. Francesco Perfetti, "La modernità di Bernanos, conservatore incompreso," *Il Giornale*, March 16, 2014. Trans. Rachel Stone.
38. Malgieri, ed., *Conservatori. Da Edmund Burke a Russell Kirk*, 275. Trans. Rachel Stone.
39. Ibid., 279. Trans. Rachel Stone.
40. Giovanni Cantoni, "Un contro-rivoluzionario cattolico iberoamericano nell'età della Rivoluzione culturale: il "vero reazionario" postmoderno Nicolás Gómez Dávila," *Cristianità* no. 298, (2000). Trans. Rachel Stone.
41. Marcello Veneziani, "Nicolás Gómez Dávila, l'oscurantista luminoso che casellava le parole," *Il Giornale*, May 13, 2013.

Chapter Five: Spanish Conservatism

1. Gabriele Fergola, *Storia della destra spagnola* (Rome: Ciarrapico, 1979). Trans. Rachel Stone.
2. Fergola, *Storia della destra spagnola*, 45. Trans. Rachel Stone.
3. Ibid., 83. Trans. Rachel Stone.
4. Ibid., 25. Trans. Rachel Stone.
5. Ibid., 29. Trans. Rachel Stone.
6. Carl Schmitt, *Donoso Cortés* (Milan: Adelphi, 1950), 59. Trans. Rachel Stone.
7. Schmitt, *Donoso Cortés*, 59. Trans. Rachel Stone.
8. Juan Donoso Cortés, *Saggio sul cattolicesimo, il liberalismo e il socialismo*, 395.
9. Schmitt, *Donoso Cortés*, 34. Trans. Rachel Stone.
10. Marco Ravera, *Introduzione al tradizionalismo francese*, 10. Trans. Rachel Stone.
11. Donoso Cortés, *Saggio sul cattolicesimo, il liberalismo e il socialismo*. Trans. Rachel Stone.
12. Fergola, *Storia della destra spagnola*, 68. Trans. Rachel Stone.
13. Ibid., 72. Trans. Rachel Stone.
14. Ibid., 49. Trans. Rachel Stone.
15. Ibid., 62. Trans. Rachel Stone.
16. Bruce Frohnen, ed., *American Conservatism: An Encyclopedia*, 761.
17. "Santayana, George" entry in *Treccani*. Trans. Rachel Stone.
18. Fergola, *Storia della destra spagnola*, 78. Trans. Rachel Stone.

19. Gennaro Malgieri, ed., *Conservatori. Da Edmund Burke a Russell Kirk*, 221. Trans. Rachel.
20. Malgieri, ed., *Conservatori. Da Edmund Burke a Russell Kirk*, 316. Trans. Rachel Stone.
21. Ibid., 318. Trans. Rachel Stone.
22. Francisco Elias de Tejada y Spínola, *La monarchia tradizionale* (Turin: Edizioni Dell'albero, 1966). Trans. Rachel Stone.

Chapter Six: Britain's Heir: American Conservatism

1.   Gerd-Klaus Kaltenbrunner, *La sfida dei conservatori*, 67. Trans. Rachel Stone.
2.   Kaltenbrunner, *La sfida dei conservatori*, 68. Trans. Rachel Stone.
3.   Freidrich A. Hayek, *The Constitution of Liberty* (Chicago: University of Chicago Press, 2011), 689 (e-book).
4.   Spartaco Pupo, *Robert Nisbet e il conservatorismo sociale*, 33. Trans. Rachel Stone.
5.   Jean-Jacques Rousseau, *The Social Contract*, (New Haven: Yale University, 2002), 173 (e-book).
6.   Gennaro Malgieri, ed., *Conservatori. Da Edmund Burke a Russell Kirk*, 242. Trans. Rachel Stone.
7.   Roger Scruton, *A Political Philosophy: Arguments for Conservatism* (New York: Continuum International Publishing Group, 2006), 194.
8.   Roger Scruton, *A Political Philosophy: Arguments for Conservatism* (New York: Continuum International Publishing Group, 2006), 201.
9.   T.S. Eliot, *The Idea of a Christian Society*, 13.
10. Malgieri, ed., Conservatori. Da Edmund Burke a Russell Kirk, 312. Trans. Rachel Stone.
11. Spartaco Pupo, *Robert Nisbet e il conservatorismo sociale*, 132. Trans. Rachel Stone.
12. Robert Nisbet, "Conservatives and Libertarians: Uneasy Cousins," The Imaginative Conservative, July 15, 2012, https://theimaginativeconservative.org/2012/07/conservatives-and-libertarians-uneasy.html.
13. Robert Nisbet, "Still Questing," *The Intercollegiate Review*, Fall 1993, https://isistatic.org/journal-archive/ir/29_01/nisbet.pdf.
14. Carlo Mongardini and Maria Luisa Maniscalco, *Il pensiero conservatore. Interpretazioni, giustificazioni e critiche*, 29. Trans. Rachel Stone.
15. Malgieri, ed., *Conservatori. Da Edmund Burke a Russell Kirk*, 386. Trans. Rachel Stone.
16. Thomas Molnar, *The Counter-Revolution* (New York: Funk & Wagnalls, 1969), 201.
17. Molnar, *The Counter-Revolution*, 201.
18. Bruce Frohnen, ed., *American Conservatism: An Encyclopedia*, 602.
19. Samuel Huntington, "Conservatism as an Ideology," *The American Political Science Review* 51, (1957), 454–61, 470–73.
20. Bruce Frohnen, ed., *American Conservatism: An Encyclopedia*, 179.

21. Barry Goldwater, *The Conscience of a Conservative* (Shepherdsville, KY: Victor Publishing Company, Inc., 1960), 6.
22. Goldwater, *The Conscience of a Conservative*, 37.
23. Ibid., 22.
24. Ibid., 62.
25. Ibid., 66.
26. Ibid., 70.
27. Ibid., 78.

Chapter Seven: Italian Conservatism

1. Giuseppe Prezzolini, *Intervista sulla destra*, 17. Trans. Rachel Stone.
2. Prezzolini, *Intervista sulla destra*, 18. Trans. Rachel Stone.
3. Armando Torno, *Il paradosso dei conservatori* (Milan: Bompiani, 2011), 6. Trans. Rachel Stone.
4. Torno, *Il paradosso dei conservatori*, 9. Trans. Rachel Stone.
5. Ibid., 12. Trans. Rachel Stone.
6. Ibid., 19. Trans. Rachel Stone.
7. Vincenzo Cuoco, *Saggio storico sulla rivoluzione di Napoli* (Rome: Laterza, 2014), 55. Trans. Rachel Stone.
8. Marcello Veneziani, *La rivoluzione conservatrice in Italia* (Milan: Sugarco, 2012), 34. Trans. Rachel Stone.
9. Eugenio Garin, *Cronache di filosofia italiana. 1900-1943* (Rome: Laterza, 1966).
10. Carlo Mongardini and Maria Luisa Maniscalco, *Il pensiero conservatore. Interpretazioni, giustificazioni e critiche*, 113. Trans. Rachel Stone.
11. "Benito Mussolini," *Il popolo d'Italia*, March 23, 1921. Trans. Rachel Stone.
12. Marcello Veneziani, *La rivoluzione conservatrice in Italia*, 98. Trans. Rachel Stone.
13. Stefan Breuer, *La rivoluzione conservatrice. Il pensiero di destra nella Germania di Weimar*. Trans. Rachel Stone.
14. Breuer, *La rivoluzione conservatrice. Il pensiero di destra nella Germania di Weimar*, 101. Trans. Rachel Stone.
15. Ibid., 108. Trans. Rachel Stone.
16. Veneziani, *La rivoluzione conservatrice in Italia*, 66. Trans. Rachel Stone.
17. Ibid., 70. Trans. Rachel Stone.
18. Ibid., 72. Trans. Rachel Stone.
19. Malgieri, ed., *Conservatori. Da Edmund Burke a Russell Kirk*, 69. Trans. Rachel Stone.
20. Ibid., 70. Trans. Rachel Stone.
21. Ibid., 74. Trans. Rachel Stone.
22. Diego Fusaro, ed., "Vilfredo Pareto," http://www.filosofico.net/pareto.htm. Trans. Rachel Stone.
23. Luciano Simonelli, *Mario Missiroli: il più rivoluzionario dei conservatori* (Milan: Simonelli editore, 2013). Trans. Rachel Stone.

24. Mongardini and Maniscalco, *Il pensiero conservatore. Interpretazioni, giustificazioni e critiche*, 74. Trans. Rachel Stone.
25. Ibid., 83. Trans. Rachel Stone.
26. Senato del Regno, Atti parlamentari. Discussioni, December 11, 1931. Trans. Rachel Stone.
27. Alfredo Rocco, *Scritti e discorsi politici*, vol. II (Milan: Giuffrè, 1938), 631. Trans. Rachel Stone.
28. Giuseppe Prezzolini, "La nostra promessa," *La Voce*, December 27, 1908. Trans. Rachel Stone.
29. Gennaro Sangiuliano, *Giuseppe Prezzolini. L'anarchico conservatore*, 237. Trans. Rachel Stone.
30. Giuseppe Prezzolini, *Manifesto dei conservatori*, xiii. Trans. Rachel Stone.
31. Sangiuliano, *Giuseppe Prezzolini. L'anarchico conservatore*, 156. Trans. Rachel Stone.
32. Veneziani, *La rivoluzione conservatrice in Italia*, 147. Trans. Rachel Stone.
33. Ibid., 162. Trans. Rachel Stone.
34. Ibid., 401. Trans. Rachel Stone.
35. Sangiuliano, *Giuseppe Prezzolini. L'anarchico conservatore*. Trans. Rachel Stone.
36. Prezzolini, *Manifesto dei conservatori*, vii. Trans. Rachel Stone.
37. Ibid., 10. Trans. Rachel Stone.
38. Ibid., 12. Trans. Rachel Stone.
39. Ibid., 13. Trans. Rachel Stone.
40. Ibid., 16. Trans. Rachel Stone.
41. Sangiuliano, *Giuseppe Prezzolini. L'anarchico conservatore*, 426. Trans. Rachel Stone.
42. Prezzolini, *Manifesto dei conservatori*, 44. Trans. Rachel Stone.
43. Ibid., 69. Trans. Rachel Stone.
44. Ibid. Trans. Rachel Stone.
45. Ibid., 78. Trans. Rachel Stone.
46. Ibid., 79. Trans. Rachel Stone.
47. Ibid., 89. Trans. Rachel Stone.
48. Panfilo Gentile, *Democrazie mafiose* (Milan: Ponte alle Grazie, 2005). Trans. Rachel Stone.
49. Paolo Granzotto, "Panfilo Gentile. L'eresia liberale," *Il Giornale*, August 11, 2005. Trans. Rachel Stone.
50. Gentile, *Democrazie mafiose*. Trans. Rachel Stone.
51. Francesco Perfetti, "Ansaldo, un eretico conservatore," *Il Giornale*, November 2, 1914. Trans. Rachel Stone.
52. Leo Longanesi, "La provincial," *Gazzetta del Popolo*, March 6, 1949. Trans. Rachel Stone.
53. Leo Longanesi, "Il successo della vita," *L'Italiano* 14 (1933). Trans. Rachel Stone.
54. Leo Longanesi, "Non ci salveranno più," *Il Borghese* 2, January 13, 1956. Trans. Rachel Stone.
55. Leo Longanesi, "Non ci salveranno più," Trans. Rachel Stone.

56. Annalisa Terranova, "L'anniversario che la destra ha dimenticato: trent'anni fa moriva l'editore Giovanni Volpe," *Il Secolo d'Italia*, August 4, 2014. Trans. Rachel Stone.

57. Dino Messina, "Montanelli, conservatore rivoluzionario. La seconda vita: 1958-2001," in *Corriere della Sera*, June 18, 2009. Trans. Rachel Stone.

58. Marco Travaglio, *Montanelli e il Cavaliere* (Milan: Garzanti, 2004), 148. Trans. Rachel Stone.

59. Travaglio, *Montanelli e il Cavaliere*, 255. Trans. Rachel Stone.

60. Luciano Lanna and Filippo Rossi, *Fascisti immaginari* (Florence: Vallecchi, 2003), 311. Trans. Rachel Stone.

61. "Ennio Flaiano, vita e opere di un marziano in Italia," *Il Giornale*, November 28, 2010.

62. Ennio Flaiano, *La solitudine del satiro* (Milan: Rizzoli, 1973), 228. Trans. Rachel Stone.